Trends & Styles

in Twentieth Century

French Literature

by Helmut Hatzfeld

THE CATHOLIC UNIVERSITY OF AMERICA PRESS
Washington 17, D. C.
1957

126247

PREFACE

THE FOLLOWING presentation of contemporary French literature is somewhat different from those already existing within and outside France. It singles out trends which are deeply rooted in problems of contemporary life or in burning questions of principles of literary art. It refers critically to scholarly research on the literary style and structure of special works and disregards the subjective appraisals of impressionistic critics. It endeavors to understand all trends and styles, which does not mean that viewpoints incompatible with Catholic principles are therefore accepted. Thus the presentation is intrinsically Catholic, without, however, the slightest attempt to treat questions which only the theologian is competent to deal with, or to criticize ideas without relation to the mind of the author who embodies them in his work. Those interested in a strictly philosophical and theological criticism of contemporary French literature should read Rev. Charles Moeller's *Littérature du XXᵉ siècle et christianisme* (Tournai: Casterman, 1953 ff.). They should consult also the periodicals *Etudes, Esprit, La Vie intellectuelle, Dieu vivant* and *Témoignages*.

As a responsible literary historian and critic, I likewise refrain from *explicit* statements of a psychological or sociological character beyond the barest necessity dictated by the works of fiction. To expatiate on such problems *per se* would necessarily lead to mere dilettantism. The literary critic is not in a position to pass judgment on the prose writers or poets in their human relations and difficulties, unless these reveal themselves through their art. Or, to repeat the well-known statement of T. S. Eliot who expresses the same idea from another angle: "Honest criticism and sensitive appreciation is directed not upon the poet but upon the poetry."

There is no doubt that the critic's task is to assess the intrinsic meaning of the literary artifact, and contribute to the understanding of it in the light of the historical circumstances that brought it into being. Literary trends therefore are illustrated by works rather than by authors. The judgment passed on these works will be mainly functional, structural and aesthetic. Any moral criticism is—as much as possible—in close connection with the artistic appraisal.

The facts given and judgments passed are illustrated by many quotations and justified in rather numerous footnotes. These footnotes constitute at the same time a special bibliography which is not repeated at the end in the general selective bibliography of works and monographs concerning the outstanding authors.

The presentation steers a middle course between a literary history and a literary essay. A history of a period in which a critic himself is living is not feasible, for he does not have a sufficient perspective. Therefore stress is not laid on chronology but on a projection of the trends into a space extending from 1900 to 1955. The choice of material and the emphasis put on it clearly show my own preferences. However, since I prefer a relative completeness to the arbitrary selection of the essayist, I feel obliged to put into their proper place even things I dislike.

The approach thus used becomes clear. The works themselves with their human or literary aspects, rather than the authors, illustrate the main trends. With the trends determining the overall principle, it became necessary to make a typical selection of works from the total output of the various authors, and sometimes also to discuss the same authors under different trends. This is particularly the case for some of the greatest writers, who follow not only one but several different lines. The disadvantage of this method is compensated for by a presentation based on the needs of our time, which it is hoped will elicit a spontaneous and lively response in the modern reader who cannot help but feel himself personally involved in the problems dealt with.

The reader may be struck by the unequal length of the analyses of the single works discussed. The reason for this is that three kinds of analysis are used: a summary analysis of their works in the case of most authors (for instance the works of Mauriac among others); a brief analysis of representative works which as morally objectionable, I presume, many people will not care to read (for instance the novels of Sartre); an extensive analysis of voluminous works that very few people will have read (for instance the twenty-seven volumes of Jules Romain's *Les Hommes de bonne volonté* and the sixteen volumes of Marcel Proust's *A la recherche du temps perdu*). For representative dramas the plots are indicated (for instance the main plays of Claudel, Lenormand, Giraudoux, Gabriel Marcel, Sartre and Anouilh).

Thus the book is meant to appeal to the educated reader who has a certain liking for French culture, and also to advanced undergraduate and graduate students specializing in French. In view of these readers the quotations are mostly given in French.

I will not close this preface without thanking those who helped, with the personal sacrifice of many, many hours and days, to make my English manuscript more readable and idiomatic, namely Rev. Father Edmond D. Benard, Professor Alessandro Santi Crisafulli and Dr. John Frey.

TABLE OF CONTENTS

INTRODUCTION

THE GENERAL SITUATION

To PRESENT contemporary French literature since 1900 as a sequence of historical developments seems to me a somewhat premature enterprise. Therefore I chose to show it as a phenomenological prism of persistent and still existing trends reducible to a unity. The unity becomes visible in the literary concept of a super-reality which transcends the individual consciousness and the external cosmos. This concept is not of a supernatural but of an empirical order and receives support from the different non-literary cultural aspects of the epoch: science, psychology, sociology, philosophy, religion, art. Literary trends are always anchored in cultural trends; they show not only particular literary style features, but also general characteristics of the culture and the epoch producing them.

Thus, conceptually, formally and culturally, contemporary French literature can be reduced to a kind of *anti-réalisme*. In whatever form this *anti-réalisme* may manifest itself, whether as an unconscious surrealism or a brutal vulgarity, it obviously deforms reality. Unconscious surrealism has, in a softer form, all the features which André Breton (1896-   ) has vindicated for it in exaggerated programs since his first *Manifeste du Surréalisme* (1924).[1] All the important twentieth century authors, including the serious dramatists, are convinced that the task of literature is not to copy life but to offer free and poetic interpretations of it.[2] André Gide (1869-1951) believed that the greatest danger to any art was the disastrous preoccupation with realistic presentation in the nineteenth century sense.[3] Twentieth century literature is a "studied affront to the self-sufficiency of the material and the obvious."[4] This tendency is not a mere opposition to a form of art, it is an opposition to a state of mind: "The rough and erroneous perception left alone," says Marcel Proust (1875-1922), "puts

1

everything into the object while everything actually is in the mind."[5]

The content of dreams and myths is supposed, through its dark symbols, to reveal the true soul of man, "an image of man that upsets us to the degree that it appears to be the real one."[6] Even the cruder realism of the existentialist novelists, using however this new psychology, is, according to the pertinent remark, of Gaëton Picon, "a metaphysical realism"; in other words it never merely seeks the *détail divers* but suggests at least symbolism or myth. Any author will agree that the "myths from the Sphinx to the Niebelungen reflected a spiritual truth infinitely more important than the ephemeral happenings which have occurred at a given moment."[7] This new "non-reality, now called the reality"[8] has nothing in common with romanticism. It is not a flight into a beautiful lie. On the contrary, it is the tendency to discover reality in disguise, a disguise whose manifest elements reveal the latent ones. This higher reality sometimes appears couched in an art of abstraction which creates e.g. an ideal Middle Ages, dateless in spirit and form, the better to catch its essence, as Paul Claudel (1868-1955) tried to do with the atmosphere created around *L'Annonce faite à Marie,* or as the great theatrical manager Pitoëff did with his *mises-en-scène,* for instance when he staged *Jeanne D'Arc.*[9]

Twentieth century literature is not anti-realistic in the sense of avoiding at any price naturalistic details so far as they are part and parcel of modern psychology. There is even a good deal of neo-naturalism whenever sex or cruelty is involved. But nobody, in these works, ever seems especially interested in eating, drinking, or sleeping. In the aristocratic society of Proust, such a natural occupation as horseback riding is never mentioned.[10] Proust himself boasts about much more: "Pas une seule fois un des mes personnages ne ferme une fenêtre, ne se lave les mains, ne passe un pardessus, ne dit une formule de présentation."[11] And Louis Carette remarks: "You may go through the whole work of Gide or Mauriac, let alone that of Proust, without finding any description of furniture or the price of a man's suit."[12]

The famous passage in *Sursis* of Jean-Paul Sartre (1905-   ):
"Un instant Mathieu mangeait, Marcelle mangeait, Daniel
mangeait, Boris mangeait, Brunet mangeait" (p. 59), does not
evoke any detail of the dinner table; it is only the springboard
for creating the simultaneous anguish of all those persons expecting the immediate outbreak of war. The same is true of the
"Hitler dormait, Ivich dormait, Chamberlain dormait" (p. 155).
Reading the ethereal Jean Giraudoux (1882-1944), one would
not even think "that he encountered in the world people that
had suffered, abandoned wives, orphans, unhappy couples, men
in the throes of anguish and death,"[13] and nevertheless he is full
of ironically presented exact psychological reality. In Paul Valéry
(1871-1945), "La recherche de l'Absolu" is the theme of reality
which seems solved in Eupalinos' architectures "which sing" or
in the dance-movements of Athikté "which think." Even the
more realistic plays in the nineteenth century sense as represented
by Charles Vildrac, Denys Amiel, Jean-Jacques Bernard are
definitely dramas of the mind and of the "unexpressed."[14] Non-
realistic also is the fact that reason has been rejected in favor of
intuition, that frenzy replaces serenity, Sade and Lautréamont
have dethroned Sophocles and Plato, the incommunicable, the
incomprehensible and the abnormal have taken over, the literary
heroes have become men without a conscience but are all the
more anguished, tortured, expecting a mysterious, undeserved
punishment in the fashion of Franz Kafka.[15] A realist of the
nineteenth century would not recognize as realistic, either, the
transposition (into the technique of literary novels) of the techniques of the movies such as simultaneanism, crossing of two different stories told at the same time; in brief, literary photomont-
age.[16] Or, to summarize the general type of twentieth century style
with Gaëton Picon: "If surrealism is a realism, its purpose is to
make visible the magic halo of the real."[17] Paradoxically, realistic is
the desperate attempt to come to grips with ultimate reality experi-
mentally—but alas—without the aid of speculation, let alone
religion: "Retrouver le contact fondamental avec la réalité
vécue, au mépris des principes et des réflexions a priori,"[18] or the

immediate intrusion into realms of the strange and the unknown: "La recherche du merveilleux en tant que réalité."[19]

The realistic-surrealistic paradox thus coming strikingly to the fore in literature has its parallel in contemporary general civilization and especially in contemporary science. Modern science, though continuing rational methods inherited from the nineteenth century, does not reject the paradoxical. Modern science restricts its experimental statements to the observable field, while its theories and hypotheses gradually abandon logic and causality. These tendencies go back to the ideas of Emile Boutroux (1845-1921) as expressed in his book, *De la contingence des lois de la nature* (1874). Albert Einstein (1879-1955) formulated the paradox that the apparently boundless space is finite. He consequently has to admit the conclusion that in a curved space a straight line, if pursued indefinitely, would return to its original starting point.[20] For Einstein and Max Planck (*Quantentheorie*) there is no separation of time and space and no separation of matter and energy. What exists is condensed energy in a space-time unit. With Jean Perrin and Lord Rutherford, one does not believe any longer in the atom as the smallest chemical unity; it is a nucleus with a system of electrons comparable to a star with its satellites and it radiates energy. With the split atom, man is ready for a warfare which may mean the end of the world. Everything is reduced ultimately to energy, vital and active itself, creating and destroying space and time.

The theoretical physicists Heisenberg and De Broglie have upset the physical principles of Maxwell together with the mechanics of Newton, both of whom believed in a separate absolute space, time and motion. To the modern monistic physicist the laws of gravitation and electro-mechanics appear identical. To the mathematician, Euclidian geometry seems outlawed by a geometry of "infinite dimensions."[21]

The discoveries of astrophysics are of a most revolutionary character. The sun is no longer the center of the cosmos but only of a galaxy, or a milky-way star-system, and there are innumerable such galaxies with suns a hundred million times as great in volume as our sun, encompassed by stars partly of a lighter matter, partly of a matter two thousand times as dense as gold. Thus groups of stars, like leaves, organize themselves into trees and these form a metagalaxy the same way as the stars form a galaxy. And all these stars are tremendously far away and move at a fantastic speed; the so-called nebulous galactic ones reach sixty thousand miles a second in their recession from a center.[22] This led Lemaître and Edington to the theory of the expansion of the universe from a single radioactive atom, an expansion still in progress. Pope Pius XII, highly impressed by this theory, intimated to his Academy of Science that it is the best translation of the biblical cosmogony into modern scientific language and supposes a creation *ex nihilo* entrusted to expansive energy, on a "primordial 'Fiat lux' uttered at the moment when, along with matter, there burst forth from nothing a sea of light and radiation, while the particles of chemical elements split and formed into millions of galaxies" (*Le prove della esistenza di Dio alla luce della scienza naturale moderna. Allocutio 22 nov. 1951*).

Chemistry has achieved the artificial fabrication of synthetic colors, synthetic rubber, nylon, chocolate, and diamonds, realizing in all these products one of the greatest dreams of industry and economics. Radio and television have taken away all distances from eye and ear. The world has become a world of shadows and dreams since, as already mentioned, the natural scientists and mathematicians proclaimed the restriction of the fundamental law of cause and effect: "Tout est remis en question. Aucune certitude possible. Deux et deux ne font plus quatre. . . . On a découvert un planète, qui s'appelle Uranus et qui tourne à contresens. Et tous ses satellites aussi tournent à contresens . . . : Les sciences dites exactes sont une énorme duperie" according to the ideas of Laurent Pasquier.[23] Biogenetics makes bold to infringe on the laws of heredity and to decide on the sex of the embryo. Biochemistry tries to erase the frontier between organic life and minerals. Medical science achieves "surrealistic" triumphs in operating on "blue" babies, in separating Siamese twins, in stopping interior hemorrhages by transfusion of the right type of blood kept in a blood bank, by replacing glands, removing lungs, dislodging brain tumors, doing surgery on the heart held in the operator's hand.

Religion, still despised by Ferdinand Buisson and Solomon Reinach, has been in a way reenthroned by the comparative study of religions in the ethnographical sense of Lévy-Bruhl as well as by the religious psychology of William James, Boutroux, Le Roy, and Carl Jung. Consequently the atheists of today have to introduce themselves as antitheists; otherwise they cannot speak to traditionally, fundamentally theistic mankind. Explaining the world as absurd and meaningless, they actually identify their attitude with a Promethean revolt. In this situation and outside the strictly theological discussion a strong Christianity versus any kind of substitutionary humanism has been defended by the Catholic personalist Emmanuel Mounier as well as by the Protestant cultural philosopher Denis de Rougemont. France lent her ear also to Karl Jaspers and his philosophical idea that everything is a *chiffre* and has to be deciphered, a proof that immanence needs transcendence as an explanation. Albert Schweitzer's not quite Christian though heroic humanitarianism has become popular in France to the point that it elicited the drama of Gilbert Cesbron: *Il est minuit, Docteur Schweitzer*. Simone Weil tried to live a life of asceticism and sanctity. She was called the saint of the unchurched.

The greater the despair of the Promethean revolutionaries against God, the more intensive became the involuntary dialogue between them and certain Catholic intellectuals: Rivière, Gide, Duhamel, Thierry Maulnier on one side, Claudel, Charles Du Bos, Bernanos, Mauriac on the other, not to mention minor names. Wavering converts like Cocteau cannot invalidate the many solid conversions and reconversions as they occurred with Claudel, Psichari, Ghéon, Dupouy, Max Jacob, Charles Du Bos, Gabriel Marcel, the Maritains and many others. The attraction to the eternal values of the Church on the part of the intellectuals who were craving for the "experience" of God and for a true community, comes from her newly rediscovered spirituality, asceticism, mysticism, Christian perfection (Garrigou-Lagrange), and the liturgical movement (Romano Guardini, M.-J. Yves Congar, O.P., Abbé Bouyer). The influence of priests like Canon Cardijn spread out into the social sphere of the youth movements of workers, students and farmers (Jocistes, Jécistes and Jacistes) and attempts have been made to bring to life the social principles laid down in the encyclicals *Rerum Novarum* and *Quadragesimo Anno* in order to oppose a Christian "socialism" of love to the brutal communism of dehumanization, flourishing in the cities, suburbs, and the Parisian banlieue. While the younger intellectuals (Malraux, Sartre, Camus) were irresponsible enough to embrace a drawingroom communism although fighting for and with the masses whom they despise nonetheless, on the Catholic side, saintly priests do not hesitate to descend into the hell of communistic and atheistic workers, an outstanding example of such priests being Abbé Pierre, the founder of the "rag-picker" colony of Emmaus. The great though somewhat belated social insight of French Catholicism, so often stressed by the late Cardinal Suhard, was restated by François Mauriac with the excellent formula: "Happiness can no longer be individual, like prayer." Acknowledging the share in the products of the earth to which the masses are entitled, but stressing no less the liberty and dignity of the human personality, Emmanuel Mounier preached his just mentioned personalism. This movement became a program for the periodical *Esprit* and men like Louis Martin-Chauffier, Stanislas Fumet, Albert Béguin and Jean Lacroix.

The primitive belief in progress collapsed progressively as an entirely unrealistic utopia since Georges Sorel's sociological study *Les Illusions du Progrès* (1922). What the nineteenth century regarded as progress is considered only social change, indifferent in itself. Sigmund Freud gave rationalism its death blow when he showed that forces of consciousness, reason, self-control, and free will are constantly threatened by the domains of the subconscious, subliminal, day-dreams, unconscious actions, traumas and passive remembrances. These forces are not susceptible of voluntary evocation and clear analysis. Freud's theory, often catastrophically applied, at least helped the fundamental French rational philosophy to arrive at a more open rationalism in philosophers like Maurice Merleau-Ponty (1906-   ), teaching at the College de France, or even at spiritualism as in Louis Lavelle (1883-1951) and René le Senne. It led furthermore to a particular kind of French psychoanalysis applied to man's reaction to the four elements throughout the centuries. This novelty goes to the credit of Gaston Bachelard (1884-   ).

Freud's subconscious as opposed to the conscious had an independent parallel in France in the philosophy of Bergson with its distinction between *souvenir* and *mémoire*. Bergson's *élan vital* and *évolution créatrice,* furthermore, represent a philosophy which tries to explain the contradictory "reality" of a stability which is in a continual change, perceptible only in the memory, where the past and the imaginable future are as "real" as the present. The changing *devenir* thus can become an unchangeable *être* in a psychological concept of time. Thus the relative becomes something quasi-absolute. The spatial physical time is replaced by a psychic-sensitive *durée,* or *temps humain.* Bergson's philosophy is accordingly a system as antilogical and irrational[24] as that of the contemporary philosopher Heidegger. His existentialism tries to find psychological ancestors in Pascal and Kierkegaard and ends ethically in the destructive *engagement* of a self-made *choix* in Sartre and Simone de Beauvoir. Also in existentialism there is the paradox that the contingent is declared absolute, and existence is considered to precede and create being, almost in Hegel's sense of the objective spirit. The neo-thomist Jacques Maritain (1882-   ), it is true, was able to prove the philosophical incompatibility of an identified *être* and *devenir* in Bergson as well as of essence and existence in Sartre. But Maritain himself subscribes in the realm of art to intuition and in epistemology to different degrees of knowledge. Thus in the realm of art Bergson's anti-intellectual statement would be shared by Maritain's creative intuitionism: "Far from detaching us from the empirical world, intuition showed us its reality and truth."[25] A truth intuitively acquired[26] is for Maritain, however, still a subjective truth; but an insight so acquired is irrefutable according to the father of existentialism, the phenomenologist Edmund Husserl (1859-1938), and even according to the Christian existentialist Gabriel Marcel. To round out the picture, we have only to add that a philosophical idealist critic, such as Benedetto Croce (1866-1952), also challenged rationalism by the theory that poetry itself is nothing else but an adequate means of discovering absolute truth. Not sharing this confusion of truth and reality, in France Abbé Bremond (1865-1933) conceived mysticism and poetry as two phenomena of experience, between which exists a certain affinity and which are superior to science as organs for contacting reality directly in the domains of *charité* and of *finesse* respectively.

The mind of the modern individual, not rooted in a collectivity of a common creed or philosophy but in an entirely pragmatic and anarchic view of life, is helplessly chaotic. Therefore, modern man, resorting to the concepts of race, nation, class, professional group, has tried to forge more complete economically and technically conditioned unities, bent on a mutual political antagonism, often leading to isolation, enslavement and mental destruction of the personality. This predicament comes from the fact that the psychic chaos of split personalities is on the outside confronted with the multiplicity of a world "knocked into fragments." Democracy is threatened by the brutally organized anarchism called communism. Nothing reflects this political situation, constantly lingering in France, better than modern art, which appears in a similar state of disintegration. The understanding of modern painting may help us to close the circle which we started with the consideration of literature. The modern painter on one hand is a prey to his inner dissociations; on the other hand he yields to the outside multiplicity of which he is so vividly aware. He indulges in "a merely mechanical association of ideas by uncontrolled introspection."[27] Despairing of finding an ordered system inside and outside, he breaks "the world of appearances into fragments . . ., rearranging these fragments according to a new order."[28] This artistic tendency is not concerned with a logical comprehension and acceptance of the world. It ends in desperate, simultaneous, unconnected juxtapositions of never-heard-of analogies, while "the actual appearance of the visible world is no longer of primary importance."[29] Opposed to the careful registering of impressions made on the spot of observation, now "the duty and task of a painter as well as a writer are those of a translator of his stored impressions,"[30] which he rearranges into an arbitrary kaleidoscope. Thus Pablo Picasso, painting a guitar, dissects the instrument in its different parts, adding the notes to play. Henri Rousseau, painting "Le Rêve," combined, in a primeval forest of gigantic flowers, peaceful natives and half-tamed lions around a naked woman reposing on a comfortable couch standing in this very virgin wood. In other words: he combines the possible elements of a virgin wood with a new impossible synthesis; very possible, however, in a dream. He even combines the dreamer with her dream.

In art, the psychic dilemma of modern disintegration leads also to the discovery of another type of "order," a mathematical world of geometrical and essential forms not directly visible in everyday reality. "L'univers du peintre devient exprimable en polyèdres et en corps ronds. Il n'est de seins, de cuisses, de joues, de chevaux, ni de vaches que l'on ne puisse bâtir de ces durs éléments."[31] In the historical evolution the painters give us much better than the writers an insight into the progressive application of the principle of realistic disintegration and surrealistic reintegration. Cézanne destroyed the picturesque and multifarious phenomena and reduced them to preconceived geometrical forms. Vincent van Gogh cut out all details which did not interest him and reduced a fictitious nature to its essentials, but so arbitrarily that cypresses are reshaped into flaming and burning beings. Paul Gauguin borrows the eye of the primitives, suppresses the third dimension and recreates a world of flat foregrounds made of unreal colors. Henri Matisse shows the way to another kind of reshaped human beings, where the athlete consists only of muscles, the mother of breasts, the dancer of legs, the thinker of a head. Caricatures of man are taken seriously for the first time in history and direct the whole sculpture from Rodin over Maillol to Archipenko. The situation in other countries is similar but lacks the extremely varied picture offered by France.[32]

The poet Antonin Artaud (1895-1948), praising particularly Van Gogh as the prophet of modern art, reveals what the poets and writers also consider as their task: "Van Gogh pensait qu'il faut savoir déduire le mythe des choses les plus terre-à-terre de la vie. En quoi je pense, moi, qu'il avait foutrement raison. Car la réalité est terriblement supérieure à toute histoire, à tout fable . . ., à toute surréalité" (*Van Gogh, le suicide de la société*). This may be an intuitive definition of the essence of contemporary aesthetics in general and certainly is valid also for literature. Similar definitions have been formulated consciously in order to buttress the surrealistic manifestos and group-tendencies. One can find them easily elsewhere.[33] What is of importance with them is the general stress on a dream-reality which is truer than any other kind of reality and which is furthermore poetic by principle. Proust has seen this: "Notre imagination, crée des fantômes qui nous sont plus précieux que les êtres réels . . . La réalité n'existe pas pour tant qu'elle n'a pas été recréée par notre pensée."[34] The judging intellect and its objects are considered as inseparable as in Rousseau's picture of the virgin wood, as inseparable as Kant's noumena and phenomena. Now, both together form the surrealistic psychic unity: "An hour is not merely an hour. It is a vase filled with perfumes, sounds, plans and climates. What we call reality is a certain relationship between these sensations and the memories which surround us at the same time, a relationship that is destroyed by a bare cinematographic presentation."[35] This aesthetic concept coincides partly with Bergson's *durée*: "Intellectualiser dans une oeuvre d'art des réalités extratemporelles."[36] As to their style, moderate and extreme surrealistic painters and writers are expressionists; they express their own intuition of an object, not by giving impressions of it, not by interpreting it at random, not by giving an abstract view of it, but "en se plaçant au dedans de l'object"[37] with sympathy and empathy.

This object in the psychological realm is a part of the subject and encompasses it, but is at the same time a counter-ego.[38] As such, or as the *id* according to Freud, it reveals the secret passions of the *ego,* as for example the heroes of the contemporary novels lay bare the souls of the authors. Marcel in *A la recherche du temps perdu* is Proust, Mathieu in *Les Chemins de la liberté* is Sartre. Each character thus represents the *id,* judging the *ego,* but with a certain intricacy justifying the *ego* nevertheless. The author who expresses his self and his Gidean *disponibilité* without restraint, without *refoulement,* without shame, renders a reality of sinful, nay criminal tendencies, frightening in their taboo-breaking "sincerity," a reality allegedly superior to the moral restrictions of life, its conventions and the censorship of conscience. He also reveals on the other hand "l'image effrayante et parfaite, toujours agrandie de l'être qu'il n'a pas osé, pas pu devenir."[39] If, however, the picture of man is drawn in contempt of the most elementary moral laws, it often appears terrible because it releases from the bottom of the soul "tous ces monstres que déchaîne la confession, . . . [parce] que tout humain qui n'est pas doublé a l'interieur par un sourd-muet est la trappe par laquelle le mal inonde le monde."[40] Not considering such extremes, Georges Duhamel defined the modern artist as "celui qui nous seconde dans la connaissance et l'expression de cette partie de notre vie qui semble, au premier abord, incommunicable."[41]

In this contemporary psychological and parapsychological French surrealism there is much talk about *transcendance* and *dépassement.* We must not be duped by this elusive semantics into a real, metaphysical transcendentalism. It is on the contrary, as Jean Wahl puts it, a trans-de-scendentalism, since man who psychologizes even God, depriving Him of His being by identifying ontological supranaturalism with parapsychologism, or by making essence dependent on existence, dethrones Him and debases himself. The *disponsibilité* of a generation philosophizing this way fortunately does not close the doors to better insights.

The provisional refusal to face a simple, given external reality has led to the constant use of three new technical procedures in French literature: The *monologue intérieur* invented by Edouard Dujardin (born 1861) in his novel *Les Lauriers sont coupés;* the-stream-of-consciousness technique stemming from the *Ulysses* of James Joyce (1882-1942); and the simultaneous narration of different events which was used for the first time in *Manhattan Transfer* by John R. Dos Passos (1896-   ).

CHAPTER I

INDIVIDUAL AND GROUP IN TENSION

ONE OF THE most tragic turns of the twentieth century is the reaction to the individualism of the nineteenth to such a degree that groups and collectivities of all kinds try to wipe out any individualism and thus provoke a desperate resistance of the person rooted in humanistic, democratic or spiritual convictions. Collectivism, before becoming a literary idea in France, was a political and an economical theory. Politically it even materialized in socialistic, bolshevistic and fascist experiments outside France. In France collectivism in general has only reached the form of a doctrine adhered to by political parties or scholars in sociology, the communist party having been recognized a danger in works like Michel Collinet, *La Tragédie du marxisme* (1948), and the state as such having remained sufficiently immune. Emile Durckheim (1858-1917) with his *Règles de la méthode sociologique,* Gustave Le Bon (1841-1931), hinting at mass-psychology, with *La Psychologie des foules* (1905), Gabriel de Tarde with *Les Lois de l'imitation,* and their master, the anthropologist Lucien Lévy-Bruhl (1857-1939), with his studies on primitive man and his creation of "La Science des moeurs," have discovered special problems inherent in the concept of collectivism: the importance of ephemeral group-formations, the meaninglessness of the individual in front of mighty and dangerously organized group-forces, and the total incorporation of the individual consciousness into a collective structure directed by a leader. Marxian theorists untiringly stress this situation as does Pierre Hervé in *Individu et Marxisme* (1948). France proved to be under this spell when Louis-Ferdinand Céline (1897-   ) created the slogan of the *garçon sans importance collective.* No less than 150 novels deal with this topic. They are concerned more specifically with the tensions between the individual on one hand, and the family, community, *équipe,* youth gang on the other, with the situation of the individual in the democratic or the totalitarian state, and finally with the reaction of different groups to the anarchic, non-assimilable and ostracized individual.[1]

The atmosphere in which the relations between individual and society, personality and collectivity are discussed, is also the climate of the poet, novelist and dramatist Jules Romains, pseudonym for Louis Farigoule (1885-   ). As early as 1903 he claims to have discovered by mere intuition what he called "La vie unanime." It was at this epoch that he realized amidst the traffic, movement and turmoil of a fall evening at Montmartre, how concrete powers literally absorbed the individuals. The stores devoured the clients, the streets made the cab drivers their obedient slaves, and in a flash, Romains recognized that cities, squares, theatres, workshops, soldiers' barracks, hikers' groups, cyclist bands are similar forces, transforming their members and participants into collective beings and monster units. In opposition to the economists and independently of them, the poet felt, however, that being devoured by a group means bliss to an individual and the possibility of existing in a more powerful form (*pour exister davantage*). Man absorbed by the collectivity thus undergoes a pantheistic, yoga-like elation according to Jules Romains. This feeling is multifariously expressed in Romains' poems of *La Vie unanime* (1908). The concrete demonstration of the underlying psychological facts is the short novel *Mort de quelqu'un* (1910). Here it is the sudden death of the railroad engineer Jacques Godard which creates a mourning collectivity around him, first the tenants of the apartments in the house of the deceased man, then the neighbors. Both of them are joined by the father of Mr. Godard who comes by train from afar. He "escaped" the fellow travellers with whom he was united by the eagerness to reach Paris. His ephemeral traveller group being dissolved by the arrival, he becomes free to be ephemerally linked to the neighbors and friends of his son. With all these persons he forms a new collective force of interest. They form the burial, before which the onlookers give way as though the ephemeral group were a concrete thing. Even after the burial, the dead Godard is kept alive in the memory of the mourners who thus are still united by him. Godard is entirely dead only when, after years, the last of the mourners has thought of him for the last time. "He was always on their lips" says Henri Barbusse (1874-1935), author of the world war I novel *Le Feu* (1918).[2]

Thus Romains' intuition does poetically verify E. Durckheim's fundamental thesis: "The social facts can be reduced to a force superior to the spirit of the individual." Furthermore Romains— without knowing it—takes up the old romantic concept of a collective soul, which, created by the German Johann Gottfried Herder in the eighteenth century, had not failed to influence Hegel and Karl Marx. But since in Jules Romains' time "the Marxian dream" has become here and there a magic super-organism, Jules Romains—if we may judge from certain chapters of his great novel: *Les Hommes de bonne volonté*—seemed attracted by *cette grande lueur à l'Est* (vol. XIX). To do him justice, we must add that after theoretical discussions of bol-shevism, the experience of communistic Russia in volume XX: *Le Monde est ton aventure,* reveals to him rather the collective strangulation of liberty: "the cities seem graveyards, the citizens beggars, harassed by inquisitorial-political agents, the countryside struck by famine, arrest, intellectual torture and imprisonment." To his unanimistic concept a better response seemed to be given by the military collectivity of men under arms and under the strain of war and defense. This unity gives Jules Romains the clue for the "contrainte de la collectivité" as a moral superreality, which faces the recalcitrant individual with "la honte, le déshonneur, l'impossibilité morale, la peur mystique, le tabou." The whole volume *Verdun* (XVI), from which this quotation is taken, illustrates the group-forces of mobilization, defense, attack of a nation in danger, educated by ideologies to justify and not to question the moral necessity of submission to the will of the community which represents the common good. Romains also points out the group-danger of a general strike as menacing the group of an organized state, drastically described in *Montée des périls* (vol. IX). His unanimism is at its best when underscoring the highest thrill of a nation in the hour of victory, when the dead and the living seem to fuse into a tremendous unity, as was the case in the victory parade in 1919 (vol. XVI). It was the parade of the *fête nationale* about which even the mystic Madeleine Sémer—she was present there—wrote in almost unanimistic terms: "For some minutes during the passing of the *poilus* the crowd had truly but one heart, one soul, and it was this that was wonderful and moving to tears."[3]

Jules Romains did not fail to explain that a curious communion or strange communication can exist first of all between man and woman. So before starting his unanimistic monster enterprise of twenty-seven novels, combined in a so-called *roman-fleuve: Les Hommes de bonne volonté* (1932-1947), he tried an intimate trilogy of bridal and conjugal love to bring out his point. The particular problem of the trilogy is that it is strongly based on the sexual element and nevertheless is seen in an enigmatic, almost spiritual fascination of the mutual belonging, inseparability and oneness of a couple. The trilogy therefore is called *Psyché* (i.e. in her traditional relation to Cupid). It describes the awakening of love in two young persons in *Lucienne* (1922), their marital union in *Le Dieu des corps* (1928) and their temporary separation in *Quand le navire . . .* (1929), a separation which produces hallucinatory mutual presences of Lucienne on the ship of her seafaring husband Pierre, and of Pierre in the room of Lucienne.

Jules Romains lacks humor in his great novels but has displayed much humor in his plays and in the smaller *récit, Les Copains*. Here seven enterprising bad boys, representing, however, "un être uniforme à sept têtes" by their energy and tricks transform the burghers of Ambert and Issoire from somnolent individuals within an ignored community into a conscientious unanimistic unity. The blissful consciousness of the individual that he possesses a group just by realizing that he is a member of it, is here humorously demonstrated.

The novel *Les Hommes de bonne volonté,* however, despite its literary failure and morally low concepts, is a rather serious enterprise, because it catches the collectivity of European society in well-chosen types in a pageant extending over twenty-five years, from October 6, 1908 to October 7, 1933. Its character as a novel is hampered by its journalistic style. Its value consists in the fact that it reflects at the same time the sensibility and reaction of the writer, as a typical exponent of the society depicted, to the great political and historical events. The whole was written in fifteen years, from 1932 to 1947. It is an undertaking of enormous difficulty involving innumerable types from the different strata of society in the thin story of two friends, Jallez and Jerphanion. Setting himself an almost impossible task, Jules Romains tries to follow the destiny of all the secondary types throughout many years and together with their groups. He is moreover eager to sketch natural and moral atmospheres. Thus he evokes at the beginning of the novel a late summer day of 1908 with all the people of Paris filling the streets from the early morning up to the rush hour. Romains centers the interest of all the Parisians around the newspapers foreshadowing the Balkan war. The difficulty begins with the interlocking of private relations, for instance that of the actress Germaine Baader with her lover, the politician Gurau. This obliges the author to follow the erotic adventures of the actress and the political career of Gurau throughout the novel. To show the political situation of the French parties, he introduces the conservative Marquis de Saint Papoul and the communistic schoolteacher Clanricard. Romains is at his best again when he gives the simultaneous picture of the evening trains reaching Paris from all directions. One of them brings the student Jerphanion who comes to start his studies at the Ecole Normale Supérieure. Romains introduces with less skill some supernumerary characters, including the real-estate agent Haverkamp representing materialism and big business, and he caters to the taste of the masses by inventing as a standing figure the bookbinder Quinette who will become a murderer. This is the content of volume one (*Le Six octobre*) and volume II (*Le Crime de Quinette*).

In volume III (*Les Amours enfantines*) Romains develops the character of Jallez, born a poet, and weak in action, by making him explain to his friend Jerphanion the story of a childhood love. One evening at the Ecole Normale Jallez and Jerphanion discussed Baudelaire's expression "Amours enfantines." At that point Jallez felt challenged to speak of Hélène Sigeau whom, as a pupil of the Lycée Condorcet, he used to meet with so many stratagems. Hélène loved him, too, with the same purity and romanticism. This lovely story is distributed in installments over the whole volume and keeps the political group developments at bay. At the same time it serves as a foil to volume IV (*Eros de Paris*) where the hideous facets of another kind of love, voluptuousness, are shown. The prodigal Germaine Baader severs her ties to the thrifty Gurau, now minister of the *travaux publics,* and becomes interested in the wealthy Riccoboni. The capitalist Sammécaud rents an apartment for adulterous meetings with the aristocratic Mme de Champcenais. Jerphanion starts a student love with a *modiste* and Jallez unfortunately finds again Juliette whom he knew after Hélène Sigeau. She is now married, in Paris, and with her he continues adulterously his former love.

Since Romains is not a Dante, he cannot vary his groups as Dante varied the circles of the Inferno, and with volume V entitled *Les Superbes,* he delays the reader endlessly with upper class adulterers and libidinous types. The countess of Champcenais gives herself to Sammécaud, "out of gratitude" because he arranges for the care of her mentally ill son whom the count does not want to have around him. Her resulting pregnancy and abortion serve as pretext to bring her in contact with her counter-group: *Les Humbles* (vol. VI). Low class types are shown here. The little Louis Bastide who tries in vain to persuade the wife of his father's employer not to dismiss him, the wise Abbé Jeanne who, rather fairly sketched, ponders on the problem of chastity and Christian perfection and tries to save the poor Bastide family from misery. The young political scientist

Jerphanion, wandering through the slums, receives for the first time an idea of the urgency of solving the social question lest a revolution may bring to grips the groups of the *superbes* and the *humbles*. But he regrets most of all, for himself, his not belonging to the group of groups: the Church. Therefore in volume VII (*Recherche d'une Eglise*) Jerphanion explains his craving for a spiritual community. He does not accept the Catholic Church despite certain modern movements culminating in the ideas of Abbé Mionnet who submits to bishop Lebaigue the problem of a modern worker parish. It is remarkable how early Romains introduced this burning problem. Jerphanion also rejects organized socialism, he ridicules the Masons after the information received from some of their adepts, he feels attracted and repulsed at the same time by secret societies.

After this ideological chapter in which Romains does not achieve anything constructive, provincial life is brought into the limelight in volume VIII (*Province*) by the appointment of Jerphanion as secretary to the Marquis de Saint Papoul living in a château situated between Bergerac and Périgueux. A whole electoral campaign is described in which the old aristocrat figures as a democratic candidate, is forced to receive the bourgeois in his château and to have the marriage of his daughter performed in the parish church and not in the chapel of his castle. The province is also used to put other strings together. The promising, modern Abbé Mionnet is called to the Velay to smooth out a bankruptcy scandal of a tramway enterprise in which diocesan investments are involved.

Volume IX (*Montée des périls*) shows again another constellation of groups. In this case it is the government with its dictatorial tendency confronted by a revolutionary labor organization, and all this despite the lingering peril of war with Germany. Romains reaches a peak in his novel with the description of the October strike of 1910 when Briand as premier remains master of the situation only by mobilizing the *cheminots* under martial law. The attempt against his life, however, reveals the strength of the organized proletariat and the syndicalism of the Banlieue-Nord.

A glimpse at the human situation shows Edmond Maillecotin working on the assembly line and his sister sinking into the slums of prostitution, while the bourgeois author Allory, known for his low morals, is flattering powerful ladies to have them sponsor his candidacy for the *Académie française*.

The groups affecting the foreign policy, France and Germany, appear in volume X (*Les Pouvoirs*) for the first time in sharp conflict following the Agadir incident of 1911. Gurau, with his new portfolio as minister of foreign affairs, now comes into the open again. Despite his absurd behavior in private life, in the metro, in the homes of rich ladies, and despite his vulgarity, he has clear ideas on the necessity of a Franco-German under-standing. But in the long run, the group of the anti-German militarists, stronger than he, prepare the *Recours à l'abîme* (vol-ume XI). The formation of the Poincaré cabinet is a certain step toward war. Artistically, the approaching danger is stressed by the presentation of Jerphanion as a soldier in Reims, and by the businessman Havercamp buying a shoe factory as an investment for war. Strikingly, Romains himself moves downhill in this volume since he seems to enjoy the description of the moral quagmire and the hell of the flesh in which a society doomed to war is living without any responsibility.

A very weak volume XII (*Les Créateurs*) shows the scientist groups at work, while Jallez, sending articles as correspondent from Germany, is devoured by nostalgia for Juliette. Volume XIII (*Mission à Rome*) centers around the French government's fear that the Vatican might side with Austria and Germany in case of a conflict. Poincaré sends Abbé Mionnet on a half-official mission to Rome to find out the situation. Although the chapter reveals Romains' lack of information concerning diplomatic customs, he prepares an impressive and unbiased scene between Mionnet and the overwhelming personality of Cardinal Merry del Val. A symbolic volume XIV (*Le Drapeau noir*) underlines the inevitability of war since the boat which brings Jallez back from a trip to London has hoisted a black flag which intimates a catastrophe. The more serious news of the moment is reflected in Jallez' moral decision to break with Juliette while Jean Jerphanion has married a colleague from La Rochelle, Odette Clisson. The serious events of volume XV (*Prélude à Verdun*) bring Romains back to his unanimistic style. Forgetting his previous *cochonneries,* he gives a truly dramatic picture of the mobilization and the tragic stalemate of the front after an indecisive, short mobile war. Jerphanion as a lieutenant discusses with his comrade Fabre the possibility of ever breaking the stalemate, while Gurau, as minister of war, meets with Marshal Joffre to see what can be done about active warfare. Meanwhile the German emperor has ordered the attack on Verdun.

The presentation of the battle of *Verdun* (volume XVI) is a masterstroke. The secretly prepared great attack on the 21st of February, 1916 is introduced by the daily inspection of the front by Major Gastaldi, accompanied by his lieutenants Mazel and Raoul, who are caught unawares by the German artillery. Then the strategic view is cleverly widened. The reader is taken to the highways around Verdun where reinforcements are moving in from all sides. Among these reinforcements is the 151st infantry regiment with the company of Lieutenant Jerphanion, coming from the Argonne front. The French civilians fleeing from the villages near Verdun are obstructing the highways. Jallez with his red trousers and his blue capote, representing the rear echelon, is sorting mended army shoes in Paris. He remains the less useful, feminine type.

Volume XVII (*Vorge contre Quinette*), after the two Verdun volumes, is rather a liability. Since Romains has not eliminated Quinette, he feels obliged to invent a juridically objectionable story. Quinette is no longer pursued for his crimes since he is now a veteran in counter-espionage. But the story turns absurd when the advocate who studied Quinette's crimes in the records of the prosecutor Fachuel approaches Quinette to learn from him the technique of murder, and, a promising pupil, from lust attempts to murder Quinette's wife. Poor also is volume XVIII (*Douceur de la Vie*) in which Jallez spends the winter of 1919-20 in Nizza writing poems. There he meets a charming salesgirl,

Antonia, with whom he enjoys a precious afternoon in Falicone, and then debases this romantic adventure by revealing it to a new mistress, the shrewd Madame Elisabeth Valavert. There he also meets Quinette and the new bishop of Digne who is nobody else but Msgr. Mionnet.

The group problem is taken up again in volume XIX (*Cette grande lueur à l'Est*) where the question arises whether the light of the Russian revolution is a dawn or a fire destroying the whole European civilization. This actually is the problem which splits up the Parisian socialists in 1922 when the West tries to form in Geneva a Society of Nations together with the Russians. Jerphanion gets ready for a trip to Russia as secretary to minister Bouitton, while Jallez, after having attended the Geneva meetings, goes to Rome to study the opposite grouping, the young fascism.

But Romains' eagerness to compose detective and suspense stories also sends Jallez from Italy to Russia in volume XX (*Le Monde est ton aventure*) and while Jerphanion with his minister reaches Moscow, Jallez at the same time happens to land in Odessa, and is arrested as a spy. Released from prison, he meets Jerphanion in Nizhni Novgorod. Returning to the postwar provincial groups in volume XXI (*Journées dans la montagne*) Romains introduces Jerphanion as candidate of the radical socialist party for deputy of his own department, Haute-Loire in the Velay. The wine merchant Grousson takes him around in his car and brings him to the Vaurevauzes farm, famous for an incestuous double murder in which Jerphanion becomes interested. Thus Romains' taste for detective stories flares up again.

Volume XXII (*Les Travaux et les joies*) is a rather meaningless filler. It seems to everybody as if they were already living *entre-deux-guerres,* as though the concern with one's own happiness were subordinate for a moment to the greater political worries. Nevertheless new moral aberrations are introduced. Havercamp has bought a château in the Touraine. Sammécaud, in his sixties, has assumed pederastic propensities, spending a time of voluptuous living with friends in Tunis. This picture is contrasted by an ephemeral group idyll: Jerphanion, Jallez, Odette and an old friend of theirs are invited to a castle, live through days of simple and true happiness in remembrance of their youth and as *hommes de bonne volonté*.

Volume XXIII (*Naissance de la bande*) shows the rise in France of fascist terror groups, and this in close combination with erotic perversion. This volume is written with a captivating *élan* and realism. A young, still decent girl, Françoise Maieul is disgusted with the cynicism of her Sorbonne professors and with the new style of secret societies like the A. A. (*Action d'abord*) in which young gentlemen and ladies not only meet for wild orgies, but sponsor the political terrorism of the ex-communist Douvrin, who, surrounded by a bodyguard, disturbs and terrorizes political assemblies. Volume XXIV (*Comparutions*) is like a technical liquidation of the destinies of persons of the novel who seem to have become superfluous. So we get a kaleidoscope: the murderer Quinette is dying in Nizza; Havercamp loses the confidence of the London bankers; Jallez at forty still starts flirtations with the neighbors of his Parisian apartment, also with Germaine Baader, now a spiritist and owner of the Renaissance Theater; the once poor boy Bastide silently works as an engineer in Africa for the French Empire; and Françoise Maieul refuses a wealthy marriage with a rich Brazilian.

In volume XXV (*Le Tapis magique*) Romains for the last time yields to his most vulgar weakness, the expatiation on erotic variations. Competing with Paul Morand he shows how Jallez while on his flying-carpet lecture tour through the whole of Europe tries to escape the hardships of life by throwing himself into one erotic adventure after the other, while his friend Jerphanion at the recommendation of Gurau has become *ministre des affaires étrangères*. Volume XXVI (*Françoise*) brings to an end the love adventures of Jallez. Having learned from Françoise Maieul that his books mean much to her, he meets her and they become engaged. Volume XXVII (*Le 7 octobre*) does not succeed in giving a clear final weave of all the threads of the story, but it is a mighty finale. After twenty-five years Paris is shown going to work again on an autumn morning. The busses are over-crowded; many use their private cars. Everybody listens to the radio news. Flying has become so usual that Jerphanion interrupts a meeting of the Radical Social Party in Vichy to take a plane to Paris where he joins a party of old friends, and is introduced by Jallez to his charming fiancée Françoise. But above all these peaceful activities there is, for the second time within a quarter of a century, the threat of a dark cloud from Germany: Hitler. This fact changes Jerphanion from a pacifist into a defender of a preventive war. Gurau has become prefect in Tours where, at a dinner, he discusses the situation of the poor lower clergy with the new archbishop Mionnet. The minds of people are confused. Jerphanion's educational product, the young marquis Saint Papoul, has become a theoretical Leninist while the work-man Maillecottin as a foreman looks upon the whole question of communism as a hoax. France has tried to appease Hitler. Jallez is sitting in the airport restaurant with Jerphanion, who flies back to Vichy and sighs: "Ce monde moderne serait tout de même quelque chose de bien épatant, si"—and everybody might finish the sentence for himself: if war were not again around the corner.

This gigantic piece of *reportage* in the form of a *roman-fleuve* may be read as the story of group-struggles in the modern world. But it is doubtful whether Romains' unanimistic ideas would come to the fore clearly from this novel if the reader were not acquainted with his earlier works, particularly his early poems. In one of them he describes the absorption of the theatrical audience, an ephemeral group literally spellbound by the actor group on the stage. And this ephemeral group is so strong that it almost resists dissolution, for the theatergoer still enjoys his group-pleasure at the moment when the curtain drops. Conse-quently the group (*la foule*), formed by its common attention to the performance, is slowly dissolved only when the impression

of the performance vanishes. The spirit of the theater group therefore apostrophizes the public leaving the theater in this way:

> Les hommes déliés, glisseront par les portes,
> Les ongles de la nuit t'arracheront la chair.
> Qu'importe!
> Tu es mienne avant que tu sois morte.
> (*Ode à la foule qui est ici*, 1909).

This "frisson nouveau," as another unanimist, Georges
Chennevière (1884-1927), calls it, was strong enough to create
the language of a new collectivity. This language reflects life,
creation, birth, growth and death as a continuous condensation,
absorption and dissolution by which either the individual is
devoured by the group or the group made conscious by the individual. As Leo Spitzer has shown,[4] stress is laid on the unanimistic
verbs of action, such as: *exister plus, exister davantage, exister
mieux, exister un peu, plus ardemment; se dépêcher de naître,
lâcher, vomir des hommes, déborder, foisonner; diluer, dissoudre,
évaporer, pulvériser, volatiliser, rarifier la ville; scier la masse
des corps en lamelles fragiles, s'éparpiller, crever, s'accroître, se
dilater, gonfler, enfler; engraisser, absorber, nouer de nouvelles
étreintes; se résumer, se ramasser, se recroqueviller, se cailler;
vibrer, trembler, frissonner, onduler, transfuser, fondre (comme
la graisse, le beurre, la neige), émaner, respirer, aspirer* (typical
mystic expressions of the seventeenth century), *arracher;* to which
I would add: *envelopper, engluer, amortir la pointe qui pénètre,
s'allonger par coulure,* and groups of substantives such as *pâtés
de maisons, pullulement des maisons, paquets de maisons,* etc.

Leo Spitzer has also given a running stylistic commentary to
Mort de quelqu'un along these lines.[5] André Cuisenier[6] and others
have made pertinent remarks on the earlier art of Jules Romains
but have failed to see the structural-stylistic achievements of the
chef-d'oeuvre where the radical unanimistic style appears only in
certain places, mainly in the introductory and concluding volumes,
and in the grandiose and central volume on Verdun. Alfonso
Reyes[7] sees in *Les Hommes de bonne volonté* an attempt to grasp
the fragmentation of life in which certain things have no conse-

quences and in which the fulfillment of destiny is uncertain. This factor hints at the necessarily symphonic and not tectonic structure of the novel. The language is simple and attempts rhetorical heights and truly poetic unanimism only in emotional situations. Vulgarity is incorporated on too large a scale even as to vocabulary: "C'était estomaquant." Journalistic style in a disturbing sequence of present tenses is combined with a real dearth of subordination of thought in the clauses. This makes the narration a pseudo-newspaper and a collection of pastiches. There are dwarf sentences: "Les élèves sortent. Mais pas elle." There are parodies of surrealism: "La main gluante coule vers le miroir." Romains skillfully intersperses the narrative with lyrical addresses, anaphoras and repetitions stressing the writer's empathy. His *monologues intérieurs* do not fail to absorb the reader. Certain words and expressions of preference, "Tout se passe comme si . . .," *frissonnement, salaud, visqueux, nausée,* anticipate the bleak world picture of Sartre. Like him, Romains is precise and renders perfectly "le grouillement tentaculaire" of the early twentieth century. As Vorge, hero of volume XVII of the *Hommes de bonne volonté,* therefore puts it, the style of unanimism "ne manquait pas d'un certain surnaturel, mais ce n'était là qu'un surnaturalisme grossier."

The rhythm changes according to the events narrated or the phenomena described. Formulas worthy of a classic moralist are frequent. Comparisons are striking in their fitness[8] and critical adequateness to certain types of persons: "Allonger le bras *comme les buveurs* que le médecin examine," "Un si mystérieux sourire . . . qu'ils étaient impatients de connaître *comme une femme* le cadeau qu'on lui apporte enveloppé." An insinuating suggestiveness envelops the reader as in "Jour d'hiver doux et feutré"; and "Le choc des poubelles qu'on ramasse." Striking metaphorical sense impressions stand out: "On entendait à chaque instant siffler la dernière syllabe de ses 'merci' " or "le tramway chansonnait constamment sur les rails." The propensity to the voluptuous is balanced by a rather robust brush used for many little tableaux. The daring use of long adverbs, as in Gide, gives the phrases a striking importance: "une manière juridiquement incontestable," "une bouche largement ouverte," "quelque chose d'exquisement scandaleux," "les toujours mêmes rues aux boutiques fermées." Antithetic frescos (Elysée and Banlieue-Nord, military and civilians on the roads to Verdun) are the *pièces de résistance* of the lavish descriptions and reappear again stylistically in dense imagistic paradoxes such as: "prêcher la révolution sociale en tenue de soirée."

Although Jules Romains' strength consists in the presentation of ephemeral groups and "milieux," in no case has he coped adequately with the group par excellence, the family. On the contrary, he debased the mother-child relation beyond imagination in his recent novel *Le Fils de Jerphanion*. The family problem was dealt with more authentically in two other less revolutionary *romans-fleuves*, namely in *Les Thibault* (1922-1940) by Roger Martin du Gard (1881-   ) in whose eight volumes the tension between two generations is analyzed in masterly fashion,[9] and in *La Chronique des Pasquier* (1933-1944) by Georges Duhamel (1884-   ), where the different destinies of the children of a good bourgeois family are described and explained by character, circumstances and social change.[10]

Les Thibault is centered around Jacques and Antoine, the sons of a stern widower and Catholic gentleman, founder of a receiving home for wayward children. Jacques has a classmate, Daniel Fontanin, offspring of a Protestant family, with whom he escapes from school. The two boys are arrested in Toulon and brought back to Paris by the police. While Mme Fontanin simply forgives her romantic son, Jacques' father confines his son to his prison-institution.

Antoine achieves the liberation of Jacques by persuading Abbé Vécard, confessor of M. Thibault père, to seek permission for the boy's return to his family. Now he lives together with his brother, a young doctor, in Antoine's bachelor-residence. Jacques starts a serious flirtation with the niece of the concierge, and has tender feelings for his half-sister Gisèle, but his real love belongs to

Daniel's sister Jenny. Jenny as well as Jacques, however, stifle their mutual love because of the pharisaic education they have received from their families.

Jacques is admitted to the Ecole Normale, but escapes from his studies and from Jenny. After wandering around for a long time, he is introduced into a revolutionary club in Lausanne. Antoine, prospering as a surgeon, enters into a passionate relationship with his neighbor Rachel. Meanwhile M. Thibault père becomes seriously ill and Antoine dedicates much of his time and art in a vain effort to cure him.

Through a novel written by Jacques in which he disguises his story as an incestuous problem, Antoine trails him to Lausanne and gets him back to Paris, this time to the deathbed of his father. The two brothers meet Gisèle there. The death of M. Thibault père, who suffers terribly, is brought about by euthanasia. Jacques breaks with Gisèle, and Antoine explains to Abbé Vécard his atheistic-hedonistic concept of life.

The outbreak of the first world war is imminent. Differing ideas on war and peace separate the two brothers interiorly. Jacques, now engaged to Jenny, and Antoine, living with his mistress Anne de Battaincourt, are called to war. Antoine is mobilized. Jacques flees to Switzerland and in a fit of generous sacrifice drops from an airplane peace manifestoes between the enemy lines. He is shot down and killed. Antoine returns after three years with a gas-poisoned lung and lives as a doomed patient in a sanatorium, keeping a diary up to his last day. He had become a friend of Daniel who returned from war as a leg-amputee. Daniel with brotherly and fatherly love takes care of the last offspring of the Thibaults, Jacques' and Jenny's illegitimate son, Jean-Paul, while Jenny and Gisèle live together with Mme Fontanin in their common grief. Jenny tries to sublimate her disillusioned love for Jacques.

Martin du Gard's picture of a family is panoramic, like Romains' *Hommes de bonne volonté,* but on a sounder, more limited scale. Unanimism is partly used as a stylistic device, but journalistic style and poetical language alternate in an even more drastic fashion than in Romains. The *Epilogue* to *Les Thibault* adds a new tragic ephemeral group to those known through Romains, namely *La Clinique des Gazés,* comparable to the more elaborate picture of the collectivity of consumptive people in the *Magic Mountain (Der Zauberberg)* by Thomas Mann.

More than Romains, Martin du Gard has stressed the religious problem, particularly in the conversations of Antoine with Abbé Vécard. He has dedicated also, however, a special volume, *Jean Barois* (1913), to this matter. This book was written still under the clouds of modernism and, although the young Barois sees the shakiness of an arranged compromise between science and faith which would take all the mysterious, revelatory and supra-intellectual elements out of the latter, his decision is for science as a substitute for religion. Martin du Gard, out of his personal serious predicament, describes rather objectively the loss of faith of the pious but rationalistic Jean, whose educators are not in a position to cope with his questions, and drive him from senti-mentalism into pragmatism without ever bringing up the role of wisdom, awe, human limits of understanding, and the inscruta-bility of the mysteries of life as the self-evident assets of religion in its relationship with science. Since in the revision of the Dreyfus case the Catholic public opinion sides rather with order as under-stood by the army than with justice, Barois feels morally entitled to become an outspoken anti-clerical. This is, however, not as easy for him as for his friend Luc, because his religious family ties are strong: his pious wife Cécile leaves him, and his daugh-ter becomes a nun. All these circumstances, and, as Martin du Gard would have it, Barois' irrational fear of extinction, bring about his death-bed conversion. It is assumed that at the stronger and more confident age of forty he had made, like Ernest Renan, a provision by which he anticipated and revoked a possible death-bed conversion out of weakness; so Cécile and Abbé Levys burn his testament.

Granting Martin du Gard's inclination to make a point for the position of the non-believer this *roman à thèse* is moderate and dignified. One-sided in its almost exclusively intellectual discussions, it offers an unusual structure, consisting of scraps of conversations, situations, unlinked impressions, with so few and so economically used elements that its clever prose sometimes seems to consist rather of dramatic dialogues with some stage directions.

Georges Duhamel in the ten volumes of *La Chronique des Pasquiers* deals in another way with the group *par excellence,* the family. This *roman-fleuve* is written, in certain passages, in the sense and form of the more programmatic unanimism of which Duhamel was once a fervent adherent, namely in the times of the common life of the writers of the abbaye de Créteil which incidentally Duhamel evokes in the fifth volume of *Les Pasquiers,* "Le Désert de Bièvres" (p. 188 ff.) and which he describes lavishly in *Le Temps de la recherche* (Paris: Hartmann, 1947, p. 29-38), but with a negative judgment on this type of community life: "L'homme est incapable de vivre seul et il est incapable aussi de vivre en société" (*Bièvres,* p. 259). In *Les Pasquiers* the problems of science, art, economics and the interlocking of all the activities of the modern world are rooted in the destinies of the incorrigible old Don Juan, Doctor Pasquier, the wise Mme Pasquier-Delahaye and the five Pasquier children, Laurent the biologist, Joseph the materialistic businessman, Ferdinand the uneducated boy, Cecile the pious pianist, and Suzanne the shrewd actress. We follow their evolution through tragic and happy days in school, apartment house, business, garden party, artists colony, concert, theater, laboratory, newspaper office and stock market. Here the whole social sector is brought into the family life. The language of the presentation is reduced to normal proportions, and the psychology of the characters is stressed. It is not marred by neo-naturalistic experiments such as spoiled the dignity of Romains' attempt. For his philosophy of life, naturally, Duhamel was branded *Le bourgeois sauvé.*[11] In presenting a family and an epoch Duhamel is fundamentally interested in individuals raised almost to classical types,[12] as seen from the men and women of the three Pasquier generations. What is absolutely original, however, is the varied reaction of the family group to one and the same event, e.g., the waiting for the news concerning the alleged testament from the *notaire du Havre,* which is a study of collective psychosis differentiated by the characteristics of each family member.[13]

Georges Duhamel, despite the fading importance of his problems, remains on the stylistic level a first class writer of the strictly logical sentence vibrating with genuine feeling. Describing the life of families of all shades he brings out the aspects, noises, and smells of a house with evocations more impressive than those of Honoré de Balzac. His imagery, never showy, is used only to bring out the psychological climate of a situation or a place. Thus he would express the sadness of a pawn shop by the following "personification": "Les vêtements pendus à des clous, à des patères, à des crocs, semblaient solliciter la compassion du fossoyeur" *(Le Désert de Bièvres).* His easily sketched sentences are heavy with meaning and are avowedly kept on a moderate level of rhythm and euphony. He uses all the grammatically admissible inversions of word order to bring out psychological shades in an unassuming manner. Grammatical possibilities are used and distinguished with care and delicacy to the point of never saying *aimer voir* for *aimer à voir,* or *de toute part* for *de toutes parts* (see René Georgin, *La Prose d'aujourd'hui,* Paris, André Bonne, 1956, p. 315-18).

The disintegrating tendencies in the still quite united family in Duhamel are relatively harmless, however, when we compare them to the recent picture of a family hell as given (after the manner of Mauriac's *Le Noeud de vipères)* by Hervé Bazin (1918-   ), grand nephew of the *bien pensant* writer René Bazin. In Hervé Bazin's *Vipère au poing* (1948), the hatred between a mother, Mme Rezeau (called Folcoche) and her children, particularly her son Jean (called Brassebouillon) simply proves that family harmony or any group harmony cannot be established artificially. The group harmony in Duhamel still reflected traditional bonds of solidarity which do not exist any more for the revolutionary views of this younger generation.

The secular solidarity, discussed until now, lacks the cosmic, moral and religious background which it has in Catholic authors like Paul Claudel and Georges Bernanos, although the motif of solidarity itself is not their central topic. Claudel, accustomed by his diplomatic service in the Far East and in Brazil, often evokes France, Europe, and other countries where he has relatives and friends, and finally all regions under the sun where God's creatures live in a fraternal union without knowing it: "Le soleil de ses premiers rayons ras troue la feuille Virginienne. ... Il pleut à Londres, il neige sur la Poméranie pendant que le Paraguay n'est que roses, pendant que Melbourne grille."[14] Thus Claudel includes in solidarity a boundless, unlimited group: "toute la surface de la terre avec l'herbe qui la couvre et les bêtes qui la peuplent ..., le coup de vent (qui) du même trait ... emporte la crache de la mer, la feuille et l'oiseau du buisson, ... la fumée des villages et la sonnerie des clochers."[15] Here unanimism includes nature, too, and becomes really a cosmic "connaissance" of all being, not only a human turmoil of the modern world.

Bernanos has well seen the tragically moral side of the problem of solidarity: "Je crois que si Dieu nous donnait une idée claire de la solidarité qui nous lie les uns aux autres, dans le bien comme dans le mal, nous ne pourrions plus vivre, en effet" (*Journal d'un curé de campagne,* p. 204). A particular kind of unanimistic feeling came from the cult of the unknown soldier, e.g., in Anatole de Monzie's *Destins hors série* (1920), where "L'anonymat total ... tend à exclure le rôle des individus pour exalter l'action des masses."[16]

André Malraux (1901-   ), fascinated by the *conquistadores* and their spirit of adventure, praises the absorption of the individual by the mass, because "L'ensemble de l'escadrille est plus noble que presque tous ceux qui la composent" (*L'Espoir,* p. 233).

André Malraux's dream of a revolutionary collective fraternity was once decidedly communistic but corrected by an individualistic anarchy. He pleads for the primacy of mass interests only, "parce qu'il y a de la misère . . . , qu'il y a ces gens riches qui vivent et les autres qui ne vivent pas" (*Les Conquérants,* 1928, p. 81). Thus, when he encounters the cravings of the masses, the individual adventurer type with leader instincts awakes them to a greater consciousness and feels bound to excite the inert crowd. Malraux, before his retreat into art, seems to look at the absurdity of this situation with interest. Therefore he delights in the terrible awakening of India and China to a conscious political life despite his concerns as a European. He is astounded that the Ghandis and the Tcheng-Dais with their idealism of passive resistance created proud Eastern masses for the first time in history, "les coolies chinois qui sont en train de découvrir qu'ils existent" (*Les Conquérants,* p. 15). His literary problem, however, is to show patriotic idealism at grips with the brutality of a more realistic kind of "liberation."

Nothing is more dramatic than the arrival of the narrator on a boat bound for Hong-Kong at the beginning of *Les Conquérants,* when the Kuomintang in Canton want to paralyze England in the Far East by a general strike and limited warfare, while the individual terrorists (General Hong) resort to a more radical *action directe* of torture. The Russian helpers as organizers of the Chinese half-bolshevik revolution must make a decision as to whom to support. In this catastrophic set-up, anarchic individualism and a blind collectivism come to ominous clashes. This antagonism is centered around two top figures, Garine and Borodine. The hero Garine is a true revolutionary anarchist, not interested in collective action, but in his personal and courageous behavior. Life to him is absurd by definition, and still less tolerable if there are no individual values. Thus in the brutal attempt of Borodine to conquer Hong-Kong for Russia against England, to Garine's mind the Chinese are being used only as tools to create an impossible collective paradise of coolies who will remain coolies none the less after a heavy price of blood, sweat, tears, death, and terror. Garine, born in Switzerland, in his dignity as an individualist and adventurer had left the *légion étrangère* in 1916 because he was disgusted by the kitchen-knife killing of enemies in the trenches. Now he has the greatest contempt for the red bosses such as Borodine, who with leader-like ambition and cattle-like instincts know only one principle: the party line. Garine in full disobedience refuses to praise the tortured and killed murderer Klein at his funeral. Were he not to flee from China and soon to die himself from an advanced ailment he would certainly be liquidated.

This first intentionally stylized journalistic account in literary history, renouncing any novelistic plot, gives a very correct analysis of the attempt of intellectuals to liberate economic slaves by making them, as far as human dignity is concerned, still more miserable than before. But in this weird picture of absurdity and lack of moral principles, there is at least the adventurer-critic who by his courage lays bare the rotten foundation on which the collective organizers of a new society try to build.

In *La Condition humaine* (1933, Prix Goncourt) the vile sham collectivity of International Communism is again given the lie by the heroic individualism of the abandoned victims of the Shanghai insurrection. The background of the critical action is the entrance of the then Kuomintang general Chiang Kai-shek into Shanghai. With the permission of Russia, he tortures and kills all the bolshevik Chinese revolutionaries who are now his prisoners. Disillusioned by this treason, terrorist Tchen tries to assassinate Chiang, but is killed himself as he throws a bomb under the empty car of the general. The revolutionary leader Kyo avoids being thrown alive into a locomotive boiler by taking a cyanide pill. His friend Kato, however, is burned to death in the engine after having given his pill to two weaker comrades. A heroic death at least means to these men release from the *condition humaine* from which ordinarily there is no escape, as there is none from hunger, sex, and death. Beyond this the individual is recognized as tragically lonely.[17]

In his 1952 appendix to *Les Conquérants* Malraux has stated his fundamental rejection of bolshevism in very plain language:

"Nous proclamons d'abord valeurs, non pas le bourrage de crânes, mais la vérité . . . : la garantie de la liberté, c'est la force de l'Etat au service de TOUS les citoyens" (p. 178). Malraux stresses struggle, even murder, to maintain the promethean liberty of man, who imposes his will on *angoisse* first by considering life itself a meaningless, absurd affair, and second by preferring even suicide to the only evil, defeat, for defeat is consenting to one's fear of death. It is a sexual weakness, a shameful and contemptible weakness. To overcome the fear of death in oneself one must overcome first the fear of killing another man and "laver l'assassinat de toute signification impure."[18] Malraux's once youthful ideology has to be considered as objectively destructive. It practically recommends: "Le meurtre sans but," "la révolution sans espoir," "l'héroisme comme drogue," "la torture comme valeur métaphysique," "un monde où l'homme n'existe qu'écrasé."[19] Malraux thus anticipates fictionally what was to become Hitler's program: the pitiless struggle of the jungle, imitated by mankind, the sadistic, self-sacrificing pride which ignores Calvary and prefers the paradoxical sacrificial killing of the savages, a nightmare more terrible than anything Hieronymus Bosch could ever imagine. Here a new mass psychology has changed all Christian values into their Nietzschean contrary. Such heroes seem to be martyrs, but are really criminals because their desire "d'engager l'essentiel de soi-même" and "d'exister contre la mort"[20] is not meaningful and transcendental, but simply brutal.

It is pathetic to see how a misinterpreted ethics does guide Malraux's heroes. Tchen starts out with a brutal, well-planned political murder before daring the suicidal assault on Chiang's car. The first seems envisioned as a daring but sinful exercise, the second as an atonement for the first. Curiously enough, though Malraux's barbaric extremism has been tempered by his flight into art, his professional domain, he has not given up his revolutionary attitude. Even his art criticism is impregnated with the idea of *révolte* as is evident in *Les Voix du silence* (1948) or, as the larger edition is called, *Psychologie de l'art* (1950). Here he contrasts the rebellion and the ascetic fight against life in Egyptian, Assyrian and Medieval art with the rejected equanimity and balance of Greek art which does not know the *condition humaine.*

Malraux, none the less, is under the fascination of the mass spirit. Introducing his short story *Le Temps du mépris* (1951) on the imprisonment of the communist Kassner by the Nazis, he explains that any worthwhile type in history was in communion with his society, possibly in a dialetical opposition, but never in an isolation from it: "L'individu s'oppose à la collectivité, mais il s'en nourrit. . . . Romain de l'Empire, chrétien, soldat de l'armée du Rhin, ouvrier soviétique, l'homme est lié a la collectivité qui l'entoure."[21]

Malraux's style is of an unusual loftiness and lightness. It has been called cosmic in view of its images of ascension culminating in that of the aviator's soaring into infinite heights.[22] His structures are perfect so that the dramatic and pyramidal composition, e.g. in *La Condition humaine,* is demonstrable down to the developments of the single motifs and the gradual intensification of the images.[23] These images shift with abruptness from the abstract to the concrete sphere and move around three predominant themes: death, agony, and torture.[24] They contain the destructive and horrifying symbols so typical of our time, the shrill sound of the whistle symbolizing anguish, insecurity, shock; the gnawing and pestilential insects symbolizing the undermining of the bases of any ideals in modern man; and the cheap trumpery ware symbolizing the ostentation of a world without values and without art.[25]

Modern civilization is uncannily evoked by particular types of epithets or equivalent phrases strikingly drawn out: "Une atmosphère de cabine de bains" (*Les Conquérants,* p. 9); "La silhouette clopinante d'un marchand de soupe" (*ib.,* p. 57); "Le roc militaire d'où l'empire fortifié surveille ses troupeaux: Hong-Kong (*ib.,* p. 10); "Une adolescence de jeune Juif occupé a lire Marx dans une petite ville lettonne avec le mépris autour de lui et la Sibérie en perspective" (*ib.,* p. 17); "nuit informe trouée ça et là de taches carrées: les échopes anamites" (*ib.*, p. 22); "Des grands paquebots illuminés, avec leurs étages de hublots dont les reflets en zigzag se mêlent dans l'eau à ceux de la ville" (*ib.*, p. 30); "cette nuit écrasée d'angoisse" (*Condition*, p. 181-2); "une épouvante à la fois atroce et solennelle" (*ib.*, p. 184).

Leitmotifs underline the seriousness of an action, as when Tchen, after committing the murder, constantly refers to his delicate conscience (*Condition*, p. 221). The *monologue intérieur* of a character appears in parenthesis within the flow of narrative. The events are left at the decisive moment in an unbearable suspense (e.g., Tchen's attempt on the life of Chiang Kai-shek) and are clarified much later by indirect means of reporting from eyewitnesses or rumors. The unity in Malraux's stylistic tendencies results from the use of the purest language, free from the crudities and banalities of Romains or Sartre, from an effortless narration abundant in excellent phraseology, in the presentation of fragments (*fiches de police*, dialogues, radio news) in an apparently unpolished form without interpretive remarks as background. Malraux within his wealth of new verbal coinages is always faithful to "la phrase claire et nette."[26]

Comparable to Malraux, Henry de Montherlant (1896-   ) seems uninterested in the success of war, or victory to avoid further wars. This latter idea, particularly associated with Charles Péguy's concept of *La juste guerre* and embodied in his great poem *Mystère de la charité de Jeanne D'Arc* (1910, see chapter six), would be unrealistic to Montherlant, the champion of a super-individualistic Nietzschean *héroisme pur*. He has sung the *Chant funèbre pour les Morts de Verdun* (1924) and he has made the statement:

> Si à la prochaine guerre Verdun est pris, quelle ironie de lui avoir consacré un monument! . . . A Verdun, j'ai vu la gloire de l'homme. . . . Peu m'importe quels étaient ses buts; peu m'importe, s'il les a atteints. . . . Que tout soit remis en question, rien n'a prise sur cette vertu humaine portant en soi son accomplissement et sa fin, donnée au monde comme l'oeuvre d'art.[27]

War is for Montherlant, as it were, the very best *art de mourir:* "Comme un sage enfant, quand sa mère l'appelle: 'Mon chéri, il est l'heure de rentrer,' je laisserai où ils en sont, mes châteaux de sable."[28] Thus one understands that the hero of *Le Relève du matin* (1920) and *Le Songe* (1922), namely Alban de Bricoule (Montherlant), enlists "pour se plonger dans les éléments," for *Le Service inutile* (1935). In peace time Henry de Montherlant finds particular sources of daring love and hate in the Olympic games and the bullfight. He thus continues with another ideology a line which had first been traced by Maurice Barrès in his *Du sang, de la volupté et de la mort,* written as early as 1894. Montherlant has a feeling for the mysterious complementary relations between death and love, both soliciting a decision from the individual. From the girl as a comrade in the fight he does not tolerate tender feelings which belong to an interior world. Therefore Alban destroys the life of Dominique Soubrier, the impossible girl-comrade and army nurse who fell in love with him *(Le Songe).* The external warrior and Viking who tries to solve the problems of a chaste strength outside the spiritual realm and remains to his great humiliation womanbound, combines "l'amour des jeunes filles et leur destruction," just as he unites "la tendresse pour les taureaux et l'extermination des taureaux," the desire of loving and killing the same object of fascination.[29] Actually the bull to be fought (*Les Bestiaires,* 1926), the enemy to be killed (*La Relève du matin,* 1920), the girl to be loved (Soledad in *Les Bestiaires*), all are similar objects of an irrational hatred-love relation, a relation which is not unknown to Hemingway's *Death in the Afternoon* (1932), where, too, "The formalized murder joins these curious lovers [bull and matador] . . . , death uniting the two figures in the emotional, aesthetic and artistic climax of the fight."[30] Behind Montherlant's superreality of force is a terrible superhuman pride, which, as Yves Gandon has excellently proved, is reflected in typically repeated expressions such as "au sommet," "C'est moi Montherlant qui parle," "Moi-Montherlant qui écris," "sentiment jovieu," etc.[31]

This individual pride, inconsiderate toward the community of men, is, however, a complex phenomenon. It certainly has something to do with the Catholic ascetic education of the author who in his youth was a *brancardier* in Lourdes. This complexity is not only the clue to his later contemptuous and cynical attack on all femininity, as in his prose tetralogy *Les Jeunes filles, Pitié pour les femmes, Le Démon du bien, Les Lépreuses* (1936-38); it is also the key to his curious alternative already mentioned, manhood or love, and has reached its oddest incarnation in the more recent drama *Le Maître de Santiago* (1947) whose hero repents having generated his own daughter even in legitimate wedlock and persuades her to "try" together with him, her father, to become a mystic. The best literary realization, however, remains the novel *Les Bestiaires* (1926). Alban de Bricoule, training himself as an amateur *torero,* has developed a serious inclination for Soledad, the daughter of the Duke de la Cuesta, owner of a great cattle ranch in Andalusia. When he wants to make a date with her, a somewhat complicated enterprise given Spanish customs, she makes it dependent on his courage to kill the wildest and most dangerous of her father's bulls, *Mauvais Ange.* Her pride, however, is no match for Alban's. He actually kills the strongest bull, but in so doing kills also his love for Soledad whom he despises for her cruelty. This nuclear scene is set in an enormous background of dissertations on the art of bullfighting, on the Mithras cult as containing the spirit of the *corrida,* the bond allegedly created by the bull between pagan and Christian traditions, on Mithraistic migrations of the soul and the doctrine of purgatory. It cannot be denied that from the braggadocio, nay the courage, energy and youthful optimism, which keep Montherlant's blasphemous cynicism at bay, comes a certain fascination to the reader.

Montherlant's style is characterized in general by a strong imagery, by a strictly logical word order and by a choice of metaphors in close connection with his original thoughts. Love for archaisms, even for *pastiche,* and syntactical liberties makes him reconstruct the classical thought-image with its maximatic and aphoristic implications: "On peut nous ôter les branches qui dépendent des hommes, mais on ne peut nous ôter la racine qui ne dépend que de Dieu" *(Port Royal)*. One may furthermore apply to Montherlant's own style what he has found in that of Saint-Simon: conciseness despite expatiation, and substance despite his simple pleasure in writing. But what distinguishes him from Saint-Simon is his poetical ability to observe and transform a landscape, a group of human beings, a situation: "On arrivait à la pièce d'eau. Des jeunes filles s'y miraient, et l'eau, pleine de leurs châles aux couleurs éclatantes, semblait une ville de papillons derrière un voile de cristal" *(Les Bestiaires)*. Like Flaubert, Montherlant is capable of imparting to such chromatic sentences an agreeable rhythm (see René Georgin, *La Prose d'aujourd'hui,* 329-331 and 195-196).

The unifying force of danger is the subject of *L'Equipage* (1923) by Joseph Kessel (1898-   ), where the spirit of comradeship in the air force officers Herbillon and Maury in the face of death is stronger than their jealousy and love for the same woman. These men, according to Kessel, belong "au royaume des âmes nues," comparable to the mystics. Kessel has an almost conservative style, apparently unsuited to his advanced views. He couches all his fresh post World War I insights into a language abounding with simple past tenses and imperfect subjunctives.[32] This style makes sense, however, if we consider that sacrifice and boldness, as old as mankind, are still behind the modern craftmanship of warfare. Here there is the secret formulated by Ernest Psichari (1883-1914): "Toutes les terres sont belles pour un jeune soldat. Toutes les aubes sont fraîches, naives, puisqu'on s'y lève joyeux, confiant dans sa force, audacieux."[33]

The second world war produced a particular situation of comradeship, that of some French soldiers split from their regiments and facing the rebuff of their English allies who had no room to take them to England after Dunkirk. It was described with some erotic injections by Robert Merle (1908-   ) in his novel *Weekend à Zuydecoote* (1949).

The ironical Jean Giraudoux (1882-1944, see chapter four) in his war books from World War I: *Adorable Clio,* and *Retour d'Alsace* (1916), as well as in his radio propaganda during World War II, knows "the elevating and purifying effects of danger."[34] "Giraudoux," says Marcel Thibaut, "a réussi à caresser la guerre elle-même." Hinting at the comradeship extended in peacetime to the sports team, Thibaut quotes Giraudoux's flippant remark: "La moitié du péché originel est peut-être rachetée . . . pour le corps par le sport."[35]

Peacetime sport as daring spirit, as a danger, and as a value is highly praised by Antoine de Saint-Exupéry (1900-1944) in his flyer novels, *Courrier Sud* (1929), *Vol de nuit* (1931), *Terre des hommes* (1939), *Pilote de guerre* (1941): "Le pilote dispute son courrier a trois divinités élémentaires, la montagne, la mer, l'orage" (*Terre des hommes,* p. 9). *Vol de nuit,* Saint-Exupéry's masterpiece, defends the spirit of sport and enterprise, and at the same time presents the serious moral problem of whether personal happiness should be sacrificed to socially important experiments of value to future generations. On this problem, Simone, married only six weeks to the daring pilot Fabien, and Rivière, director of the Toulouse-Buenos Aires airline which is exploring the possibilities of night flights over the Andes, are at odds. She, of course, cannot understand why her husband must crash and die for commercial greed. In a thunderstorm, he had to mount to a high altitude, lost his direction and ran out of gas. Rivière, on the other hand, will not, because of losses of single lives, stop the night flights and thus lose the competition with maritime transportation. The story, which also shows the flyer torn between the love for his wife and the duty to his task, poeticizes the episode of the establishment of the French airlines in Argentina during the twenties, an enterprise which was confided to Saint-Exupéry himself. The author has used the profile technique in a stupendous way. He takes the reader in turn to the cockpit of Fabien's plane moving through the starry sky, and to the apartment of Simone who, watching the skies with fear and trembling, incessantly rings the phone of the administration of the French airways. By a third switch the reader is taken to the office of Rivière who is waiting for cables and news from airfields together with air mail from Europe and information from all the planes en route. When Fabien stops giving any sign of life, he simply removes the little flag symbolizing Fabien's plane and its route from the map; apparently coldblooded, but no less heartbroken than Simone, he has to encourage, with the decision of a leader, new pilots to the still uncertain enterprise.

The style is pregnant with symbolic imagery culminating in the hand of the pilot on the wheel which represents the same spirit of strong guidance that emanates from the energetic character of Rivière. The symbol of grasping, possessing, losing the cities over which the pilot flies reflects his destiny.

The new spirit of sports which will be discussed further in the next chapter was also propagated by Jean Prévost (1901-1944) who wrote *Plaisirs des sports* and *Dix-huitième année,* and by Gilbert Prouteau in his *Anthologie des textes sportifs de la littérature* (Défense de la France, 1948).

The war and sport spirit assumed a particular form during the resistance movement in Hitler-occupied France. It is the top-ranking poets rather than the novelists who lent their pen to this new and serious form of patriotism in which the love of France and the hatred of the oppressor have an equal share. This movement produced in Henrijk Keisch's song *Les Partisans français* a kind of a New Marseillaise: *Ami, entends-tu le vol lourd des corbeaux?* which contains arousing strophes like this:

> Montez de la mine,
> Descendez des collines,
> Camarades!
> Sortez de la paille
> Les fusils, la mitraille,
> Les grenades.

To this group belongs Louis Aragon (1897-   ) who, known for his surrealistic vagaries since 1930, now raged against the Vichy regime in his quatrains: "J'écris dans un pays dévasté par la peste . . . Où . . . Hérode régnait quand Laval est dauphin."[36] Paul Eluard (1895-1952), sobered by the tragic events after his period of surrealism, joined Aragon, who was in the same situation, with his *Chant Nazi* and its refrain in the Villon style: "Ainsi chantent, chantent bien, les bons maîtres assassins." The more gentle Pierre Emmanuel (1916-   ) meditates on the horror of the system of the hostages (*Otages*): *Ce sang ne séchera jamais sur notre terre.* Georges Ribemont-Dessaignes, author of *Ecce homo* (1945), offered the most desperate and hopeless complaint: "O le désert qui s'ouvre . . . , O paradis perdu . . . , le temps barbare est né." He asked in a series of apparently joking variations throughout eight stropes: "Qu'est-ce donc que tout ce rouge?" (*un coucher de soleil? une averse de roses? une bouche fardée? un pourpre cardinalice?*) until he reached the climax with: "C'est le sang de l'homme qui coule." The publisher Pierre Seghers (1906-1957) accused "le massacre des innocents" (*Octobre*) and dreamed of final rest and peace in Paris (*Quand le cap des misères changera ce nom . . . Quand le train d'Arpajon retrouvera les Halles*).[37]

The experience of Hitlerism during the German occupation and the Vichy regime also produced direct fictional repercussions such as the novel of Maurice Toesca (1895-   ), *Le Soleil noir* (1946). He tells the story of a girl, Anneliese Muller, who, engaged to a gestapo officer, Kraus, sacrifices her brother Bernhard as a traitor to the nazi party. The vicissitudes of a French village during the occupation are described by Jean-Louis Bory (1921-   ) in his rather colorless tale *Mon village à l'heure allemande* (1945). The alleged depravities committed by the nazi soldiers with minors are stigmatized in the novel *Paille noire des étables* by Louis Parrot (1906-1948).

The most dignified examples of the resistance to Hitlerism are the short stories of Jean Bruller (1902-   ) who writes under the pseudonym of Vercors. *Le Silence de la mer,* reminiscent in a sense of Maurice Barrès' *Colette Baudoche* (1909), shows the resistance in the reserved attitude of a French girl who rejects even the serious and respectful homage of a noble young German officer Werner d'Ebrennac, billetted in her parents' home. Despite her love for him, she never responds to his cultured and literary monologues except by a heartbroken "Adieu," when after months he tells her that by choice he is going to return from his *poste de commandant* to his former field division.

One of the most tragic collective units was that of the prisoners of war. Among those who wrote about it is Francis Ambrière (1907-   ) who in his *Les Grandes vacances* (1946) describes the life of prisoners in seven stalags, stressing their escape projects, the comforting letters from their wives, and their resistance to German orders.

The individual solitude and abandonment of the inmate of the prison camp is treated by Marc Blancpain (1909-   ) in *Le Solitaire* (1945), and by Paul Tillard (1914-   ) in *Mauthausen*. Jacques Perret (1903-   ) was even serene enough to treat the theme of captivity with humor in his novel *Le Caporal épinglé* (1947).

The tortures of the camps are stressed by David Rousset (1912-   ) in his novel *Les Jours de notre mort* (1947). Rousset also wrote an essay on the subject, the title of which became a slogan in France: *L'Univers concentrationnaire*. He offers a slightly camouflaged description of all the horror of a camp where the SS fuehrer with provokingly shiny boots tests the solidity of the gallows, mixes up the garments of his naked victims under the disinfecting showers, shouts menaces throughout the camp and brutalizes the inmates day and night.

Pierre Gascar (Prix Goncourt 1953) invents *Les Bêtes,* the ghastly story of the prisoners of war who steal from a neighboring circus the meat destined for the animals. When the nazis shoot the main culprits in this affair, their corpses are thrown as a restitution to the animals. In *Le Temps des morts* Gascar deals with the mass extermination of the Jews and the nazi soldiers salving their conscience in this gruesome occupation. The mass rape of German women by the conquering Russian invaders finds a treatment in Jean Cordelier (1912-   ), *Les Yeux de la tête* (1953) where a French ex-prisoner of war is killed defending his German sweetheart against such a bolshevik monster.

Another recent form of community spirit, developed in connection with the resettlement of transferred groups, mainly ethnic groups living together and migrating under political pressure, is reflected in Pierre-Henri Simon's novel *Les Hommes ne veulent pas mourir* (Paris: Seuil, 1953). It is here that the adaptation of a village of Banat Germans of Yugoslav nationality to the new living conditions of a camp near Stuttgart produces the revival of this community as "Neudorf" after the aged, the sick and the non-cooperative members have died or gone away. A love story centers around Hans, the unphilosophical man of enterprise, and the schoolmistress Elsa, who is seeking the meaning of life. She desperately tries to find a middle road between Christianity and communism, but is doomed to die of cancer. There is finally the ghastly group of European emigrants and refugees in America described by Michel Mort (1914-   ) in his novel *Les Nomades* (1951).

The older generation confronted with the new social and political forms of individual-absorbing groups said its word in critical rather than fictional form, but the reaction of each of its authors is different. André Gide (see also chapter three) since his *Voyage au Congo* (1927), where he saw the exploitation of the colored people by the white man, and until his *Retour de l'URSS* (1936), where he saw the barbarism of mass-organization based on conformistic lies and mere materialism, dreamed of an ideal superreality of more "human" modern masses. In this ideal society, truth and social justice would prevail and the curious absorption of the individual and the reciprocating reabsorption of the community by the individual, corresponding to Jules Romains' vision, would become possible. These ideas may be found in Gide's *Journal intime* (1934-36) and *Nouvelles Nourritures* (1935). In Russia he believed he at least saw "l'utopie en passe de devenir realité" (*Retour de l'URSS*, p. 15). Gide's view is equivalent to Malraux's, who, when connected with the Spanish Civil War, wrote that "Les hommes unis à la fois par l'espoir et par l'action, comme les hommes unis par l'amour, accèdent à des domaines, auxquels ils n'accéderaient pas seuls" (*L'Espoir*, p. 233). Gide's unanimistic conception of the collective spirit is revealed by his style: "L'individu se fond ici dans la masse, est si peu particularisé qu'il semble qu'on devrait, pour parler des gens, user d'un partitif et dire non point: des hommes, mais: de l'homme. Dans cette foule, je me plonge, je prends un bain d'humanité" (*Retour de l'URSS,* p. 37). Although Gide retracted and recanted his communistic leanings in his *Retouches à mon retour de l'URSS,* the collective problem obsessed him to the point of obstructing his art until his death: how to reconcile the inalienable right of the individual to self-development, and the urgent necessity for the diminution of the misery of the masses.[38] Gide created the formula which was to fit Camus, Saint-Exupéry, Montherlant, even Sartre: "Je sympathise avec l'individu; je m'éperds dans la multitude" (*Journal* II, p. 94).

Georges Duhamel, too, as early as 1928, in his *Voyage de Moscou,* was in a certain way fascinated by the communistic reality. His corrections, however, are considerable. After having complained that illiteracy subdues intelligence, he has many objections of a moral order: "Je n'aime pas cette atmosphère de délation mutuelle . . . qui semble un souvenir de la terreur. . . . Je trouve tout a fait pénible d'entendre des hommes sérieux et sages baisser la voix et murmurer: . . . 'Mais n'y a-t-il personne derrière moi?'."[39] A collective superreality seems bound to remain a spiritual domain.

Romain Rolland (1866-1944), the author of the now antiquated *Jean-Christophe* (1903-12), in which he was striving for Franco-German friendship, was led by an extreme pacifism and a fanatic anti-fascism, to give communism a chance in the fourth part of his cyclical novel *L'Ame enchantée* (1922-32). In this part, called *L'Annonciatrice,* Marc, the son of the heroine Annette, marries the Russian political agent Assia as a symbol of an eternally revolutionary France linked to any popular movement of "liberation." Marc, who himself becomes a bolshevik agent in Italy, is killed in a brawl with fascist adversaries in Florence. Although ideological problems are paramount in Rolland who fought for peace during World War I and for justice during the mock trial of Van der Luppe, 1933, there have been repeated attempts, at least in Germany, to appreciate him as a literary artist whose style is informed by music[40] and to analyze his narrative technique.[41] A *Société des amis de Romain Rolland* is publishing a periodical to assess critically the merits of this author and his works.

That the younger generation in France has become more or less communistic is no secret, although many of them are reluctant to submit the dignity of human thought to the brutality of a party line, as is shown by many plots in the contemporary novel and drama. If the fad of French literary communism must be given an ancestry, it may be found in the enthusiastic poems *Hourra l'Oural* (1934) by Louis Aragon, mentioned already among the poets of the resistance.

Socialism as a noble *mystique* of altruism and human solidarity versus socialism as a compromise and a materialistic *politique* was a preoccupation of the peasant poet Charles Péguy with his strong Catholic heritage (see chapter six). In his insisting on *mystique* versus *politique,* he developed a style in which repetition, permutation and concentration have the effect of hammering the ideas of the author into the mind of the reader. His ideas are condensed in his prose treatise: *Victor Marie Comte Hugo* (1911). As the man sacrificing his individuality to the nation, he addresses his convert friend Ernest Psichari, the "centurion" in Africa, in this style of interlocked wreaths, carpet designs and *emboîtements:*[42]

> Vous . . . qui dans une maison glorieuse des travaux de la paix avez réintroduit la guerre et l'antique gloire guerrière . . . Latin, Romain, Français, vous qui de tous ces sangs nous faites un sang français et un héroisme à la française. . . . Pacificateur, Edificateur, Organisateur, Codificateur, Justificateur . . . vous qui imposez la paix par la guerre . . . vous . . . faites la paix par les armes (*Victor Marie Comte Hugo*).

If in Péguy the social and the military spirit tend to merge, Ernest Psichari (1883-1914), like Péguy a heroic victim of World War I, goes still further. In *L'Appel des armes* (1913) he even states that "l'armée était la seule réalité que le monde moderne n'avait pu avilir, parce qu'elle n'appartenait pas au monde."[43]

This conception of the collective spirit of daring sacrifice in the army was implicitly contradicted by *"la douceur de vivre"* as an ideal for the individual. Péguy and Psichari identified the military spirit with the ascetic spirit of the Church, became converts, fought and died on the battlefield as a kind of hero-martyrs. Those who survived the struggle of World War I came back rich in heroic experiences. Philippe Barrès in his *La Guerre à vingt ans* called war "un sombre et sublime univers où l'esprit approcha du fond des choses." Henry de Montherlant, having seen both world wars and the *entre-deux-guerres* as well, distinguishes between war and peace as "ce qui compte et ce qui ne compte pas,"[44] but, as we have seen above, for quite different reasons.

CHAPTER II

THE VOICES OF SEX, EARTH AND CLAN

IT BELONGS to the very essence of twentieth century realism to perceive nature neither by a romantic exaltation of the soul nor by an intellectual analysis of the mind, but by the senses and the instinct, or better by the whole personality. This is an instinctive existentialism *avant la lettre,* and is the key to pan-sexualism as well as racism in French literature. The proper pioneers along this line were such outstanding women writers as the Comtesse Anna de Noailles (1876-1933) and Gabrielle Colette (1873-1954), the latter recently honored by an edition of her *Oeuvres complètes* in fifteen volumes (Flammarion).

The Comtesse senses with her womanly heart *Les Forces éternelles* (1921) of nature. She identifies her own cravings with these forces. Her own carnal troubles and fear of death appear to her like calls from the earth, as we can see in *Les Eblouissements* (1907). She knows nature by a kind of total participation and communion, by actually becoming one with it:

> Etre dans la nature ainsi qu'un arbre humain,
> Etendre ses désirs comme un profond feuillage,
> Et sentir, par la nuit paisible et par l'orage,
> La sève universelle affluer dans ses mains.

This so-called *naturisme* of the former Rumanian princess Brancovan, Mme de Noailles' maiden name, may be partly a direct outcome of her Rumanian soul, at least of her knowledge of the primitive eroticism of the popular Rumanian songs called *doinele,* one of which has been reported by P. Morand:

> Que l'ourse fasse ses petits
> Et que fleurisse l'osier,
> Car j'ai eu mon plaisir avec Elle.
> (*Bucarest,* p. 229).

Sidonie-Gabrielle Colette experienced the same animalistic link between man and nature as did Mme de Noailles. Therefore she was able to write fascinating animal stories (*Dialogues des bêtes,* 1905; *La Paix chez les bêtes,* 1916). Likewise her human creatures show the instinctive life of animals as is the case with the uneducated youths and children of her novels *Chéri* (1920), and *Le Blé en herbe* (1923). They are free from any moral hamperings or ethical considerations. "Colette a chanté un hymne dionysiaque à la nature, à l'instinct, à la volupté, à la vie."[1] Her message, open to human tragic possibilities although resulting from sensuous, even decadent situations where one ought not to expect them, is best conveyed by *Chéri* and *La Fin de Chéri* (1926). The two-volume novel is a study of pure animality in the society of the demimonde, to which belong Fred's (Chéri's) mother, Mme Charlotte Peloux, as well as her friend Léa. Léa at forty-three gives up all of her lovers since she has fallen in love with Chéri who is nineteen at that time. After six years of a debased intimacy their curious love relation is gravely disturbed by Chéri's marriage. He belongs, however, so strongly to Léa that he neglects and estranges his wife Edmée, and in a "bonne entente monstrueuse" keeps on returning to Léa again. Meanwhile Léa has grown older; she is now forty-nine, he twenty-five. War breaks out. Chéri, returning after some years of military service, finds Léa an old woman, fat, gray and wrinkled. In his despair he spends days and nights in the home of another old courtesan, La Copine, simply gazing at her collection of Léa's photos dating from the time when she was young and beautiful. Pondering over these pictures and the bygone "happiness" he had experienced with her, and also disturbed by the idea that he may not have been her great love but just one of many lovers, he lies down on a couch, takes his revolver and kills himself.

After the recent literary immorality of Jean Genet, Louis-Ferdinand Céline and Jean-Paul Sartre, that of Colette seems almost redeemed as "le plus lucide témoignage de l'asservissement de la créature a l'instinct."[2] Colette's analysis of the animal instincts in man is far away from any demimonde romanticism of the Dumas and Augier type. Colette's *naturisme* is to be compared rather with the scientific attempts to interpret love and death in the world of animals as serious phenomena of instinctive life.

In André Demaison, *La Vie privée des bêtes sauvages,* or Léon Binet, *Scènes de la vie animale,* or Maurice Maeterlinck (1862-1949), *La Vie des abeilles, La Vie des fourmis* and *La Vie des termites,* the frontier between man and beast seems to be eliminated. In these works it has been demonstrated that male flies execute a wild dance before their females in order to win their favor, male birds offer their brides a gift (some food) before their union, female firebugs coquettishly attract the males by signaling with their light, bees and mantises kill their males after the wedding night to continue their love with other males after their "crimes passionnels."[3]

Jean Giraudoux, introducing the animal-picture book of E. Bourdelle, makes the suggestion that human life is bound to be enriched by the influence of animals. "Il semble que la vie humaine . . . ait besoin autour d'elle d'un induit pur et brut qui est la vie animale. . . . La tension vitale s'accroît, aux dépens de la tension humaine, quand le lion circule autour des cases."[4]

It is this idea that Colette also embodies in most of her motifs and in her style. She uses the cat as a symbol of the female type because the cat does not care any longer for her kittens or anything else as soon as she hears from afar the amorous call of the tomcat, "l'appel du Matou," which she understands with all its implications:

> Mes dents courberont ta nuque rétive, je souillerai ta robe, je t'infligerai autant de morsures que de caresses, j'abolirai en toi le souvenir de ta demeure et tu seras, pendant des jours et des nuits, ma sauvage compagne hurlante . . . jusqu'à l'heure plus noire où tu te retrouveras seule, car, j'aurai fui . . . las de toi, appelé par celle . . . que je n'ai pas possédée encore . . . et tu te réfugieras dans un long sommeil tressaillant de rêves où ressuscitera notre amour, . . . viens! (*Les Vrilles de la vigne,* from *Les plus belles pages de Colette,* Flammarion, 1930, p. 35.)

And just as this cat resembles a woman, so the well educated and still innocent Vinca from *Le Blé en herbe* resembles a cat, when she suggests in her jealousy to Phil that he should have seduced her and not another woman. And Léa, called by Chéri Nounoune, is also a cat, caressed by this name, and Colette herself "soupçonne qu'elle pourrait être chienne" and said: "Je pense à épouser un jour un énorme chat." Actually in one novel, *La Chatte* (1933), she did present herself as a cat, and in another one, *La Vagabonde* (1910), reflects on her music-hall adventures as those of a kind of strutting animal. This kind of animal-like and uninhibited eroticism is not accompanied by any comic Rabelaisian flavor or ironical refinements of civilization. Incidentally, Emile Verhaeren (1855-1916) was also exposed to this *naturisme* when he revived the Flemish spirit of his fellow countryman Peter Paul Rubens during the first decade of this century. Verhaeren gives the theme wider scope by rooting the animal instincts of men and women deeper in blood and soil. This is the case with his collections of poems called *Les Flamandes, Les Forces tumultueuses* (1902), and similar troubled works.

Colette beyond her fundamental insight into instinctive life has a masterful grasp of the language. Her marvelous nature evocations play a structural rôle. When a short time before Chéri's planned marriage he and Léa clash for the first time, the old *demimondaine* becomes overwhelmingly aware of the difference of age between her and the spoiled young pimp. Colette at this moment associates Léa's autumn of life with the autumn in nature and thus transforms a vulgar scene into one having human dignity:

> Léa tourna les yeux vers la fenêtre. Une pluie chaude noircissait ce matin d'août et tombait droite sur les trois platanes, déjà roussis, de la cour plantée.
> —On croirait l'automne, remarqua Léa et elle soupira.
> —Qu'est-ce que tu as? demanda Chéri.
> Elle le regarda, étonnée: Mais je n'ai rien, je n'aime pas cette pluie *(Chéri).*

Colette's sentence, says Desonay, sometimes light, sometimes developed, is curved and cambers like the spine of a cat.[5] It expresses with a thriftiness of adjectives and a minimum of highlights all the sensations and nuances of life, and achieves with its restraint in the description of daring scenes something like "la sainteté du style." Colette rejects technical terms, slang and foreign language expressions. Her choice of words and critical shades of meaning subjectively never imply any connivance, but only sensuality considered "natural."[6] Colette's to-the-point images have a wide range in which appear visual, auditory, and olfactory elements separately and in synthetic combinations.[7] Her style closely follows the changing tone of narration, expressing vivacious sensations, colorfulness, combined with precision and poetic musicality. There are passages savorously overdone of an apparent but not real virtuosity.[8] Colette's message has been enthusiastically defined by André Gide who shares her viewpoint in *L'Immoraliste* (1902) and *Nourritures terrestres* (1897). In the latter he states:

> Une éparse joie baigne la terre. . . . Chaque animal n'est qu'un paquet de joie. . . . Tout aime d'être et tout être se réjouit. C'est de la joie que tu appelles fruit, quand elle se fait succulente; et quand elle se fait chant, oiseau. . . . Que l'homme est né pour le bonheur, certes, toute la nature, l'enseigne. C'est l'effort vers la volupté qui fait germer la plante, emplit de miel la ruche, et le coeur humain de bonté.[9]

Fortunately Gide, who sometimes was wiser than Colette, gave also the criticism of this statement:

> J'éprouve que chaque objet de cette terre que je convoite se fait opaque, par cela même que je le convoite et que, dans cet instant que je le convoite, le monde entier perd sa transparence, ou que mon regard perd sa clarté, de sorte que Dieu cesse d'être sensible à mon âme.[10]

Naturisme virtually includes the theme of pan-sexualism. It finds its most impressive representation by women, who are by definition nearer to nature than men: "Mme Marie Dauguet parle de l'ivresse d'exister, Mme Hélène Picard se dechaîne dans son *Instant Eternel*."[11] According to those authors, to use the words of Germain Nouveau:

Tout fait l'amour

. . . .

Même le pas avec la route,
La baguette avec le tambour.

Même le doigt avec la bague,
Même la rime avec la raison,
Même le vent avec la vague,
Le regard avec l'horizon.

Such pan-sexual but still poetical views foreshadow the erotic, factual cynicism of the midcentury which is the sad heritage of the disillusioned generation left by World War II. It comes drastically to the fore in *Les Corps tranquilles* (1948) by Jacques Laurent (1919-   ). This drawn-out novel depicts the disgusting behavior of the couple Anne Coquet and Monique Chardon who interpret their sex life as a simple physiological necessity such as eating or defecation, so that they lose all the human dignity which still prevailed in the suffering of Léa and Chéri.

An attitude steeped in instinctive life without any moral considerations, if it spreads from the individual to the nation, leads to situations with dangerous pagan implications: "un culte du soleil et des étoiles, un culte des ancêtres, un culte des arbres, et . . . ces naives dévotions aux mystères sacrés de la vie des corps."[12] The pagan earthy-spirit made its first appearance when Maurice Barrès (1862-1923), following Count Gobineau (1816-1882), pointed out in his *Les Déracinés* (1897) that all tribes and races, modern Frenchmen as well as any tribe in the jungle, are primarily, fundamentally and exclusively rooted in their soil. He thought that everyone who would not feel that way is a decadent. The sap of the soil and the vital forces of the race are identical. They are its very existence. Beyond them there cannot be anything else but vain ideologies. Therefore the Parisian professor Bouteillier who had studied Kant, but lost his anchorage in his tribal soil, can only poison the souls and weaken the bodies of the seven sound youths from Lorraine who are confided to his guidance. These boys are lost if they do not reject the philosopher's ideas as alien and foreign to them. Actually they did not receive any moral foundation and got involved in crime. At the tomb of Napoleon I, "professeur d'énergie," they reject philosophy to the advantage of national action based on racial instinct. This is the meaning of *Les Déracinés*.

But Barrès, who in many quarters is erroneously considered a champion of the Church, goes farther. He suggests that the tribal forces of the soil will advantageously cope not only with all ideologies, but with all spiritual forces, which are looked upon as artificial modifiers of the sound substance of a nation, self-sufficient and able to guide itself. Barrès with this "intuition" was consistent and temerarious enough to consider Christianity as a philosophy which was merely capable of maintaining these forces of the soil. He leaves no doubt that "la prairie" is older than "l'église," "the grove" opposed to "the chapel." Long before Christianity there existed many chtonian hills with allegedly magic qualities, like the one depicted by Barrès in *La Colline inspirée*. In this story Mount Sion-Vaudemont in Lorraine is said to have excited pagans to mysterious rites and cults earlier than it inspired Christians to their devotions. Therefore it could still inspire the heresiarch and ex-priest Vintras in the nineteenth century to establish a heterodox cult. Paganism, the Church and Vintras, without knowing it, simply were serving the forces of the soil. The Celtic forces are the oldest in France. Therefore their "vieux dieux depossédés" reappear throughout the centuries, their goddesses become the beautiful saints; the blood of Velleda is older than that of Jeanne D'Arc. With this teaching, Barrès established the "Mystère en pleine lumière." No philosophy, no metaphysics, no supernaturalism is needed for him. "Il préférait rechercher la permanence des forces instinctives, même vagues: cela lui semblait, au moins, encore réel."[13]

Barrès' views, in spite of some stronger accents on the cultural side of the picture, were unmistakably shared by conservative critics like Charles Maurras (1868-1952), Pierre Lasserre (1867-1930), Ernest Seillière (1866-1955), Jacques Bainville (1879-1936), Robert Brasillach (1900-1945). Their France is the old Gallic France with the order of a Roman civilization and the genuinely absorbed spirit of a Catholic (in the sense of a Latin) culture.

In Léon Daudet (1868-1942), Barrès' closest follower, the forces of nature stifle the other forces entirely and are betrayed even by his language. "La sève du langage monte en lui" says Yves Gandon, because he finds him to be "épris jusqu'à une panique ivresse de la vie."[14] Just this has been the case, only on a more individual basis, with Mme de Noailles and with Mme Colette. The English author David Herbert Lawrence has best described the "panique ivresse" of an earth-bound race feeling: "You look at the strong body of a trunk. . . . The only thing is to sit among the roots and . . . not bother. . . . All the old Aryans worshipped the tree. . . . Here am I between his toes . . . and I feel his great blood-jet surging . . . a rootlust" *(Fantasia of the Unconscious).*[15] This rootlust is the key to the work of Jean Giono (1895-   ).[16]

Giono intends to write the eternal epic of his little Provençal clan in Manosque through fables the people will enjoy just as, he thinks, Homer intended the epic of Ithaca in his *Odyssey* *(Naissance de l'Odyssée,* 1930). Rootlust pushes him on, however, to a more animalistic eternalization of the race as reflected in the mirror of an epic myth. There is a force unleashed on men and animals which drives them to uninterrupted procreation: "La fureur d'exister eternellement qui avait donné l'odeur aux brebis et faisait battre les béliers, me dévorait aussi." This unconscious desire of an immanent eternal life of the race, envisioned less brutally from Jean de Meung to Walt Whitman, seems to Giono the most indestructible force in history. Therefore in the symbolic city of *Le Chant du monde* (1934), called Ville-Vieille, the inhabitants celebrate still today "La Mère du blé." Two thousand years of Christianity with all its softening effects, education, compromise and substitution of values were not able to kill Ceres or Cybele or the Magna Mater. The daughters of the village have still the spirit of the bacchantes and give terrible proofs of it. They serve "la divinité des sèves et des forces." In *Le Grand troupeau* (1931), the wives of the absent warriors or their young widows run half-mad because of their forced abstention without any spiritual or merely rational mastering of their desires. In

Regain (1930) the heroes Panturle and Gedemus move in a kind of fertility spell around Arsule. These erotic-racial forces, however, are only one side of the pagan earthy spirit of Manosque. The other side is brutality and destruction: "Tout est trop mou," says Giono in *Le Chant du monde,* "tout est trop femme. Et qu'on se casse la gueule un peu, les uns aux autres."

That Giono's naturalism has a highly symbolic power may be best seen in his novel *Batailles dans la montagne* (1937). Here there is described a terrific inundation in a mountain valley with the all-devastating torrents, the heavy atmosphere and the muddy smell before and during the catastrophe, the fear and the running wild of animals, including a dangerous bull, and the helpless despair of men, but also the receding of the water and the calming down of nature. But what nature symbolizes happens also in the human sphere. Boromé, the rich owner and old bull in human shape of the "ferme du Chêne Rouge," after having had forty-four children from twenty-eight women, feels lonesome on his alpine seat and hires Sarah as a helper. She comes with her fifteen-year-old daughter Marie and becomes his wife. Down in the valley, however, she loved the much younger and vigorous Saint-Jean, forty years old like herself. After Saint-Jean has proved himself an indomitable hero during a storm by dynamiting rocks to release the water at the right places, and by killing the village bull which endangered everybody's life, he appears on "Le Chêne Rouge" to take Sarah from Boromé. He is ready for a fight with the old man when the innocent question of Marie: "Qu'est-ce que vous faites-là" calms him down just as the wild storm was calmed down. Saint-Jean silently retires to the village, overcoming his stormy passion and making a sacrifice for the peace of Sarah and Boromé.

In this novel where the uncanny effect of a bleak light in a ghostly night cut by the shadows of heavy clouds is described, Giono vies in impressionistic and convincing traits with Pierre Loti: we believe with him the deserted mountains populated by "des personnes faites de pluie et de soir." Giono's artistry makes us believe in the sincerity of his *Précisions* (1939) in which he distinguishes between his own ideology of the sources of the soil and that of Adolf Hitler, although he shares with him the individual and racial intoxication by blood, "le sang [qui] ne s'arrête pas de battre, et de fouler, et de galoper, et de demander avec son tambour noir d'entrer en danse" (*Que ma joie demeure,* 1935, p. 185). Giono is such a stereotyped romantic of rootlust that since his first great novel *Un des Baumugnes* (1929), he has not added anything new to the pattern. His recent attempt in *Le Hussard sur le toit* (1951), a novel of the cholera, probably to compete with Camus' *La Peste,* starts a new trend.

Mixing brutality with a keen imagery in a slipshod French which is not authentic peasant language, the style of Giono is marred by a "maniérisme barbare" and by overdone sensuous phrases, by a prolixity of showy details, by an animism which is more *précieux* than natural, by a halucinatory picturesqueness which gives the sensation of "the sudden baring of a leg."[17] These mannerisms and *éclairs* represent his "normal" rootlust style in which the river Durance reflecting the light of the sun is metaphorically called "cette garce [qui] fait sa risette blanche" and the life of men "cette grande saumure dans cette épaisse boue"[18] upon an earth where "le glacier pose sa joue contre la belle joue du ciel" (*Batailles dans la montagne,* p. 169), et "le ciel se poudre d'un sable d'argent qui étouffe les étoiles" *(Naissance de l'Odyssée).* On the other hand, he is also capable of giving by rapid enumerations the impression of ghastly fatality.

A parallel but more refined case of earthy inspiration is Charles Ferdinand Ramuz (1878-1947). He really extols his Swiss village Gully-sur-Lausanne in the Vaudois canton, and "the holiness of the earth."[19] In his many works he identifies himself, by a fascinating empathy, with his peasant countrymen of almost magic beliefs overlaid with poorly understood Christianity. *Derborence* (1934) tells about the disappearance of a village of that name, described in a leit-motivistic form: "le mot chante doux" —"triste et doux"—. It is the story of a catastrophe in the mountains comparable to Giono's *Batailles dans la montagne* which appeared three years later. The newly wed Antoine Pont has been buried under falling rocks, while his wife Thérèse is expecting her first child. The destructive and constructive forces of life come in conflict in the fate of Antoine, who though digging himself out of the débris cannot overcome for a long time the obsession that he still has to find his fellow worker, old Seraphin, who was really killed in the accident. Ultimately the constructive forces of life triumph. The thought of his heir to be born cures Antoine. When he breathes the alpine air again, he thinks:

> Ça entre, ça a un goût et un parfum, ça descend dans le corps, ça coule dans l'estomac, ça circule dans le ventre. . . . Le corps tout entier entouré de soleil maintenant . . . (p. 129).

In *La Grande peur de la montagne* (1925) Ramuz describes an epidemic among the cattle in the mountain pastures. The desperate peasants of the village interpret it as a diabolic spell and resist the return of the animals from the mountain in order to avoid contagion for the cattle in the village. The situation is unbearable to Victorine who is thus separated from her lover, Joseph. She tries secretly to ascend the mountain during the night to see him, but has a fatal accident. Joseph, also agitated on his part, enters the village against the law, coming down from the mountain pastures, and finds in Victorine's house people at her wake. Not comprehending the tragedy, he murmurs: "Ce n'est plus elle, on me l'a changée." Thus his madness begins. The superstitious in the village feel definitely assured of the "revolt of the mountain" when a horrible thunderstorm drives the cattle, running wild, and their remaining herdsmen down from the pastures to the village. There the superstitious and the rationalists fight a bloody battle in the cemetery after the burial of Victorine.

The range of Ramuz' presentation of earth and clan is narrower but more human than that of Giono, sharing this quality with the so-called earlier regionalists (René Bazin [1853-1932], Henri Bordeaux [1870-   ], Henri Pourrat [1887-   ], Alphonse de Chateaubriant [1872-1951]), but he exhibits real skill in varying the primitive reactions to the catastrophes of nature in *Si le soleil ne revenait pas* (1937); to evil in *Le Règne de l'esprit malin* (1917); to the redeeming power of a maiden in *La Guérison des maladies* (1917), topics which in themselves give his peasants a note of human dignity.

Frenchmen are so deeply convinced that Ramuz has done a disservice to the French language, was incapable of writing a good story, and treated problems far away from the French literary interests, that Henri Peyre, for instance, devotes only a footnote to him in his history of the contemporary French novel.[20] Nonetheless, the general discussion of the style of Ramuz has been considerable. French critics find it "âpre et raboteux,"[21] and reduce his procedure to a formula: "stylisation lente et mono-tone, mais cependant par larges traits, avec soudain un épisode poignant."[22] Swiss sympathizers find that his indiscriminate use of the pronoun *on* acts like a weird power subduing man to things, and gives his style a magic force.[23] French critics resent the inclusion of Vaudois expressions in Ramuz' literary language,[24] but the Swiss Pierre Kohler, more profoundly and in a more positive way, has seen the greatness of Ramuz' style in a stream-of-consciousness technique in which heroes and author merge.[25] Ramuz' central art consists in the successive destroying and recre-ating of space in slow-motion-picture technique with magnifying devices, the insisting on particular details, the hammering on the reader with series of relative clauses and the simultaneous narrat-ing of different actions by a motley of changing narrative tenses.[26] By stylistic means Ramuz reveals an unknown psychology in a new world.[27] His landscape description is outstanding since he depicts mountains, streams, and lakes not only as they are linked to men and animals and to the changing atmosphere, but also as they are reflected in the minds of wanderers climbing or descending the Alps, and he stresses the silence or sounds of human activity, of beasts or birds[28] as actually experienced or heard. He is such a perfect painter that he can challenge the real artists of the brush, impressionist as well as cubist, mainly Cezanne[29] whose geometric landscapes he likes and best imitates.

The rootlust spirit is also responsible for the trend to look into the roots of other peoples, Jews, Arabs, Negroes, Chinese. The brothers Tharaud, Jérôme (1874-1952) and Jean (1877-1953)—

Jérôme once was secretary to Barrès[30]—try especially to study Judaism and Mohammedanism. The eternal Semitic forces of soil and blood, according to them, produce the Oriental religious spirit. They are good observers but very bad interpreters since they see the unique and naturally inexplicable Semitic mono- theism and the mysteries of the redemption through late borrow- ings from Greek myth: "La même profonde imagination a tou- jours inspiré les Sémites de Syrie. Sur les rives du fleuve Adonis, comme au bord de la Kadicha, on s'est représenté le divin sous une belle forme humaine qui succombe en apparence à la mort. Mais . . . toujours le Dieu ressuscite."[31] Stronger than this insidi- ous attack which reduces the Resurrection to a Semitic fancy, is the statement that the differences in creed among the Semites in Syria are not a struggle for truth, but a force of the soil: "La secte, le schisme, l'hérésie sont une floraison naturelle de l'âme."[32] According to Jean and Jérôme Tharaud, the Jewish destiny is due only to racial factors. The Jew Theodor Herzl, a newspaper correspondent in Paris who has almost forgotten his Jewish roots, becomes one day, under the spell of the injustice in the Dreyfus case, "le prophète du Boulevard" with the self-created mission to lead all the Jews back to Palestine, "le rôle de guide d'Israel, tenu autrement par Moïse" (L'An prochain à Jérusalem, p. 92). Jewish colonization, however, according to the Tharauds, is bound to fail because of "l'impuissance d'Israel de changer sa vieille âme pour devenir un paysan" (ib., p. 151).[33] The blood of their race makes the Jews messianic dreamers: "C'est le même sentiment, l'éternel espoir d'Israel d'entrer dans la terre promise; c'est l'antique instinct de la race qui présente à tous ces gens leurs imaginations, leurs rêves comme des réalités prochaines. La vieille force d'espoir qui a guidé les Patriarches Abraham, Jacob et Moïse, n'a encore rien perdu de son antique puissance" (J. et J. Tharaud, A l'ombre de la Croix, Plon, 1920, pp. 42-43). The Tharauds rather naively also spread an idea which became dear to the nazis, as well as to all "freethinkers," namely that the Jews are the racially conditioned "vieux peuple qui inventa l'angoisse du péché, le Dieu toujours en courroux, le rachat par la pénitence et le jeûne" (ib., p. 255).

Just as messianism, according to the Tharauds, is an eternal force of the Jewish blood, so magic, according to Paul Morand (1898-   ), is an eternal force of the Negro blood. It is the dominating voodoo, which was reintroduced by Occide, *Le tsar noir*, in his Haitian soviet republic, replacing all other forms of religion because: "il lui suffisait de subsister animalement parmi les chèvres et les porcs . . . replongé . . . dans l'immense matrice de la terre" (*Magie noire,* 1928, p. 38). The famous dancer Congo, modeled, it seems, after Josephine Baker, has acquired all the accomplishments of a refined culture and is able to bewitch Paris, but is a helpless victim of the voodoo, living in a tragic fear of spell and *envoûtement.* The eternal forces of Africa are no less efficient in the almost white-looking Miss Fredman from Fifth Avenue, who prefers to become one of the many wives of an African chieftain rather than to play the rôle of an emancipated woman among the white passengers of a cruise ship who abandoned her purposely on the African shore. The liberals who treated race questions in French literature without believing at all in instinctive racial forces are, to say the least, much less interesting. Luc Durtain (1881-   ) in *Dieux blancs, hommes jaunes,* describing the terrific difficulties between French and natives in Indochina, thinks that such race antagonisms are only misunderstandings which can be removed on a natural basis and by conventions: "Il a terriblement simplifié le problème de l'antagonisme Orient-Occident en le ramenant à un conflit de mythologies."[34] The Negro missionary problem has been brought into the limelight by Maurice Genevoix (1890-   ) in his novel: *Fatou Cissé* (Flammarion, 1954). Fatou is the maid-servant of a white French family. She refuses to follow them to Europe, gets married to an old Negro, loves the ancient superstitions in spite of her Catholicism, and aspires only to saving her morally endangered son Luc who, educated by the missionaries, is succumbing to the bad influence of one of his classmates.

The cultural tension between bonds of race and tribe on the one hand and the advantages of French civilization on the other, which reflects in a way also the crisis of French colonial policy today, comes clearly to the fore in the works of the French Negro poets themselves. The movement was started thirty years ago by René Maran with his naturalistic novel *Batouala* and is continued by authors such as Léopold Sédar Senghor from Senegal (1906-), Léon-G. Damas from Cayenne (1912-), and Aimé Césaire from Martinique (1913-).

Despite the terrible example of Hitlerism, the more the French authors become materialistic the more the spirit of the earth seems the only religion left to them. Even the most prominent among them, Albert Camus (1913-), born in Mondovi in North Africa, considers himself rather a part of the larger Mediterranean world than of *Chrétienté:* "C'est un destin bien lourd à porter que de naître sur une terre paienne. . . . Je me sens plus près des valeurs du monde antique que des chrétiennes. Malheureusement, je ne peux pas aller à Delphes me faire initier!" (*Nouvelles littéraires,* le dix mai, 1951).

The rootlust and the spirit of the earth have also become responsible for the tendency of modern man to commune with the elements, as in bathing and sunbathing, a practice almost unknown to Latin nations before World War I. The cult of water, sun, and open-air was so unfamiliar to the French up to the twenties that Paul Morand did not hesitate to describe his surprise at these developments in health and sport. He cannot, however, look at these activities without a feeling of voluptuousness: "L'époque des athlètes . . . et des jeunes filles nues. . . ." "Sur les degrés en amphithéâtre de la piscine," he continues ironically, "s'ordonnent, . . . d'admirables nudités brunes que contemplent, avec envie, a mille mètres dans le ciel, du haut des avions . . . les hommes d'affaires et les politiciens trop pressés pour s'arrêter et qui perdent leur vie" (Paul Morand, "Nourritures solaires," in *Le Réveille-Matin,* Grasset, 1937, p. 208). Morand's critical contempt is counterbalanced by utterances in which the existential pleasure in swimming and bathing is genuinely praised and truly lived and experienced, especially by Mediterranean authors like Paul Valéry (1871-1945) and the just mentioned Albert Camus. The latter, e.g., writes:

> Tout à l'heure quand je me jetterai dans les absinthes
> pour me faire entrer leur parfum dans le corps, j'aurai conscience
> . . . [de] ce soleil, cette mer, mon coeur bondissant de jeunesse,
> mon corps au goût de sel, et l'immense décor, où la tendresse et la
> gloire se rencontrent dans le jaune et le bleu (*Noces à Tipasa*,
> p. 20-21).

Camus surprisingly maintains that this type of *esprit de sport*
easily acceptable to more primitive populations in North Africa
becoming familiar with the French brings out the significance of
a situation which is pagan in kind:

> Pour la première fois depuis deux mille ans, le corps a
> été mis nu sur les plages. . . . Aujourd'hui la course des jeunes gens
> sur les plages de la Méditerranée rejoint les gestes magnifiques des
> athlètes de Délos (*Noces*, p. 62).

At the same time Camus declares that these open-air activities
have nothing to do with the program of the "naturistes, ces
protestants de la chair" (*Noces*, p. 58) which means that they
preached a cult of sensuality and a kind of hedonistic dogma.
This borderline seems thin, however, if one considers the behavior
on the beach of Meursault, Camus' *"Etranger."* (See chapter five.)
It seems that a civilization permeated by eroticism, as is the
French, has no possibility of integrating the spirit of calisthenics
and gymnastics with a serious love of nature as is the case with
the nordic nations.

CHAPTER III

INTROSPECTION. NEW ASPECTS OF LOVE.
ACTE GRATUIT

The main achievement of French literature from the days of the *Roman Courtois* down through Montaigne, Racine, Pascal, La Rochefoucauld, Mme de Lafayette, Choderlos de Laclos, Stendhal and Flaubert is the psychological scrutiny of the soul and its reactions to love and ambition. The age of Freud, therefore, was bound to become a challenge to French literature. Names like Proust, Mauriac, Gide, Duhamel, Green, Lenormand and a phalanx of minor authors actually stand for the artistic discovery of the subconscious which revealed the very depths of the human soul. They become masters of introspection. Entirely new aspects of love relations, particularly abnormal and conjugal relations, were analyzed for the first time. The uncontrollable urges in man, particularly the irrepressible impulse called *acte gratuit,* the demoniac attraction of despair and suicide, the yielding to the absurd and destructive forces in life were lavishly described. And it was all done in literary forms and styles of unusual esthetic effectiveness.

The outstanding writer of the century along the lines just mentioned will remain for a long time Marcel Proust (1875-1922). The sixteen volumes of his *roman-fleuve, A la recherche du temps perdu* (Gallimard, 1913-1928), the first draft of which, *Jean Santeuil,* was made known only in 1951, are a mine of the most subtle cases of soul searching. Only a few authors have been capable like him of developing the realm of the unconscious into an esthetic-pseudometaphysical system with an adequate style. Proust set the pattern for a whole series of important writers such as D. H. Lawrence, James Joyce, Virginia Woolf, May Sinclair, Dorothy Richards and the Chilean author Magdalena Petit.[1] Marcel Proust discovered anew the reality of vague, unaccounted-for remembrances which Plato had once interpreted, in his anamnesis myth, as recollections of an earlier incarnation of the individual soul, and which modern psychology calls the *déjà-vu* experience. For Proust this involuntary *souvenir* is the only guarantee of the existence of the individual personality, a truer reality than that guaranteed by the conscious identity. By means of *souvenir* a person is able to bring any past experience back to mind in a transfiguration which did not exist in its once material reality. Dipping a biscuit, called a *madeleine,* into the tea (*Du côté de chez Swann,* I, p. 62 ff.) reminds Marcel of all the cosy tea hours with great aunt Léonie at Combray, nay of more, of all the sweetness surrounding his youth, enhanced by a new sensibility in the moment of remembering those early impressions.

Stumbling over unevenly cut flagstones (*Le Temps retrouvé,* II, p. 7) brings back in a flash the uneven pavement once seen and touched in Saint Mark's baptistry in Venice. But together with the pavement reappears all the once experienced beauty of this town: the colors, the sounds, the perfume, the friends, in short *le temps perdu* becomes *le temps retrouvé.* In this way the unconscious becomes the storehouse of esthetic treasures which only the magic rod of associative memories is able to recall to life and to enhance in a kind of beautiful superreality. Such a *souvenir* even makes all discouragement vanish and change into a feeling of happiness. This is bliss. Similar remembrances are evoked by a once heard music, such as "la petite phrase" of Vinteuil (*Swann,* I, p. 271), the sonata (*A l'ombre des jeunes filles,* I, p. 7), the andante, or septet of Vinteuil (*La Prisonnière,* I, p. 263 and II, p. 79, 234). With music the phenomenon is more involved. The musical phrase which always can be evoked to musical life in more objective form with the aid of all types of instruments and orchestras, resting not only in the subliminal memory, but in the forever fixed notes of the composer, has something like a life, an existence of its own, an eternal existence. Accordingly the transfigured experience, treasured up in the subconscious and unpredictably brought to mind, is the participation in such an eternity, is the great surrealism of *A la recherche du temps perdu.* It is *le temps retrouvé* for a moment experienced as eternity. The transfigured moment contains eternity insofar as past, present and future are, in the Bergsonian sense, contained in it and abolished at the same time.[2] Immortality thus becomes understandable and even possible according to Proust's reasoning (*Albertine disparue,* I, p. 153) which is, however, a surprising attempt to reduce a metaphysical-moral problem to aesthetic neutrality.

The moment of such a transfiguration cannot be chosen. Marcel realizes the death of his beloved grandmother only when long after the event, he stoops to arrange his shoe laces during a second stay in "Balbec" (*Sodome et Gomorrhe,* II, p. 170). At that moment all his love and tenderness for the old lady with whom he had shared earlier the pleasures of this summer resort are unexpectedly, unpredictably reexperienced. All this is only understandable after an insight into the events of this great novel.

Subdivided into seven books, the work exists now in two editions, one in sixteen volumes and the other in three folio volumes, both published by Gallimard. Another *édition* in three volumes is available in the Bibliothèque de la Pléiade. *A la recherche du temps perdu* is made up of the refined, though rather amoral, recollections of the author (Marcel), steeped in dreams and emotions, art and literature, music and eroticism, landscape and travel. The author, awakening in the morning and daydreaming of the past, enjoys the youthful vacation days of Combray (in reality Illiers) where from the estate of his paternal grandparents one path led to the aristocratic château of the duchess of Guermantes, the other one to the villa of the Jewish art lover Swann.

Therefore book one is called *Du Côté de chez Swann.* Marcel remembers one day when Swann was a guest of his parents and his mother failed to give him, little Marcel, the goodnight kiss. That night he was unable to sleep until the mother came late in the night to stay with him until morning. In this mood of *tendresse* Marcel recalls also the summers with his beloved grandmother, his suffering old aunt Léonie eager for any kind of gossip, and her maid Françoise, strongly moral and devout, like a pillar of ancient France, who was later to be inherited by his parents; but most of all he thinks of Swann. Thus in the first book the important dimensions of the novel are given: the separation and the interplay between social highlife and intelligentsia as well as the feminine mood of a particular tenderness. In other words, Proust, the half-Jew, resents his exclusion from aristocratic society and suffers from the intellectual onesidedness without a social compensation in his own group. He reacts to this situation with a sensitive analysis. Therefore he first discusses Swann.

Swann once had a very objectionable love affair with his present wife, the former *demi-mondaine* Odette de Crécy, now mother of Gilberte. Gilberte, however, was once the ideal childhood love of Marcel himself. The affair between Swann and Odette is described at length. Swann's enthusiasm for a woman who has many liaisons at the same time, who is a shameless liar, and who uses Swann's money to invite other friends to Bayreuth offers Proust the occasion to treat the problem of whether vulgarity and lack of education can be mitigated by a kind of elegance, taste, and the bewitching attitude of a coquette. But the chief interest flowing on the structural level from the liaison Swann-Odette to the later liaison Marcel-Albertine is linked to another question. Is not love a self-centered jealousy by which one love partner is eager to deprive the other love partner of freedom out of selfish pride in possession? Thus Swann tries to surprise Odette with her other lovers because he cannot trust her declarations. Swann debases himself further by meeting her in the inferior bourgeois salon of the Verdurins where all conspire against him. The reader, however, is not too much aware of the situations so painful for Swann since they are balanced by fascinating analyses of states of mind and harmoniously inserted descriptions of nature such as the hawthorns of Méséglise on the Swann estate.

Book two, *A l'ombre des jeunes filles en fleurs,* describes the summer young Marcel is spending at Balbec (in reality Trouville plus Cabourg), a fashionable resort recommended to the Prousts by the diplomat M. de Norpois. Through him Marcel, before his departure, makes the desired acquaintance of the writer Bergotte who is kind to Marcel's first literary essays. Marcel is also encouraged for the first time to go to the theatre to see the actress Berma in her great rôle of Phèdre. Balbec offers Marcel sensations of another kind: travel, sunrises, new landscapes, the elegant hotel, the aristocratic people at the dinner table, the maître d'hotel, the distinguished guests such as the Marquise de Villeparisis from the Guermantes family, the nephew of the Duchesse de Guermantes, Saint-Loup, and her brother-in-law, the baron Charlus. His greatest fascination, however, comes from a group of young girls whom he almost loves collectively, since their youth, their gestures, their silvery voices, their ethereal bodies impress him as though they were goddesses from Greek mythology. They assume prismatic aspects of attraction, cycling, swimming, dancing like the changing sea which is their constant background. Marcel sees his feelings transformed into art by the seascapes of the impressionistic painter Elstir. It is in Elstir's *atelier* that he meets Albertine for the first time. He falls in love with her but her enigmatic, cool behavior makes him doubtful whether her friends Andrée or Gisèle would not be preferable, which makes him leave Balbec without any particular regrets at the end of the season.

Taking Marcel back to Paris, Proust continues the social diptych which he has sketched since Combray. Now he stresses the aristocratic side of the Guermantes, using the representatives of the family whom Marcel met in Balbec as a bridge. Thus book three, *Le Côté de Guermantes,* fulfills Marcel's ambitious plan to infiltrate high society. For this purpose he visits Saint-Loup in Doncières where he serves as a cavalry sergeant. Saint-Loup is supposed to give him an introduction to his aunt, the duchess. Marcel sleeps one night in the barracks, dines with the corporals, discusses war history and military tactics, meets Saint-Loup's mistress, the actress Rachel, and leaves with Saint-Loup's assurance that he will get an invitation to the duchess. But Marcel "makes" first the easier salon of the Villeparisis. He is received in a friendly manner at one of their parties, meets high nobility mixing with artists and scholars, and discusses literature, fashion, scandals, and politics, particularly the Dreyfus case which is just up for review in court. Here the positions clash; the diplomat Norpois is loath to have to talk to the Jewish intellectual Bloch about it, and the duchess of Guermantes leaves the room when Odette Swann appears. The arrogant behavior of the brilliant and pedigree-conscious Baron Charlus, who assures Marcel ostentatiously of his friendship, intrigues him. In addition to social events, Proust also inserts intimate human happenings. There is a tender description of the grandmother suffering a stroke while walking along the Champs Elysées. She dies within a few days. Albertine appears suddenly on a Sunday afternoon in Marcel's room and consoles him. He starts a love affair with her.

There follows the great dinner of the Duke and Duchess of Guermantes, prepared since Marcel's trip to Doncières. Marcel is too eager to see the Duke's collection of Elstir paintings, gets lost in the beauty of the pictures, and makes the nobility wait for him hungrily for three-quarters of an hour. Aware of his *faux pas,* he is all the more fascinated by the aristocratic patience, tolerance, elegance and friendly manners which entirely camouflage his bad behavior. He discovers with pride the greater interior liberty of his admired duchess when compared to the narrowness of the other nobility present, the Comte de Bréauté, the Duc de Châtellerault, the Prince de Foix, and the Courvoisier family. Even when conversing about the unpromising topic of genealogy she is brilliant; her famous *bons mots* are made public by her husband to the applause of the society gathered in the drawing room.

Since his acquaintance with baron Charlus, the idea of *Sodome et Gomorrhe* (book four) has entered Marcel's mind like a poison. He makes the unpleasant but indisputable discovery that many members of this society are homosexuals or lesbians, and that not only the admired Baron Charlus, but also the adored Albertine seem involved. He still does not know any details. One day he witnesses the fertilization of a flower by a messenger beetle.

By coincidence, immediately after this observation, he surprises Baron Charlus hovering around the tailor Jupien like this beetle around the flower. Listening to their ensuing talk there can remain no doubt about the nature of their relations. It is remarkable with what biological seriousness Proust treats cases on the fringe of crime and tragedy.

Thus he comes to the second great reception, that of the Princess of Guermantes, with a sharpened moral insight. What he sees at the summit of his social initiation is a weird and unhealthy atmosphere alleviated only by the plump and socially ambitious Mme de Sainte Euverte who tries to invite the very distinguished guests of the Guermantes to her own party. Confusing the exact chronology in his memories, Marcel skips as a contrast to his second stay in Balbec, this time with his mother. At the remembrance of his grandmother and at the desperate thoughts which he, an unbeliever, has about death and the dead, he becomes deeply melancholy. His gloom is relieved when he again meets Albertine with whom he feels more in love than ever. He becomes passionately jealous at her slightest flirtation with Saint-Loup, but most of all at her tenderness with girls, particularly her closest friend Andrée. His suspicions, never alleviated, make him torture Albertine in order to discover all her excuses. Marcel lavishes presents on her, takes her with him to Paris and makes her his mistress and permanent prisoner.

The title of book five, *La Prisonnière*, implies a kind of moral criticism. There is in fact criticism from Françoise, the old servant and Marcel's censor, who is shocked that Marcel loiters away whole mornings in great intimacy with Albertine, listening to the noises coming from the street and commenting on the musical character of the street vendors' cries. All this is described with a penetrating cultural understanding. The objectionable situation is almost forgotten in the evocation of the Parisian winter days, so snugly comfortable with the morning fire kindled, the water running in the bathrooms, and Albertine's trying on her dresses made after patterns delivered by the duchess of Guermantes. But since Marcel cannot introduce Albertine into high society he becomes room-bound, irritable, introverted and tortured by jealousy. Albertine goes her own way. Without any consideration for dignity, Marcel has her watched by her friend Andrée and by the chauffeur, thus creating a situation of mutual mistrust. On one occasion he sends Françoise after her to get her home at once. Such incidents bring Albertine to the verge of breaking with Marcel. Promising more dresses and jewels, and a yacht, he takes her out for a ride to Versailles. Unfortunately they start a game consisting in the search for moon poems in French literature. While Marcel knows innumerable examples, Albertine tortures her brain to find even a few. She feels culturally, socially, and literarily offended. The next morning her apartment is empty. "Mlle Albertine has left," Françoise announces with triumph and satisfaction to the thunderstruck Marcel.

It is difficult to see why Proust uses two volumes for the analysis of Marcel's unquenchable, morbid jealousy in book six, *Albertine disparue*. Marcel, inconsolable about Albertine's absence, tries by all means to get her back. To him she is still the unknown girl whose essence he failed to discover. In a kind of transfigured *souvenir* he dreams of all the days spent in common with Albertine in Balbec, in Paris, in museums, theatres, art studios, musical soirées, promenades, excursions and he discovers that the strongest element even in all these recollections is still his jealousy. Even after Albertine's death from an accidental or suicidal fall from horseback, Marcel remains a victim of his morbid jealousy to such an extent that he makes inquiries in Balbec, in the Touraine, in all places where Albertine had lived in order to have proofs of her suspected unnatural relations. But he remains caught in a net of lies and contradictions just as he was while she was living. To forget her entirely he travels to Venice with his mother. The world of his youth, however, of which Albertine was a symbol, has disappeared. Marcel is also aware that class society is bursting at all its seams. Marcel's first love, Gilberte Swann, has married Saint-Loup and is deceived by him. The niece of the vulgar tailor Jupien has been adopted by Baron Charlus and is given in marriage to the aristocrat Cambremer as a true and genuine Guermantes. And, the highest disgrace of all, the gossiping Mme Verdurin becomes the last Princess of Guermantes by her second marriage to the Duke of Duras.

Thus in book seven, *Le Temps retrouvé*, Marcel ponders on the good days of yore, existing only in the transfiguration of his mind. The first world war has changed the face of Paris completely. The cowardly Bloch pretends to be a patriot and blames the aristocrat Saint-Loup for still speaking respectfully of Kaiser Wilhelm, but while Bloch tries to escape the draft, Saint-Loup dies a hero. Charlus has fallen to the lowest depths of human moral decay and indulges in the most obscene masochistic perversities. Marcel has grown old. Walking to a reception of Mme Guermantes-Verdurin, after having for long years avoided society, he stumbles on an uneven flagstone in the courtyard of her palace, and in a flash there rises before his mind the uneven flagstones of the Battistero of San Marco in Venice, his mother standing before a gothic window, the canals and the sun and the sea, but transfigured, just as Combray had been recalled when he dipped the *madeleine* in a cup of tea at his aunt Léonie's suggestion (at the beginning of the novel).

Waiting in the library of the Guermantes until he is called in, he finds a volume of *François le Champi* by George Sand and he remembers the days when his mother read to him from this book. Later when he touches a starched napkin and hears the sound of a spoon against a glass, Balbec and the hotel, grandmother and the girls, everything comes back to his spiritual eye, but is enjoyed in distance, tranquillity and beauty. Now he understands the difference between time and eternity, between life and art, between activity and contemplation, between crude experience and literature transforming reality. Finally he enters the drawing room where he finds that his once adored beauties are decaying human wrecks. The hard reality makes him realize that transfiguration is possible only in art and poetry. The once brilliant Duchess of Guermantes has lost her memory and talks nonsense, her husband tries a last disgusting flirtation with the "sterilized rose" Odette, who seems ageless under innumerable layers of paint. Gilberte looks already as vulgar as her mother. The prostitute actress Rachel, Saint-Loup's ex-mistress, dominates the drawing room, reciting fables of Lafontaine and patronizing the daughter and son-in-law of the once renowned star, Berma. An old *demimondaine* leaves early to be punctual for her appointment, as she says, with the Queen of Spain. She seems, however, rather to hasten to her grave as does this whole society with its *temps perdu*. But Marcel still clings to life to give the world the message of a possible *temps retrouvé,* an era found again in a timeless poetry transcending life.

It is regrettable that Proust shared this message with his double, Marcel, to such an extent that in his last hour he was unaffected by the famous Abbé Mugnier who talked to him about another message, that of Christ. Relatively speaking, however, Proust's creative message is of a great artistic value. His way of introspection materializes in literature as a prototypical possibility of refining and fathoming to their very depths the experiences of nature, love and art under the magic wand of *souvenir.* He is a sorcerer similar to that peculiar patient of his Dr. Cottard, who needed merely to be touched on the temples in order to be awakened into a second existence.

Proust as a great artist finds an adequate personal style which leads him from the appearance of things to the essence of things, to use his own terminology. To cover impression, recollection, transfiguration, past and present, reaction and sensibility, it must be a style of digressions and retardations, a complex style mirroring a complex world of reality and dream. E. R. Curtius, who analyzed Proust's style,[3] shows how his global sentence holds together in masterly fashion the disparate elements. Leo Spitzer's[4] still closer probing distinguishes, according to Proust's psychological method of intuitive condensation, analysis and contemplation, three sentence types of "explosion," "dissection," and "description." The syntactical elements, according to Spitzer, paint in an almost onomatopoeic manner the movements of the soul. The frequent parentheses betray how much remains to be said by a man who in his rich views and agonized sensibility can never exhaust life. Subjunctives and indirect discourse are the corollaries to a sick man's silent introspection. The most ordinary words and expressions assume an aura of mystery from special situations. The anti-realistic atmosphere is filled with the negative prefix: *in*. It occurs in adjectives such as *irréel, immatériel, impalpable*. The secret of recapturing the past, on the other hand, is confided to the prefix: *re* in *retrouver, rechercher, reconnaître*, etc.

The introduction of new characters into the story follows the principle of the narration itself: from dream to clarity, from haze to full light, from the vague sketch to the overrich portrait.[5] The sentimentality and passion for social superficiality are redeemed by the latent irony and humor of the comments,[6] a presentation which entails even intonation, sentence structure, pastiche, situation, inverted use of cause and effect, mock-mythology and mock-euphemism. Comic elements are also used to prevent the poet from feeling any sympathy for certain persons whom he wishes to degrade to automatons.[7] There is furthermore a flight into the loftiest comparisons taken from the realm of music to dissolve the elements of time into a quasi-eternal condition.[8] To catch the invisible world the visible one is literally telescoped into analogies and parallels;[9] or, as Germaine Brée puts it, the blooming apple trees suggest the sea, all the seasons, the Japanese engravings, the dresses of ladies, the love in springtide and the atmospheric changes.[10]

The two main motifs, love and time, already present in the youthful draft of the work called *Jean Santeuil*, coalesce in the mature work in the symbols of flower, bird, hair and sea.[11] Proust, by circling the ineffable and unfathomable delicacies of the soul even in perverted mankind, came closer than any other author to "that immaterial something."[12] His style, slow, refined, *précieux*, prolix, has categorically all the qualities of a so-called edifying style,[13] and actually has been compared to that of Bossuet.[14] The logic of his endless subordinations recalls the style of Descartes.[15] Although he imitates the classics to the point of following them with "la règle des trois adjectifs," his imagery, heavy with intensive life and poetic shades, makes him one of the most modern authors.[16] The structure of the novel is loose and unfinished; some parts are more elaborated, some less and the pieces of the original fragments of this suit of motley are visibly sewn together despite some recurring Wagnerian motifs which make us believe we are confronted with a willed, complicated tapestry pattern.[17] Nonetheless, at least for the first part, as far as the banal Odette motif and the lofty Vinteuil sonata motif are concerned, there is applied the structure type of the sonata allegro; as its exposition, development, recapitulation and coda could be proved.[18] Jean Rousset has suggested a chiastic structure of the novel insofar as Odette is stronger than the *petite phrase* of Vinteuil in conquering Swann, but the septet is stronger than Albertine in conquering Marcel (*Revue des Sciences humaines,* fasc. 79, 1955, pp. 387-99).

Proust was capable of transposing his intuitive philosophical insights, even though they were only of a hedonistic kind, into the spatial concrete. This alone would qualify him as a great symbolist.[19] Cycling girls are transformed into goddesses or nymphs, the Princess of Guermantes in her fur coat into a rare beautiful bird, a hawthorn into a girl dressed for the May procession.[20] The many parentheses in the lavish and lush evocations of all kinds contain marvelous landscapes and interiors, gestures and attitudes, portraits and snapshots in static, dynamic, pictorial and sketchy fashion.[21] Impressionism is one of the driving forces of Proust's style and makes him describe nature and men like paintings, as he learned from Ruskin;[22] witness also his marvelous direct descriptions of existing paintings in their own style.[23] The landscapes, seascapes, skyscapes, according to the mood in which they are steeped, receive the quality of observation, remembrance, psychology, eroticism, dream, and often many or all of these qualities together.[24] They have the fascination of the paintings of Vermeer.[25] Scientific phenomena demanding accurate description find in Proust a masterly analyzer.

Neurasthenia, uremia, physical and sexual abnormality, and apoplexy are minutely analyzed.[26]

By his experience, Proust is actually capable of creating a super-person *retrouvé* behind the personality continuously *perdu,* not so different from *anima* behind the *animus* of Claudel and the *moi nu* behind the "personalité muable et accidentelle" of Paul Valéry.[27] Proust in his intellectual aspect resembles very much Valéry as "un rationaliste qui surtout s'inquiète du subconscient ..., les choses enregistrées cessent de [le] solliciter des qu'elles le sont. ... Nécessairement, tout le conscient projette ses forces sur l'éternelle et merveilleuse arrivée de l'insoupçonné."[28]

Very important in Proust's view is the linking of timeless art and letters as they are personally experienced in a moment of history to something magic and strange. Swann never would have been able to love Odette de Crécy, if he had not found her features in the figure of Zephora, daughter of Jethro, on a Botticelli fresco. Marcel loves his grandmother all the more since she uses expressions of Madame de Sévigné in her letters. Professor Cottard makes old locutions relive by restoring their literal sense beside the metaphorical (*Du côté de chez Swann,* I, p. 288). That the presenting of at least two planes of life is the *sine qua non* for the discovery of a higher truth nobody could explain better than Proust himself: "La vérité ne commencera qu'au moment où l'écrivain prendra deux objets différents, posera leur rapport, analogue dans le monde de l'art à celui qu'est le rapport unique de la loi causale, dans le monde de la science, et les enfermera dans les anneaux nécessaires d'un beau style, ou même ainsi que la vie, quand en rapprochant une qualité commune à deux sensations, il dégagera leur essence en les réunissant l'une et l'autre pour les soustraire aux contingences du temps dans une métaphore, et les enchaînera par le lien indescriptible d'une alliance de mots" (*Le Temps retrouvé,* II, p. 40).[29] Albertine (*La Prisonnière*) is for Marcel mysterious like the sea, her eyes the mirror of her inscrutable soul. He unites these two different planes saying that, when Albertine closes her eyes to sleep, it is as though one were to bar the view of the sea by drawing the curtains.

The inexhaustible mysteries of people's souls and the many possible motivations they are subject to remain impenetrable even to the closest observer. Why did the rather bold Albertine refuse Marcel the goodbye kiss in Balbec (*A l'ombre des jeunes filles en fleur,* II, p. 231). Ignorance? Prudery? Coquettery? Perversity? All together? None of these reasons at all? Does Marcel really love Albertine whom he keeps as his *prisonnière* or does he not rather love her company, her gossip, her changing attitudes, her slippers, symbols of her captivity? Or perhaps he loves to consider her as an unconscious plant especially when she is sleeping. There are still other possibilities. He may love the triumph of keeping others from possessing Albertine, or the words of love he has spoken to her. He may love in her through the old, familiar expressions of love, his dear mother and grandmother. Or finally does he not perhaps love himself in his jealousy? Albertine remains a mask, husk, shell and cover of an unapproachable interior, which causes suffering, tediousness, and, most of all, jealousy confused with love.[30]

Proust's magic realism always presents itself as a world of exquisite beauty. He is in this comparable to the painter Pierre Roy who also enhances reality to a rich, full, and tender beauty of dreamlike remembrances and evocative power through bewildering colors and a clear outline immediately understandable.[31] In Roy's *The Music Room,* known reality changes into "a charm of intimate revelation" like Vinteuil's *petite phrase* which reappears in his Septet "like a girl clothed in silver and dripping with bewitching harmonies, light, sweet like transparent veils, only it was not any longer a little dove's cooing, but something like a mystical cock's cry, the sharp calling of an eternal morn." The famous *aubépin* of the hedge of Méséglise gets its magic importance from its inseparability from the perfumes of early summer and the religious aspect of May, month of Mary, and from the holy jubilation of Corpus Christi day, and therefore becomes "l'arbuste catholique et délicieux." Just as Claudel's Violaine, even when she is a leper, remains in a lasting magic spell of virginal beauty "la fiancée a travers les branches," so does Proust's "petite bande de Balbec" with the sweet names Aimée, Octave, Gisèle, Rosamonde, Albertine, and their silhouettes set against the magic background of the blue sea captivate the reader forever. In spite of the questionable vicissitudes, in which the girls become involved, one feels with them always "à l'ombre des jeunes filles en fleur."

The force which transforms and transfigures space and time in Proust's work is art as a high realization of life's values. Therefore Albert Thibaudet has seen very clearly that Proust's psychological achievements are not concerned with practical considerations or specific morals. Says Thibaudet: "Le plan de désinteressement où Proust a transporté l'analyse psychologique m'a paru correspondre au plan de désinterressement où Mallarmé et Valéry ont essayé de purifier paradoxalement la poésie."[32] But there is still something else in Proust. He is in a higher sense more "classic" than Gide not because he expresses a maximum of thought and psychology by a minimum of linguistic means, but just because of his fundamental method: he remembers old impressions in perfect tranquillity.[33]

The fascination Proust's novel still produces cannot be invalidated by such judgments as that of D. H. Lawrence who calls it "Water-Jelly" or that of George Moore who says Proust is "Ploughing a field with knitting needles" or that of F. L. Lucas who derives only a pessimistic message from it:

> Vain our deluding arts; all, all in vain.
> We kiss the pale lips we have raised again.[34]

No cultured person can help but be interested in the three themes Henri Bonnet has singled out for understanding Proust: Society, Love and Friendship.[35] After having given Proust all the honors due to him, and after having granted him even a certain liberty in his realm of the *factibile* where the laws of the *agibile* sometimes seem not to enter, we may check his exploitation of the subconscious with that of others to whom the moral laws seem of a more vital importance, but whose art falls behind their good intentions.

The subconscious has been a super-reality to Christianity from Saint Paul and the Fathers of the Church down to medieval philosophers and the great mystics of the sixteenth century. Had Protestantism, The Enlightenment and Liberalism not covered these depths of introspection with silence and negation one would not have needed Dr. Freud to rediscover them. Nineteenth century authors, however, even those with Catholic formation and tendencies, do not see this dark zone at all. Therefore Paul Bourget (1852-1935) presents all his psychological problems as external cases of conscience capable of being decided by reason alone. Today one would find it a rather childish explanation that the *Disciple* (Robert Greslou) of an obnoxious philosopher (Adrien Sixte) realizes by experiment his master's teaching, and seduces his pupil Charlotte in order to study the mechanism of love, something which probably never happens; or that Mme Albert Darras becomes aware of the wrongness of remarrying after divorce only when she has a discussion with a Jesuit *(Le Divorce);* or that the Christian death of the officer Le Gallic opposed to the subjectively senseless suffering of the unbelieving physician Ortègue could reveal *Le Sens de la mort* (1906). Bourget had forgotten the knowledge still familiar to Racine, Madame de Lafayette, and even Choderlos de Laclos, the knowledge of "the two souls in man's breast," the psychomachy of the passions and its always unpredictable outcome.

The twentieth century tried to detach psychology entirely from philosophy, from logic, and from ethical demonstrations. Thus it became the concern of the psychiatrist. The psychiatrist's field, however, is by definition the subliminal and the "libidinal." Literature was to profit from the study of the subconscious contradictions in man revealed by his dreams. "Ainsi un nouveau merveilleux est né, le merveilleux psychique, une nouvelle évasion nous est offerte, l'évasion intérieure. . . . Où trouver un pittoresque plus sûr et cocasse que celui de nos rêves?—des paysages plus illimités que ceux de l'introspection?"[36]

To understand fully what is implied here, one needs only to contrast the archaic psychology of Bourget with modern psychology which can be exemplified by two authors deeply rooted in Catholic wisdom, but loath to teach or demonstrate, François Mauriac (1885-) and Julien Green (1900-). Both are concerned with the analysis of paradoxical conditions in the behavior of certain human beings whose attitude defeats any attempt at rational understanding.

Mauriac, according to Samuel Silvestre de Sacy,[37] is the investigator of the "coeurs inquiets." His first serious approach to them is *Le Baiser au lépreux* (1922). Noémi d'Artiailh "corps dru, séraphique visage, tête brune et bouclée d'ange espagnol," married to the disgusting cripple Jean Peloueyre for reasons of family prestige and money, withers away at the side of the love-hungry poor man whose embraces horrify her. They observe but never discuss their mutual sorrow. One day Jean goes to Paris. Why? To relieve her of his presence, or perhaps persuaded by the parish priest who tries to heal the terrible marriage which he had arranged. Suddenly Noémi calls him back. Why? Is it because she is now sure that her ascetic training has given her the strength to love him when he is present since she tried to love him in his absence? Or is it because she is afraid she is losing her self-control and is falling in love with the doctor who does not hide his tender feelings for her? Or was it the pastor's idea to call him back without the initiative of Noémi?[38] Jean Peloueyre, having returned, sees that Noémi is not able to overcome her disgust. He begins to visit a consumptive friend, perhaps in order to contract tuberculosis himself, a way out for one who is of no use. After Jean does contract tuberculosis, however, Noémi strives all the more to become "une épouse selon Dieu," and she reaches this goal the way old French Catholic generations did it, by struggle, with the help of grace. What actually occurs in her the reader himself has to explain. Is she a neurotic? Can a neurotic gradually develop charity and renunciation? Or even more, is her victory so great that now she really loves the dying husband? And has he the conviction of being loved or does he feel the humiliation of being pitied? Noémi refuses the doctor's hand after Jean's death. Is she ostentatiously proud or conventional according to the family spirit, or practical to keep the income from the rich Peloueyre estate which would be threatened by remarriage, or is her inner dignity at stake after widowhood which now must appear to her as something valuable, as a way of life? The reader has to decide. We here are certainly in the realm of a rich depth psychology similar to Proust's.

Maria Cross in *Le Désert de l'amour* (1924) drives the immature Raymond Courrèges almost into despair, making him feel that he will never satisfy the passion he has partly aroused in her because he is an unimportant young animal. She finds it impossible to love him because of certain negative and immature traits in his character. Thus she and he become the prototypes of human isolation. The same problem of human isolation visibly destroyed the family life of all of the Courrèges. Old doctor Courrèges neglects his wife since he, too, loves Maria Cross, one of his patients, but he likewise is rejected. But finally this light woman —*une femme entretenue*—becomes the mysterious and most unexpected link between father and son who find their father-son relations again restored through the shared defeat in the sinful love of the same woman. Such are the secrets of "la vie des sens et la lointaine présence de Dieu."[39]

Mauriac with his Catholic awareness of sin, temptation, flesh and the devil peers into all the possible subconscious seeds of great sins. Laure, for instance, in the drama *Le Feu sur la terre* (1951), loves her brother Maurice in such a way that she is ready to destroy all his relationships with other women, with the exception of the neighbor Caroline Lahure whom she would like him to marry without love so that she herself might be able to dominate both of them. When the choice of Maurice, however, tends to Andrée, she tries to hinder their marriage in the Church and so its indissolubility. The father in the drama *Les Mal Aimés* (1945) loves his daughter Elisabeth to such a degree that he selfishly opposes her marriage, and thus drives her sister Marianne into the arms of Elisabeth's lover with the result of a marriage being fraught with the possibility of adultery. In the novel *Génitrix* (1923) the mother, Félicité Cazenave, fights for the exclusive love of her son Fernand against his wife Mathilde to the point of virtually causing her death. But precisely thus she loses the love of Fernand.

In the Catholic atmosphere of Mauriac's novel the complexes are created by the falling back from a higher call to a lower level of life. This is already the case for the ex-seminarian Claude Favereau in *La Chair et le sang* (1920), who, living with his peasant parents on the estate of the wine merchant Dupont-Gunther, falls into a sensuous love with May, the daughter of the proprietor.[40] This is also the case with the ex-seminarian Blaise Coûture who in the drama *Asmodée* (1937) tries to exercise a spiritual influence in the château of Mme de Barthas, but instead seduces the governess, makes Emmanuèle, the daughter, forget her spiritual vocation and desires the *châtelaine*. The erotic despair of sanctimonious old maids dominates Brigitte Pian in *La Pharisienne* (1941), and Madame Agathe in *Galigaï* (1952). Vice versa, spiritual dispositions change the characters exposed to a hostile world into heroism as is the case with Rose Revolou in *Les Chemins de la mer* (1939), and Xavier, again a seminarian, in *L'Agneau* (1954). Rose Revolou comes closer to God when abandoned by her fiancé Robert Costadot after the financial ruin of her parents. Xavier becomes a sacrificial lamb himself when he helps the poor forsaken orphan Roland, mistreated by his foster parents Jean de Mirbel and Michèle; Xavier is apparently killed by Jean out of hatred, jealousy and revenge. This type of spiritual heroism has haunted Mauriac since *Préséances* (1921) in which Augustin, repudiated as a lover by Florence because of his illegitimate birth, finds his life's fulfillment in his service in the African desert, like Ernest Psichari and Père de Foucauld. A conversion from a debased state is the repentance of Gisèle de Plailly in the too suggestive novel *Le Fleuve de feu* (1923), or of Fabien in *Le Mal* (1925), an erotic victim who finally breaks his shackles as a slave of the divorcee Fanny, unworthy friend of his dignified mother.

Unexplained subconscious urges coalesce with a kind of satanic possession or at least resistance to grace in such a character as

Thérèse Desqueyroux (1927) who tries to liberate herself from a mediocre husband. Thérèse Desqueyroux has good qualities which are destroyed by the marriage experience with an unbeloved and not even respected husband who feigns to be upset by the liberties of a music hall but whose conjugal behavior makes him appear to Thérèse as a hypocritical brute. Mauriac tries to understand her temptation and her crime, not to justify it or to condemn it. Thérèse makes her husband take an overdose of sedative pills by falsifying the doctor's prescription. The juridical prosecution of Thérèse for attempted murder is hindered by the family for reasons of honor. Thérèse, however, is punished by the family. She is kept in strict isolation on the family estate. This revengeful humiliation makes the serious repentance of Thérèse psychologically impossible. After years of suffering she is released and escapes to Paris. It is with a trembling empathy that Mauriac watches for signs of a true repentance and of a reopening of Thérèse's heart to grace.

Therefore Mauriac tries to reintroduce her on her way to a possible serious recantation in *Thérèse chez le docteur,* a short story of the collection *Plongées* (1938), and in *La Fin de la nuit* (1935) which carries the account of her life to the point of death. Thus her contrition after ten years of interior resistance to God might have coincided with her death. Mauriac, without in the least condoning the crimes of Thérèse, arouses our sympathy for this new Phèdre, this new Mme Bovary, who was not strong enough to cope with circumstances into which she was brought by the usual family policy of combining money, timber and vineyards through marriages. The story, told in retrospect and by flashbacks, which in 1927 was a new technique, succeeds through its reflections on the sufferings of the sinner Thérèse in evoking that pity and fear which constitute the catharsis of great tragedies.

Gabriel Gradère in *Les Anges noirs* (1930) is guided back to God by the saintly priest Alain Forcas, but in a more clumsy literary fashion. In Mauriac nobody is pure, but is at best purified, as he declares. The ideal mothers like Mme Blanche Frontenac in *Le Mystère Frontenac* (1933), and Mme Thérèse Dezaymeries in *Destins* (1928) are far from being stainless. They are subconsciously jealous of and domineer their children.[41]

Mauriac's interest in the subconscious as the hideout of the passions is explained by his burning exploration of Bossuet's *Traité de la Concupiscence* which he expanded in his *Souffrances et bonheur du Chrétien* (1930). In Mauriac's view of the sexual urges everything is dangerous, even the legitimate affections of friendship and family: "Dès qu'elles tournent à l'amour, les voici plus qu'aucune autre criminelles."[42] Therefore he stresses also the complexities of possible cases of latent incestuous love. In *Ce qui était perdu* (1930), Hervé de Blenauges, laughing at the tenderness with which Tota treats her brother Alain Forcas, drives Tota's husband Marcel into despair, Tota into adultery, and Alain into leaving home to become a priest. Mauriac exploits the psychological effect of the climate of Gascogne which, sultry and heavy under a burning sun, produces wood fires and the smell of burnt pines, and arouses the slumbering elements of evil in the soul.[43] Thus there also looms the possibility of virtual incest in the relation of Mme Pian's stepson Louis with his sister Michèle whose love for Mirbel he betrays to the stepmother in order to have it forbidden *(La Pharisienne)*.

Mauriac's introspection has a Christian meaning different from that of Freud, a meaning which he himself has formulated:

> La présence de la Grâce dans un homme se mesure à
> la netteté du regard dont il se juge *(Ce qui était perdu)*.[44]

The style of Mauriac excels in deeply searching interior monologues and exciting dialogues as well as in fascinating landscape descriptions of the Gascogne, Bordeaux and Les Landes. The descriptions represent slight but not tiring variations of an endless theme. Therefore Mauriac lends himself easily to the critical art of the *pasticheur*.[45] Ernst Bendz has carefully analyzed the vocabulary and metaphors of his "hot, insistent, excessive, lyrical and rough" style. The metaphors of sinfulness and destruction are unbelievably high and drastic: *ordure, cancer, lèpre, boue, plaie, sang, gibet*. Flight from hostile persecution, the Christian's search for protection from world, devil and flesh are reflected in metaphors such as *meute, guetter, épier, rôder, détraquer, embusquer, pourchasser, brouiller les pistes, mettre les limiers en défaut, se tapir.* Even the seascapes seem sinfully contaminated by *marées, épaves, varechs, effluves.*[46] Mauriac's assimilation to the manner of Bossuet and Pascal is considerable. His unusual introspection leads him to use many forms of represented thought and speech which fuse with the narration into a kind of stream of consciousness.[47]

The rapidity of his narration makes him prefer asyndetic constructions. Any kind of neologism is avoided, the semantics conforms with the exact lexicological values of the words; one single but well chosen metaphorical word gives a sentence an unbelievable plenitude: "Une lourde pluie inattendue, traversée de soleil, *cingle* les feuilles" *(Le Fleuve de feu).* Well-balanced binary symmetries and rapidly formulated strong antitheses alternate with ternary syntactical or rhythmical word groups. In this regard Mauriac's prose is very reminiscent of that of Barrès. His language, in conformity with the higher society he describes, is strictly literary without any stylistic vulgarity. He is proud of exquisite literary patterns which he imitates in restrained doses, for instance the juxtaposition of two quasi-synonymic expressions or the discriminating use of an imperfect and a *passé défini* in the same sentence according to the usage of Flaubert (see René Georgin, *La Prose d'aujourd'hui,* Paris, 1956, p. 327-329). He uses comparisons sparingly and if he uses them it is for serious purposes: "Dieu est ce chasseur qui relève les pistes et qui guette sa proie à l'orée du taillis." His religious sentiment produces an almost imperceptible solemn verse within his prose, even his diary prose: "D'où descend cette paix qui ne vient de nous, à l'heure où s'allongent les ombres?" *(Journal),* actually a kind of distichon consisting of an alexandrine and an octosyllabic verse (Georgin, p. 175).

Julien Green (1900-   ) is comparable to Mauriac in that he shows a similar Christian dignity when speaking of sinners. His heroes apparently are victims of a materialistic world, but they are all the more drastically invaded by *un je ne sais quoi* of a supernatural anguish and hope. It is this that makes them so true to life. In *Léviathan* (1929), the terrible prison of his senses will be the undoing of Paul Guéret, the tutor of the children of Mme Grosgeorge. He will turn out to be a murderer. He rejects the advances of Mme Grosgeorge and prefers to her the prostitute Angèle whom he persecutes with sadistic jealousy. Surprised by an old man when he is beating her, he kills the inopportune witness. But when he happens to see suddenly the starry sky through his window, "brusquement quelque chose lui fit battre le coeur, un élan confus vers cette immensité silencieuse qui semblait l'appeler à elle" (p. 45). The prostitute Angèle in the service of the laundry-brothel of la mère Londe is a debased creature indeed. But she too retains an idea of human dignity and wants to be regarded as a decent woman by those who do not know her. She sometimes enters a church and thinks of her imaginations of Paradise which she used to entertain as a child and "elle se demandait confusément, si le bonheur n'etait pas dans ces illusions des premières années" (p. 111). Although Paul has beaten and disfigured her, she hides his greater crime to the police because she is aware that among all the men she has met, he alone loved not her body but her human personality. When Paul is discovered nevertheless and condemned to death, Angèle, asked why she did not denounce him, says she feared his revenge. Thus hiding her soul from the madding crowd the debased girl attains a certain greatness, while the jealous bourgeoise Mme Grosgeorge who betrayed him to the police is despicable in her "honesty." Angèle soon dies.

Green knows so well the psychology of the lust-stricken and libidinous that he pictures the power of sensual temptation as a fiendish urge. In *Le Visionnaire* (1934), Manuel, the ugly, sick young man, yearns to be loved in spite of his ugliness. But he rejects the idolatrous, seemingly maternal love of his fifty-year-old aunt. When in his plight he tries to embrace his fifteen-year-old cousin Marie-Thérèse and her girl companions, he only arouses scandal in the house and the town. So he invents a hallucinatory romance, imagining that the viscountess of the neighboring castle loves him, and after the death of her father comes in the night to his room to love him so tremendously that she dies in his embrace. This dream event was the last jotted down in his diary by Manuel who then dies himself from this traumatic shock. Marie-Thérèse, who found the diary after his death, has no difficulty in surmising the connection of the events. The imaginary viscountess was supposed by Manuel to have often had hallucinations of death, such as visions of horsemen with embroidered white cotton uniforms, speaking a strange language, riding through vast prairies; or a carriage with dangerous horses running down a hill and endangering her life (pp. 213-14). Marie-Thérèse with regard to Manuel's notebook asks herself,

> si le visionnaire, après tout, ne jette pas sur cette terre un regard plus aigu que le nôtre, et si, en un monde, qui baigne dans l'invisible, les prestiges du désir et de la mort n'ont pas autant de sens que nos réalités illusoires (p. 273).

These are exactly the questions of Jung and Adler.

The personal visionary power of Julien Green himself was made known by the publication of his lengthy and explicit *Journal*. Therefore we look with particular interest at his novel *Minuit* (1934). Here we are confronted with people living in Fontfroide, a kind of mental sanitarium, but we are confronted at the same time with symbolized human passions. The only sound person among the mental patients seems to be the girl Elisabeth. After the death of her mother she was confided to her aunts. Antagonized by their eccentricity, Elisabeth gives herself up to the doorman Serge whose brutal sexual instinct seems to her the only acceptable passion since it makes no attempt at a false or biased justification. The other inhabitants of Fontfroide are all under the insane spell of M. Edme who thinks he can only breathe at night, and in order to have company for his whim sells to the other patients as the highest wisdom, the secret of moon-adorers of old, that night is superior to day and a link to the invisible. His credit is enhanced by the propaganda of his mother and of Mlle Eva who has fallen in love with him. Edme's hypocritical rhetoric makes him a prophet in the eyes of M. Agnel, who for his part cannot live without a leader, without an idol. Mme Angeli tries to break the thraldom of M. Edme's night-watchers. In order not to lose her sleep, she invents a story about having to make the one o'clock train to meet her husband some-where. This novel of the world of the insane sheds much light on the other novels and also on the tormented soul of Julien Green. A fervent convert in his youth, after a lost vocation and a critical attitude towards Catholicism, he returned seriously as a mature man to his Catholic convictions.

Green's over-all pattern, the fusion of hallucination and crime, also characterizes Miss Fletcher in *Mont Cinère* (1926). Mis-treated by her greedy mother, after maddening privations, she marries her mother's gardener to get her freedom. But no less dominated by her proletarian husband, she becomes so unbalanced that she burns down the Virginia house with all the family inside. There is still *Adrienne Mesurat* (1927) running wild after having been rejected by the doctor for whose sake she practically killed her tyrannical father, pushing him down the stairs when nobody else was around. Madness is lurking everywhere; when Green, similar on this point to the painter Vincent van Gogh, "presents a restaurant proprietress seated peacefully among her clients, he distorts her otherwise placid features by tracing in her eyes a gleam of demoniac curiosity. When it is a woman watching over her sick nephew's bed, he stresses the atrocious satisfaction she experiences at the young man's plight," says M. H. Stansbury, hinting at *Léviathan* and *Le Visionnaire*.[48]

Green, who came close to an evident visionarism in certain moments of his life, declared:

> Certaines réalités ne me semblent vraies que si le fantas-tique les grandit. . . . Ce don de voir ainsi m'est accordé, puis retiré, puis rendu sans que je sache pourquoi. Parfois des années passent sans que l'exercice m'en soit possible; enfin il vient un jour où, l'heure et l'endroit étant propices, je retrouve cette faculté se représentant faiblement par l'esprit (*L'Autre sommeil*, Paris: Gallimard, 1931, pp. 131-133).

The stylistic principle of Julien Green is not only an uncanny fusion of thought and action, but of the real world and the dream world which normally are unbridgeable in reality. These two worlds, however, coalesce in the sensibility of highly nervous personalities. The esthetic advantage of using this fusion lies in the element of suspense because the action, contrary to the method of Proust, branches out from a sharply delineated view into a haze of hallucinations where the fringes of the actual and the dream-reality can no longer be distinguished. This upsets the logical calculations of the reader; Bernanos does much the same thing. Green, giving to all of his novels the same structure, fails nonetheless to reach a truly interesting presentation. This is so because the moral elements involved in any human action are necessarily minimized when the individual who performs it is neurotic and cannot be made responsible for it.[49]

To Mauriac and Green may be applied what A. J. Dickman stated about Henri-René Lenormand's theater: "La réalité n'est pas la réalité de la vie civilisée, mais la réalité du moi profond, de l'inconscient plus ancien que le conscient."[50] Subconscious reality is to Mauriac and Green nothing other than a revelation of the struggle "entre l'homme et son hôte inconnu, qui est lui-même son véritable Moi," the source of his "inquiétude." That is the reason why this kind of literature reflects "La méthode psychonalytique qui tend précisément à lier au rationalisme de surface l'inconnu provisoire du rationalisme de profondeur, à démasquer l'hôte mystérieux,"[51] an idea, incidentally, dear to Pirandello. The introspective writer realizes that "Nothing comes from ourselves but that which we draw out of the obscurity within us and which is unknown to others."[52] This is what these writers learned from Proust.

François Mauriac has asked some questions about the working of the subconscious worthy of a Hamlet and a Dostoevsky:

> Au fond de toute créature humaine, Dieu décèle-t-il le même grouillement confus? Que signifie: Chasser les mauvaises pensées? Ne pas prendre conscience de ce qui est tout de même en nous? . . . La pudeur des sentiments joue dans nos vies un rôle plus redoutable qu'aucun vice.[53]

One understands the depth of Mauriac and Green if one compares their statements and analysis with the "sounder" but superficial way of André Maurois (1885-   ). Maurois reduces the subconscious to the inferior rôle of a force crystallizing impure thoughts through dreams in order to make the sound soul the purer. He has symbolized this idea very wittily in his *La machine à lire les pensées* (Gallimard, 1939). Here the adulterous thoughts in the dreams of a professor seem to prove that such uncanny thoughts never take place in his conscious life, that they are only foam. Whereas Maurois thus sides unconsciously with the optimists who believe in psychoanalytic therapeutics and dissolve sins into complexes to be healed by the doctor, not the confessor, writers like Bernanos, Mauriac, and Lenormand are strictly opposed to such fancies. Bernanos shows in *La Joie* (see chapter six) that the alleged madness of Chantal's grandmother is nothing else than sin, pride, and lust of domination symbolized in the gesture of refusing to give Chantal the keys of the house in which the grandmother once reigned, and where she now has nothing to say. She is not healed by the plausible psychoanalyst, but by the severe charity of her saintly granddaughter who compels her to repent and to surrender. It is the same remedy which the Curé de Campagne uses on the countess *(Journal d'un curé de Campagne)*.

François Mauriac, as the deepest connoisseur of the soul's quagmire of guilt and shame, after having shown the criminal woman Thérèse Desqueyroux poisoning her husband and trying to steal her daughter's lover *(La Fin de la nuit)*, finally presents her on the doctor's "divan de cuir . . . , où tant de milliers de malheureux avaient balbutié, ânonné des mensonges, à la recherche du secret de leur vie qu'ils feignaient de ne pas connaître"[54] *(Thérèse chez le docteur)*.

Henri-René Lenormand (1882-1950) labels certain psychoanalytic therapeutics unequivocally criminal in his drama *Le Mangeur des rêves* (1924). The brutal doctor Luc de Bronte tries to heal his victim Jeanine from a vague fear fostered by dreams. She might have been guilty of the death of her mother when still a child. Triumphantly he explains to her that she must not take that seriously because her dream fragments only prove that she loved her father and hated her mother on the basis of the so-called Oedipus complex. This revelation shocks the girl so terribly that she commits suicide.

Lenormand does not at all dissociate his depth psychology from moral, even Christian principles. In *Les Ratés* (1920), a drama of fourteen scenes, the protagonists are a married couple, two poverty-stricken actors simply called Lui and Elle who understand perfectly that their profession does not necessarily exclude a certain happiness. But since He suffers from their poverty nonetheless, She tries to remedy the situation by selling herself first to a *certain Monsieur* in Bar-le-Duc and later to many others. He, however, cannot be at all happy with sinful money, although She seems less frustrated than He by the situation, considering herself as a victim for him. Out of dignity, love, jealousy, revenge, pride, shame, despair, guilt—He says he does not exactly know why—He first becomes unfaithful to her with a prostitute, then becomes addicted to drink, and finally kills her and himself because He finds it impossible to live, love and exist in a debased condition.

Lenormand's *Les Trois chambres* (1931) is a symbolically constructed dramatic triad of love involving two women and a man. Under the mask of maternal affection, the wife Florence tolerates the temporary desire of Rose for her husband, the writer Pierre, an artist of the Don Juan type. The arrangement does not work, and Rose drives Florence into suicide merely by telling her a dream she had:

> Je me voyais sous la forme d'un oiseau, livrant bataille à un autre oiseau . . . Les deux harpies étaient accrochées l'une a l'autre par les griffes, se lacérant à coups de bec. Le combat avait lieu au-dessus d'une fosse à fumier, dans laquelle chacune essayait de précipiter l'autre. A la fin, l'oiseau Rose devenait plus forte que l'oiseau Florence et le faisait disparaître dans la fosse (Acte II, p. 71, Edition *Théâtre complet,* vol. VIII, Albin Michel, 1935).

In Lenormand's *L'Homme et ses fantômes,* Roger, "l'homme couvert de femmes," is disgusted by the inner weakness of all women in whom he unconsciously seeks a strong protecting motherhood. He prefers at last the stronger love of his friend. He is recognized in the age of Freud as a character in which the hermaphroditic youth structure prevailed, whose homosexual elements are freed after the heterosexual have proved a failure, having attracted only hysterical women, not strong mother-types. Lenormand analyzes also a tragic case of an incestuous father-daughter love in *Le Simoun*[55] under delicate conditions, the father Laurency struggling, the daughter Clotilde unaware and innocent, the suffocating heat of Ghardaia in Algeria acting as pander. Finally Clotilde is killed by her rival Aiescha. Certain utterances unwittingly made by the unfortunate father such as "Tu es ta mère," or "Oui, ma petite Yvonne" (the mother's name instead of the daughter's, what Freud would call "Fehlleistung") are enough to give Aiescha the boldness to call Laurency his daughter's bridegroom, and to unleash the catastrophe.

The mobilization of the subconscious forces of the soul, weakened by disturbed health from life under exotic and tropical conditions, plays a different rôle in the drama *Le Temps est un songe*. Here Nico and his sister Riemke seek relief from the strain of the climate of Java by taking a vacation in their native Holland. Nico is supposed to marry Romée, Riemke's friend. But Romée, before knowing Nico, had the hallucination of somebody drowning himself in a pond, and swears that the face of the drowned one resembled Nico. Nico had actually attempted to commit suicide at fifteen, trying in vain to hang himself. Hearing Romée's remark, he is driven irrevocably to his death in the pond.

Lenormand's renown will not rest with his prose work. Among his short stories *Les Coeurs anxieux*, one will find, however, such a strongly built and shocking tale (reminiscent of Barbey d'Aurevilly) as "La plus malheureuse." The most unhappy one is a leper woman whom the English eccentric Shodds finds among the prostitutes of a volcanic island of the Antilles. His disgust induces vomiting and fever, and his death within twelve hours. Lenormand's stories in general, however, are thematically related to the dramas.[56]

*   *   *

The greatest achievement of depth psychology in contemporary literature is the newly discovered love psychology of the couple, unknown to earlier periods. While the nineteenth century needs the eternal triangle to analyze love and hatred between man and woman, the twentieth analyzes the couple isolated within its relations of hatred or love, and generally unhappy. There exists a fundamental hate between the sexes: "Nous ne sommes méchants qu'avec ceux que nous aimons" says M. Proust (*La Prison-nière*, I, p. 151). As we actually have seen in Proust, the lie dominates the relations between the lovers Marcel and Albertine, Swann and Odette. The hatred between marriage partners has been denounced in Gide's *Les Faux monnayeurs* (Part I, c. 12, p. 168). In Colette's work a rather important place is given to the theme of conjugal disillusion[57] not because of a third person intervening, but for a reason every ascetic writer of the Middle Ages would have subscribed to: "On n'échange rien dans l'étreinte," i.e., human love is frustrating. In an ideological drama like François de Curel's (1854-1928) *La Danse devant le miroir* (1914), Louise explains to Régine: "Lorsque l'accord de deux amants est parfait, chacun d'eux se voit dans un miroir, se prend pour l'autre et se contemple avec ivresse sans s'apercevoir qu'il est seul" (Acte II, sc. 3). But the more modern analysts go much farther.

The problem of the fundamental misunderstanding between man and woman is elaborated in a series of novelistic and dramatic plots. One of the pioneers to treat such a topic is the Belgian Vicomte Henri Davignon. His Catholic sensibility led him to establish a tension between the eroticism of a husband and the ascetic restraint of a wife in their conjugal relations. This is actually a problem which would not appear with such acuteness outside the Catholic sphere. In Davignon's novel *Un Pénitent de Furnes* (1925) Reginald Camerlinghe after many years of a happy marriage, at forty, became again a kind of fiery lover of Maria, his own wife. As she, on a higher spiritual level, seems not to respond, and not to approve of his unquenchable passion, he begins to hate her, the more so as Maria has spent considerable sums in helping a wounded soldier, Pierre Pharazyn, to start a fishing enterprise. Out of jealousy and wounded pride he repudiates her. Later he recognizes his own error: "C'était confondre l'appel de la concupiscence avec la vertu conjugale" (p. 126). To his utter humiliation this insight came to him by grace when he went to bear the penitential cross in the famous Furnes procession, for expiating the sins of Maria whom he had suspected of being unfaithful to him. The reaction of Maria to this entirely unwarranted suspicion is terrible. Although she had always loved him and him alone she now rejects him. Thus his jealousy seems healed by her dignity. Both, however, feel guilty: he for not understanding the interior attitude of his wife; she, on her level, for not accepting on principle all humiliations. Besides, having a delicate conscience, she is not entirely sure that her feelings for Pharazyn were only motherly. Thus they decide to separate for a higher aim. She becomes a Poor Clare and he a Benedictine Oblate. The conjugal tragedy based on the clash of two different levels of spirituality thus is solved by grace.

But conjugal relations become more tense outside the Catholic milieu since solutions through grace are not sought. Jacques Chardonne (1884-) and Jacques de Lacretelle (1888-) reverse Davignon's situation. They illustrate the tendency in man to sublimate the love relationship, misled by the apparent modesty in woman, and woman's reaction to this sublimation as an affront to her femininity. Men think like Dante that they adore the angel in woman; women feel, like Kleist's Penthesilea, that they would rather be dust than not be physically attractive to the male. Thus in Jacques Chardonne's *L'Epithalame* (1921), Albert Paearis kills Berthe's love because he wants to love her "pour ses vrais mérites," and not for her womanhood. Of course, Berthe behaves in such an irresponsible, illogical, and upsetting manner that her contribution to the destruction of love equals his.

Jacques Chardonne's *Claire* (1931) depicts the apparent happiness of a couple, Jean and Claire. But they are not well matched. Jean, at forty-five, having been married earlier in Singapore and having known superficial girls like Lorna, a boarder at his mother's home, marries the tender, beautiful, proud and poised Claire. His solicitude for young Claire is directed towards keeping her beauty intact, defending her against danger and death, and conquering her personality by a somewhat ambiguous attitude which is between voluptuousness and friendship. She, however, is not satisfied. Although not built for childbearing, she tries desperately with the help of doctors to have a child. The pregnancy, finally occurring after five years of married life, produces an internal hemorrhage and she dies in despair.

The style of the serious novels of Chardonne is chaste and dignified in characters, dialogue and action, an exceptional situation in modern love stories.[58] As to the vocabulary he always chooses the most decent, appropriate and harmonious word which conveys at the same time elegance and clarity combined with measure and discretion. Any kind of neologism is carefully avoided. He has expressed his own stylistic ideal as "fine shades in grey." His sentence is short and smooth. His psychology typical of a moralist is given here and there a thin frame of nature description, e.g., spring: "Déjà voici le bleu chaud et . . . ce ton oublié de sombre velours, où l'ombre dort." The epithet is reduced to a minimum. Any superfluous element is eliminated. Chardonne has been underrated by the critics ideologically as well as stylistically.

In Jacques de Lacretelle's *Amour Nuptial* (1929) the heroine Eline cannot understand that, when she has fallen ill, her husband loves her still as much and even more than at the time when she was able to be his wife physically. She scoffs at his sublimation. The more he adores her the more she hates him, afraid to be only pitied, and jealous of non-existing women whom she supposes her husband loves.

A specialist in fundamental matrimonial misunderstandings, but without posing any particular problems, is Paul Géraldy (1885-   ). He has shown that an argument over trifles can destroy a marriage because there is no bridge between the intellectual (male) and the emotional (female) approach to any small problem, a truth scientifically elaborated by Carl Jung.

In the drama *Robert et Marianne* (1925) both partners are subjectively convinced that they love one another, and no one could
doubt the conscious sincerity of their conviction. But the subliminal antagonism of the sexes "makes every word that the
man utters with the objective of reassuring his wife only a
further evidence of the gulf that lies between them."[59] Paul
Géraldy has spoken more explicitly about this tragic situation in
his *Notes et Maximes* on love where he makes this statement:
"L'amour n'est que l'amour de soi, et c'est peut-être sa grandeur.
Mais on n'en convient pas, et c'est là sa misère."[60] He has also
dedicated a whole sequel of poems to the problem, *Toi et moi,*
and he makes this sharp "Meditation":

> On croit qu'on est éperdu
> de tendresses,
> Mais dès qu'il ne s'agit plus
> de caresses,
> On ne se comprend en somme
> qu'à demi . . .
> Si tu étais un homme,
> serions-nous des amis?[61]

Géraldy's matter-of-fact cynicism finds a parallel in the marital
novels of Marcel Jouhandeau (1888-   ). These fictions seem
to bare his own struggles with the recalcitrant "Elise," mainly in
his *Chroniques maritales* (1938), written in concise and classic
language. He has also repeated the theme of the *Princesse de
Clèves,* namely the faithfulness of a woman to her husband
despite her love for another man, but the accent given to the
motif is very different from that once applied by Mme de Lafayette. The young woman considers herself rather at fault for not
following her lover. Her reason for remaining faithful is simply
to maintain her reputation in the provincial town of Chamina-
dour, which represents the author's home town, Guéret. The
title of the story consequently is *La Faute plutôt que le scandale*
(1949). The most popular of Jouhandeau's novels is his first,
Monsieur Godeau marié (1933) where, with a regrettable parody
of mysticism, Godeau astounds his Elise by telling her that his
disgust with her has detached him from the world and the flesh.

Claude Mauriac was very clever to present the works of Jouhandeau as an *Introduction à une mystique de l'Enfer* (Grasset, 1938). He wanted to say by this slogan that Jouhandeau's clear-sightedness led him only to a devilish egotism instead of leading him to God. Claude Mauriac implied, however, that if motivated by charity, M. Godeau-Jouhandeau would be on the right track. Jouhandeau is not detached and simply ridicules, by a selfish restraint on his part, the unrestrained abandonment of a woman to a love partner. In doing so, he shows a shrewdness rather than sublimation. In André Maurois' (1885-   ) *Climats* (1928) a gentle husband mentally tortured by his first wife becomes the tyrant of his second. The desperate struggle for an impossible platonic friendship is delineated in *Le Vent noir* (1947) by Paul Gadenne (1907-   ).

If Marcel Proust has declared love to be "le risque d'une impossibilité" (*A l'ombre des jeunes filles en fleurs,* III, p. 94), Paul Claudel has seen through the whole problem of love in the same way. According to him woman is to man by definition "La promesse qui ne peut être tenue" *(Le Partage du Midi).* The promise cannot be kept because God is standing between all lovers and demands their love for Him, the only object of absolute love. "There is no room for two," for God and the earthly mate.[62] But love can be a detour to charity through suffering. Yse and Mesa in *Le Partage du Midi* find in their adulterous love the means of learning to suffer, to renounce and to die. Marthe in *L'Echange* learns from the infidelity of her husband that being unappreciated, repudiated, insulted in spite of one's love is the best way to perfection. Violaine in *L'Annonce faite à Marie* needs her burning love for Jacques Hury, his defection and the jealousy of her sister as the material of a sainthood. Doña Prouhèze in *Le Soulier de satin* never would have realized what love really means had the desire for an unattainable lover, Don Rodrigue, not shown her what terrible dimensions of longing and suffering are becoming to the human soul, and had her marriages with unloved husbands not taught her that sacrifice and mortification develop out of hatred a superhuman love of which she never would have believed herself capable. Thus love cannot be enhanced by sublimation, but can only be renounced and thus shifted to the higher level of the love of God (see chapter six).

François Mauriac subscribes entirely to Claudel's dramatized love theory when he says: "Ce qui déshonore l'homme ce n'est presque jamais son amour, fût-il le plus charnel, mais ce par quoi il le remplace. Il le remplace . . . jusqu'au jour où il decouvre enfin que cet amour usurpait lui-même une place destinée à un Autre."[63] Mauriac still seems in the authentic tradition of Saint John of the Cross when he says: "Tout amour humain se dresse contre l'unique Amour" (*Dieu et mammon,* p. 128), and "Le Dieu des chrétiens ne veut pas être aimé, il veut être seul aimé" (*Souffrance et bonheur du chrétien,* p. 25). The problem here is not whether Mauriac is a "Jansenist," a "rigorist" or a "pessimist," as various critics have emotionally characterized him, but whether his analysis is correct. There certainly is full agreement between Mauriac and Claudel on the meaning of conjugal love as a sacrificial detour to the Love of God; therefore the critics, even the Catholic ones, are wide of the mark in accusing both authors of degrading marriage as a sacrament. The dignity of sacramental marriage and its important natural and supernatural rôle cannot detract from the hierarchy of values according to which even marriage must not be a barrier to the higher calls of grace. We have rather to decide here whether the problem as put by Claudel and Mauriac is serious, and good literature. It is this by all means, since it is not based on speculation but on observation. And therefore the exquisitely refined psychology of Proust seems to buttress Claudel's and Mauriac's philosophy: "L'amour nous pousse non seulement au plus grand sacrifice pour l'être que nous aimons, mais parfois jusqu'au sacrifice de notre désir lui-même" (*Le Temps retrouvé,* I, p. 169).[64]

An attempt at sacrificial renunciation by a girl who is caught between pride and mysticism was illustrated early by Emile Clermont (1880-1916) in his novel *Laure.* Laure yields her suitor Marc to her beloved sister Louise. She is able to live with the married couple for six years without revealing the secret of her unconquerable love for Marc. Louise, sharing the spirituality of Laure, elicits, however, the secret from her (Edition Grasset, p. 313) and, thunderstruck, tries to detach herself from her husband in order to give up the advantage she has over her sister; that, of course, destroys her marriage. Finally Laure tries to overcome her previous weakness by a new pseudo-mystical effort to reconcile husband and wife.[65]

War situations brought special conditions to modern love psychology. In Paul Raynal's much discussed drama *Le Tombeau sous l'arc de triomphe* (1924) a soldier comes back from the front for a short furlough of some days to marry his fiancée Aude. The wedding is fixed for one of these days; surprisingly a telegram calls him back the very first day. A short night separates him from the departing train. The chaste Aude, overcoming all her inner resistance, gives herself to him that very night. Her "generosity" measures up to his. He had not told her the reason for his immediate return to the front: in order to get his furlough at all, he had volunteered for a suicidal mission during the impending attack, which now was ordered earlier than expected. His father criticizes the young couple severely. He is rebuked for his civilian morals by the soldier's "morals of the front." But when Aude is no longer sure of herself and reproaches the soldier from whom she will be parted forever for having accepted her sacrifice and for not believing in chastity and in Christ, he answers in a melodramatic fashion: "Mais je lui ressemble. Il fut, comme moi, consumé d'amour, et il mourut, après avoir pleuré, en rêvant qu'il sauvait les autres" (Acte III, p. 275). The soldier's father consoles himself by continuing to enjoy the presence of Aude who takes good care of him.

A kind of answer was given to Raynal's play which illustrates the concept of the importance of an heir as a guarantee of an "immanent" immortality, by Gabriel Marcel's *Le Mort de demain* (1932). In this work the wife of a soldier on leave under spiritual inhibitions feels incapable of granting conjugal love to a human being whom she can only imagine and anticipate as the dead of tomorrow, whom she wishes to appear absolutely pure and detached before God (see chapter six).

The second world war with its displacements and migrations often reduced people deprived of everything to rely entirely on the bliss of being a couple. This situation often lost sight of inspired Jean Anouilh's *Eurydice* who is praised with the words of Orphée:

> Je ne croyais pas que c'était possible de trouver le camarade qui vous accompagne; dur et vif, il porte son sac. . . . Un petit copain muet qu'on met à toutes les sauces, et qui le soir est belle et chaude contre vous. Pour vous seul une femme, plus secrète, plus tendre que celles que les hommes sont obligés de traîner tout le jour derrière eux. . . . Ma farouche, ma sauvage, ma petite étrangère (*Eurydice,* p. 355).

But happiness is not possible without an extreme purity: Orphee must lose Eurydice, even this Eurydice.

Conversely on a less philosophical level Paul Eluard (1895-1955) praises the happiness of a problemless conjugal love as experienced by all those who return from wars (he took part in World War I, II and the Resistance) and rediscover what their wives mean to them:

> Toutes les femmes heureuses ont
> Retrouvé leur mari—il revient du soleil,
> Tant il apporte de chaleur.
> Il rit et dit bonjour tout doucement
> Avant d'embrasser sa merveille.
> (*Poèmes* 1914-18 from Paul Eluard,
> *Selected Writings.* A New Directions
> Book, 1951, p. 2.)

He becomes the poet of unproblematic and poised conjugal love in his *Phénix* (1952):

> Si je te parle, c'est pour t'entendre,
> Si je t'entends, je suis sûr de comprendre.
> . . . .
> Si je te quitte, nous nous souviendrons
> Et nous quittant nous nous retrouverons.[66]

This triumphant conjugal love is shared also by Louis Aragon (1897-   ). Comparable to what Emile Verhaeren wrote thirty years earlier, Aragon praises the constancy and serious maturation of a conjugal love of long standing:

> Dix-huit ans je t'ai tenue, enfermée
> Dans mes bras comme Avignon dans ses murs,
> Dix-huit ans comme un seul jour parfumé,
> Comme mon amour t'enclôt dans son armure,
> L'automne a déjà ses rouges ramées,
> L'hiver est déjà sous l'or des ramures.
> Mais que peut l'hiver, mon enfant aimée,
> Si demeure en nous le divin murmure,
> Si, quand le feu meurt, monte la fumée
> Et garde la nuit le goût des mures!
>
> *(La Diane française)*.

*   *   *

A sophisticated psychology made acceptable for the first time in literature unnatural forms of love. These are described chiefly, as we have already seen, by Proust and Lenormand, but also by Bourdet, Gide, Roger Peyrefitte and Montherlant. The tragedy of the invert is increased by the social taboo, which becomes a terrible injustice if no actual sin is committed and there is involved only a psychological predisposition caused by such an unfortunate biological status. In Edouard Bourdet's (1887-1944) *La Prisonnière* (1926), Irène de Montcel, educated without a mother's care, struggles in vain against the chains of her Lesbian inclinations despite the loving help of Jacques d'Aiguines, her suitor who adores her. André Gide in *Corydon* defends the human dignity of the victim of sexual inversion, his sins included, to the paradoxical and the sacrifice of Gide's own reputation. His drama *Saul* has to be interpreted in the same sense.

Friendships between college boys were made a literary topic by Amédée Guiard in his novel *Antone Ramon* (Bloud et Gay, 1914). Although novels of this type have become a fad and are for the most part worthless, there are a few with a certain literary merit. Such is the case with *Les Amitiés particulières* (1945) by

Roger Peyrefitte (1907-   ), the tragic story of the boys Georges and Alexandre which ends with the suicide of Alexandre at fifteen. The author cannot be exonerated, however, from the reproach of looking for scandals and indulging in diatribes against Catholic boarding schools. This is confirmed by his typically anticlerical novel *Les Clés de Saint-Pierre* (1955). The same topic was extended to pupil-teacher relations by Henry de Montherlant in his drama *La Ville dont le prince est un enfant* (1951, Gallimard). Here the plot is very subtle: Abbé Pradts, insisting on the dismissal of sixteen-year-old André Sevrais from school because of his allegedly disastrous friendship with the fourteen-year-old Serge Sandrier, is convinced by his superior that his own sympathy for young Sandrier goes too far, and that he must consent to the sacrifice of detachment in dismissing Sandrier likewise. René Etiemble (1910-   ), the shrewd communist critic and Rimbaud scholar, writing in an easy and appealing style, produced a particularly nasty novel in *L'Enfant de choeur* (1937). Here he describes how André Steindel, an entirely unbelieving and debauched young boy, pupil at a Catholic school, serves Mass with theatrical cant and deceives his masters, but due to his intelligence becomes the outstanding and most promising pupil while he has the most degraded natural and unnatural sexual relations culminating in incest with his mother. No story could be more vulgar.

* * *

The subconscious tendency of man to anarchy led psychologists to the belief that the subliminal *Id* is superior in importance to the conscious and rational *Ego*. In the schizophrenic personality the *Ego* is very often subdued by an enigmatic force which seems to push it to a domineering, unpredictable behavior. This unexplainable force bewitched the authors and led them to study how it dominates the *Ego*. The rationalists speak in this connection of an irresistible urge, the believers even of the devil.

André Gide (1869-1951) seems to have been aware as early as Freud himself of the most harrowing urge of all, the *acte gratuit, la fatalité intérieure,* i.e., the unmotivated crime rooted perhaps in a subliminal and unhampered curiosity. Dostoevsky's hero Raskolnikov had already killed a widow to see "how it works," but he did it nevertheless in a dire need and with philosophical speculations, and he did penance for his crime in the prisons of Siberia. Gide's Lafcadio in *Les Caves du Vatican* (1914) pushed his companion Florisoire out of the train between Rome and Naples only to see "how it works." He is a complete cynic. Lafcadio continues his trip like a paranoiac who in his irresponsible acts is unhampered by the censorship of a conscience, and does not know how to be sorry for anything he has done. Gide seems amazed and delighted that such a thing exists, that there are apparently free actions unconcerned with moral implications and he sees in this the fatality as well as the extreme liberty of human action, a *coincidentia oppositorum*.

Klaus Mann in his book on André Gide seems perfectly correct in interpreting also *La Porte étroite* (1909) not as an ironic presentation of religious sacrifice, not as a traditional treatment of renunciation in love, but as a glorification of Alissa's *acte gratuit* by which she abandons her fiancé Jerome to her sister Juliette. Such an act has a right to be absurd, foolish, sublime, or mean, but remains in all of the cases "gratuitous energy."[67]

The monstrous children in *Les Faux monnayeurs* (1926) steal, seduce, kill and commit suicide just "pour voir" and seem to Gide, psychologist of *L'Immoraliste* (1902), interesting for that very reason.[68] In the rôle of Uncle Edouard, Gide keeps a diary of the crimes of a youthful gang which counterfeits money, but worse, falsifies life by abandoning all moral standards. Edouard's nephew Olivier Molinier and his friend Bernard Profitendieu, both sons of judges, corrupt a whole boarding school. Their friend Vincent is the most irresponsible of all and declares he feels pushed by the devil. Two immoral women, Lady Lillian Griffith, finally killed by Vincent, and Laura Douviers, the adulterous wife of one of the professors, are the centers of attraction for these boys in the poisonous atmosphere of the so-called respectable boarding house Vedel-Azais where the old M. La Pérouse tries to protect his grandson Boris while without his knowledge his daughter is corrupting all the boys. Two of them, Strouvilhon and Ghéridani-sol, persuade little Boris to show by an *acte gratuit* that he has the courage to kill himself and Boris shoots himself with a revolver handed over to him by these two monsters. Olivier becomes so horrified that he himself makes an attempt at suicide, La Pérouse is felled by a stroke, the boarding school is closed, after the newspaperman Passavant had interested the boys even in unnatural vices.

How can the immoral and amoral interest of Gide in such happenings, in such terrible, gratuitous crimes which he rather tries to understand than to condemn, be accounted for? Gide's theories on the *acte gratuit* are laid down in his *Souvenirs de la cour d'Assises* (*Oeuvres complètes,* vol. VII, Paris, 1934, II, p. 29). He believes that most of the criminals commit only an *acte gratuit.* Gide practically secularizes but in an irresponsible manner the old *mysterium iniquitatis.* When André Gide, unsatisfied with his own trifling commentary on his novel (*Le Journal des faux monnayeurs*), came back to the sterner language of his calvinistic youth, the *acte gratuit* appeared to him a fiendish possession just as it appeared to his boy hero Vincent:

> Je sens en moi, certains jours, un tel envahissement du mal qu'il me semble déjà que la mauvais prince y procède à un établissement de l'enfer,[69] or:

> Vincent se laisse lentement pénétrer par l'esprit dia-bolique. Il croit devenir le diable. . . . Il sent vraiment qu'avec Satan il a partie liée.[70]

Gide's Christian language makes it perfectly clear that his discovery of the anarchic-amoral superreality in juvenile delin-quency is nothing else but a detour to reach a part at least of the forgotten Christian reality, "the contemporary substitute for original sin and damnation."[71] One cannot indeed say of Gide what has been said of the American writer John Dos Passos, that he "has glimpsed only the crust of disintegration . . . not looked beneath the surface where sin organizes or decay begins."[72] Gide, "en proie à la curiosité du mal," as Henri Massis says, is the rediscoverer of the tremendous superreality of Hell, partly

—and this is unfortunate—as the Devil's advocate by rendering sin and crime immune to moral condemnation. It is not the right place here to confront him with Bernanos, who makes the same rediscovery from a mystical viewpoint. The names which Gide gives to his hellish realities do not change the fact that the *acte gratuit* is crime, and the "curiosité du toujours neuf" a metaphysically negative phenomenon.

The style of André Gide, aiming at simplicity and therefore often called classical, nevertheless seethes with latent emotion. This comes out not in sensational imagery but in key words such as *amour, désir, tendresse, ferveur, passion, extase, volupté, ivresse, frémissement*. Gide can also express insistence by using unusually long and unusually placed adverbs such as: *obstinément douloureux, morbidement doux, habiter éperdument un paysage, ôter brusquement les souliers*.[73] Thus there certainly is something emotional, political, doctrinal which deprives Gide's style of its so-called classical purity. Therefore R. Etiemble speaks of his style as an atticism modified by Stalinism.[74] The style of Gide, according to G. Antoine ("Le rôle impressif des liaisons de phrases chez André Gide," *Studia Romanica, Gedenkschrift Eugen Lerch*, Stuttgart, 1955, p. 22-81), reflects the protean character of his author in a rhythmical linkage of the sentences which is at the same time a syntactical break. Writing mainly on the basis of syntactic coordination, Gide subordinates semantically and psychologically a half or a third of the sentence nevertheless. In the following asyndetically linked short sentences, the second presents a finality with regard to the first, the third a consequence of the second:

> Je sortis. L'air glacé du jardin me calma; j'y restai quelque temps.

Gide cuts his ideas in such a way that before a new sentence he abruptly inserts a clause with *de sorte que* which rhythmically permits a pondering pause. Others he begins with the intention of creating different effects of monotony, surprise and symmetry by the solemn biblical Et, the pathetic-lyrical Et of the romantics, and the particularly rhythmical Et of Flaubert. Additional means of achieving this ambiguous, condensed *liaison* are asymmetry, suspense, reprise, anaphora, inversion, suppression of personal and reflexive pronouns, and the combination of modifiers in form of phrases and clauses:

> J'ai vu cette eau monter, lourde de terre, tiède, et qu'un rayon de soleil jaunissait.

Thus dissonant harmonies are everywhere. Sometimes, an inverted sentence alone can link by its clashing diversity two normal ones:

> J'ai fait de grands efforts pour causer. Est arrivé Quinton. Je suis parti.

A dichotomy also appears in the structures. Gide's fictional technique alternates between narration and commentaries on all aspects of life lived in its fullness. Such a two-pronged approach produces confused actions which coalesce only in his strictly narcissistic writings.[75] Of course, the chameleon-like André Gide is well reflected in his "mirror-technique" and in his "prise de vue multiple" which is strongly reminiscent of Aldous Huxley's procedure in *Point Counter Point*.[76] His structural method shared by many moderns has been compared also to that of a conductor who dissects for his orchestra members the different movements of the score.[77]

The *acte gratuit* has more disastrous consequences in other writers. It can end in fullfledged diabolic consent to all perversities and obscenities, treacherous crimes and inhuman betrayals, and lead to dehumanization. This is the case with Jean Genet (1909-   ), a skilled but highly immoral writer from the underworld whose work has been irresponsibly published in the book series of the Nouvelle Revue Française. In his *Notre-Dame-des-Fleurs,* Mignon, the pederastic lover of Divine, alias the gangster "Notre-Dame," out of "une gaminerie née du dedans" exclaims in highest exaltation: "M'inhumaniser est ma tendance profonde." Later Mignon is killed by Divine and Divine is beheaded after having lived a life of homosexual monstrosities and in the constant temptation of suicide resulting from it. Diabolic blasphemy is not absent as is evident already from the choice of names: Divine refuses to flee from the police and prefers capital punishment to the penitentiary. He feels like a Satan who would behave like a Saint: "Je suis ... Bernadette Soubirous ... avec le souvenir d'avoir tutoyé la Sainte Vierge" (*Oeuvres Complètes:* NRF, vol. II, p. 167). Here we are confronted again with French literature at its lowest level. It is evident that delight is derived from human degradation, as is the case in the autobiographical novel *Le Sabbat* (1946) by Maurice Sachs (1906-1945). Sachs tells us all the sexual and other aberrations of his life, his conversion from Judaism and relapse after having entered the seminary, his impoverishment and self-debasing activities—which actually ended with his selling himself to the Nazis. He was hanged in Hamburg by an aroused populace.

Albert Camus, the explorer of the absurd, opens his *Mythe de Sisyphe* with the statement of diabolic revolt: "Il n'y a qu'un problème philosophique vraiment sérieux: c'est le suicide" (p. 15), or in another formulation: "Je me tuerai pour affirmer mon insubordination, ma nouvelle et terrible liberté" (*Le Mythe de Sisyphe,* p. 144). So the highest form of the *acte gratuit* appears to be suicide. It became a terrible reality with some dadaists like René Crevel (1900-1935), Vaché, Rigault, and others who killed themselves. Suicide is recognized as the typically diabolical act by Georges Bernanos in *Sous le soleil de Satan* (1926), where Mouchette cuts her throat with a razor very calmly and with poise as it seems: "le menton jeté en arrière, sa gorge tendue, . . . elle n'y jeta pas la lame, elle l'y appliqua férocement, consciemment" (p. 222). It is interesting to find a parallel to Bernanos' description of suicide in a Russian author. The half-insane woman in the novel *And Quiet Flows the Don* by Mikhail Sholokhov, the Soviet writer: ". . . picked up a scythe by the handle, removed the blade (her movements were deliberately assured and precise) and throwing back her head, with all the force and joyous resolution that possessed her, she slashed her throat with its point."[78] Anna Valentinona in Paul Morand's *Nuit turque* (from *Ouvert la nuit,* p. 101) announces coolly in Constantinople that she is going to hang herself in Paris. The suicide of Colette's *Chéri* (see chapter II), coldly executed, is described as follows:

> Il n'avait pas besoin d'exaltation pour prendre le petit revolver plat sur la table. Sans se lever, il chercha une attitude favorable, finit par s'étendre sur son bras droit replié qui tenait l'arme, colla son oreille sur le canon enfoncé dans les coussins . . . et il ne connut plus rien de la vie au delà d'un effort de l'index sur une petite saillie d'acier fileté *(Fin de Chéri)*.

Those who do not commit suicide in despair are restrained only by a modern Hamlet-like hesitation: "There's the rub!" Thus Mauriac's Yves Frontenac, abandoned by his love, says: "Pourquoi nous a-t-on appris à douter du néant? . . . L'irremédiable, c'est de croire, malgré et contre tout, à la vie éternelle. C'est d'avoir perdu le refuge du néant" (*Le Mystère Frontenac*, p. 270).

The *acte gratuit* appears also in less extreme forms. In Jules Romains' *roman-fleuve* Edmond Maillecotin, despite his moral bent, feels sometimes like snatching a handful of nuts from "une jolie voiture des quatre saisons" or even a more precious piece of jewelry from a goldsmith's show window (*Montée des périls*, p. 125). The hero of *Barnabooth* by Valéry Larbaud (1881-   ) (see chapter four), although he is a millionaire, cannot leave Florence without having yielded to the impulse to steal something from a store.

The *acte gratuit* in the works of Georges Duhamel, the humanitarian physician, is fundamentally different from the *acte gratuit* in Gide's brutal form. In a world of anarchy or senseless "duty" Duhamel agrees with Claudel's idea expressed in *L'Otage* that: "Il n'y a plus rien de gratuit entre les hommes" (Acte I, sc. 2, p. 70). Duhamel, concerned about the lack of sacrifice and love, would rather have men rely on their instincts than on their loveless rules of behavior. This seems to be the key to the sympathetic though pathological Salavin, hero of Duhamel's five stories called *Confession de minuit* (1920), *Le Club des Lyonnais* (1929), *Deux hommes* (1924), *Journal de Salavin* (1927), and *Tel qu'en lui-même* (1932). Salavin's *actes gratuits* are the reaction of an unquenchable need of liberty and the desire of a handicapped young man to surpass himself. They result from contradictory psychological complexities, but remain acts of implied fatality, and stupid attempts to liberate oneself. Is Salavin an *agent* or a *patient* when he says: "Ça a été plus fort que moi"? Does he recognize the aimlessness of the act? Montherlant, who at least envisages an objective sacrifice, formulates the idea thus: "Dans le fond je crois que je me sacrifie à quelque chose qui n'est rien, . . . je me précipite dans l'indifférence de l'avenir pour la seule fierté d'avoir été si libre."[79] Likewise, to prove his human pride and independence, Salavin as a "pre-existentialist" boxes his boss's ear and loses his job, leaves his wife just to show what he is capable of, cares for the sick in a hospital to prove to himself the possibility of a "sainteté laique." These acts are, of course, of different value, but they are all gratuitous in intention and absurd under the circumstances. Thus Salavin builds up a system of neurotic obsessions. Feeling attracted by the white arms of Mme Lanoue, his friend's wife, Salavin flees from an imagined imminent adultery. Having been helped by his friend Edouard Loisel, he feels humiliated and accuses him of misunderstanding the extent of his poverty. Salavin pays from his own funds a sum of money embezzled by his subordinate in the bank and becomes responsible for the further criminal actions of this employee. His vain attempt at using the mishaps and catastrophes of his life to become a kind of saint is repeated with more seriousness and with a constant view to the passion of Christ by Jacques Larnaud, hero of the eight-volume-novel *La Mort est un commencement* (1941-1951) by Paul Vialar (1897-   ). Vialar seems more successful with his recent *Chronique française du XX° siècle.*

Duhamel describes the *acte gratuit* in other works beside the Salavin series, but there he presents it as a strong actual temptation without clear moral implications, and the logical appeasement of such a temptation. In a volume of his *roman-fleuve Les Pasquier* which we already know, namely *Les Maîtres*, Sénac explains how tempting it is to feel like killing a cat when in caressing it, one feels its windpipe and it is only necessary to tighten a little. In the same novel, Laurent Pasquier explains his experiences when working beside Catherine Houdoire in the laboratory:

> Je contemple ce beau visage mélancolique, et, soudain, en moi, dans les profondeurs de moi, se prend à remuer une force violente et terrible qui est comme un démon. . . . C'est un besoin de saisir cette douce et aimable femme, de la saisir aux hanches ou aux épaules, de la couvrir de caresses et de baisers. . . . Et pourquoi? Je te le demande. Pour me délivrer du démon en l'assouvissant et pour, de nouveau, pouvoir considérer le monde en général et Catherine Houdoire en particulier avec le regard le la très pure amitié. Tu le vois, tout cela n'est pas simple (*Les Maîtres,* p. 144).

Here the *acte gratuit* comes near to a self-therapeutic cure which psychoanalysts ascribe also to poetic creation. Laurent Pasquier tears the first one-thousand franc note he gets in his life into pieces and throws it into the river as a liberating action (*Vue de la terre promise,* p. 35) to prove to his greedy brother Joseph that he does not serve Mammon.

Julien Green, like another Salavin, notes in his *Journal* under the date of October 25, 1934, that he felt compelled in a theatre to stretch out his hand and pull the opera conductor by the sleeve. Despite these humorously presented milder cases of gratuitous acts, they border, nevertheless, on despair. Julien Green puts this very question into the mouth of one of his characters: "Est-il jamais venu à l'esprit de quelqu'un que l'enfer tout entier puisse tenir dans un salon de province? C'est pourtant dans cette pièce que maman a tenté de s'ouvrir les veines avec un éclat de verre quand papa l'a menacée d'un divorce" (*Varouna,* pp. 243-44). Such a magic from hell envelops Jean Cocteau's novel *Les Enfants terribles* (1929), comparable on a lower level to Gide's *Faux monnayeurs.* In Cocteau's fiction, behind the apparently harmless games of the *chambres enfantines* there lurk, clad in dreams and *paradis artificiels,* all the subconscious passions of the adult; and a jealous sister, Elisabeth, after having irked all her comrades by her rather disgusting *actes gratuits,* kills her brother Paul out of a monstrous passion of incestuous jealousy, because he had fallen in love with Agathe, the intruder. Everywhere fiendish crimes appear as acts of liberty without any moral implications. This neutralization of an ethical phenomenon corresponds to Gide's theoretical question: "Mais qu'est-ce donc, que la morale? Une dépendance de l'esthétique!" (*Chroniques de l'Ermitage. Oeuvres Complètes,* vol. IV, p. 307).

The style of Jean Cocteau is remarkable. His are the most unexpected comparisons and brilliant images, his the well balanced sentence. His virtuosity makes him lean to the playful and the *précieux.* His vocabulary is restrained. His statements are short and vigorous. Cocteau has defined his style himself in *Le Secret professionnel:* "C'est cette manière d'épauler, de viser, de tirer vite et juste que je nomme le style." Cocteau has a power of metamorphosis. His allegories exhale a magic power of transformation. The room of the *Enfants terribles* invaded by the outsiders looses its family anchorage and becomes an imperilled ship simply by the following metaphorical suggestion: "Ce fut seulement à partir de cette date que la chambre prit le large. Son envergure était plus vaste, son arrimage plus dangereux, plus hautes ses vagues."

CHAPTER IV

FORMS OF EVASION:

EXOTICISM, FANCY, DREAM

FOR A Frenchman who is so fond of his country and so bound to it, leaving the boundaries of France has always meant a flight into romantic and exotic experience. Since Rimbaud's prototypical escape, leaving France has even had metaphysical implications. It has meant a detour to spiritual realms, an obsession, exemplified also by Gide's hero of *Le Retour de l'enfant prodigue* (1907), who after returning to his father's house and not finding happiness, does not hesitate to help his younger brother escape too. In the twentieth century the object of exotic escapism is a fantastic flight into unknown "wonderlands." Sometimes the exotic land is only America seen as a paradise of skyscrapers by Luc Durtain (1881-   ) in *Quarantième étage* (1927), or by Paul Morand in *New York* (1888-   ); sometimes it is merely non-French Europe seen as an attractive moving picture with "fast trains and beautiful women" changing according to the quickly changing countries as in Paul Morand's *Tendres stocks* (1921), or Valéry Larbaud's *Barnabooth* (1913), the history of a rich Peruvian traveling for reasons of vanity. The interest in the mentality of foreign peoples, as it was evident in the works of Pierre Loti, is here pushed to the background or entirely absent, in favor of fantastic sentimental landscapes and wishful assimilations. Morand (*Ouvert la nuit*, 1922; *Fermé la nuit*, 1923), "c'est le cosmopolitisme sans nostalgie . . . , Larbaud, c'est la recherche systématique du depaysement par le cosmopolitisme."[1] In all these cases, however, the discovery of unknown new realities is supposed to fill "l'irremplissable Vide" (V. Larbaud, *Poésies d'A.O. Barnabooth*).

In *Amour, mon beau souci* and *Amants, heureux amants*

(1923), Valéry Larbaud feigns the mentality of a *roué* of the eighteenth century, who is at the same time a sorcerer in a fairy world where modern Manons, bewitching sweet fairy-like creatures such as Queenie Crosland, Gertie, Rose Lourdin convincingly make beauty *un beau souci* and stifle any doubt as to whether *amants* could be anything else than *heureux amants*. These unreal girls are not living in London and Naples but in a reshaped realm of imagination according to their imaginary existence in a *monologue intérieur*. What these authors are looking for is a "strange new land—a poetic reality," as Carlos Lynes says with special regard to Gide.[2] This author sees Africa as a race and a landscape turned into something especially solemn and beautiful for his, Gide's, sake.[3] Gide, indeed, finds here what others are looking for in dreams: "L'étrange." Jules Romains similarly calls an American creation such as Manhattan, "un morceau exemplaire d'irréalité américaine" (*Quand le navire . . .*). The major surrealistic element, however, lies in the art of travelling itself. Therefore Roland Dorgelès exclaims "Partir! partir . . . Qu'il est grisant ce mot, on dirait une porte qu'on ouvre sur le monde . . ." (*Partir*, 1926, p. 155). It is the old *Partir* theme of Baudelaire and Mallarmé, taken up vigorously and turned into a kind of dream experience, as underscored at the end of the book: "C'est la fin du voyage. . . . On a dormi, on se réveille."

The *Voyage au bout de la nuit* (1932) is also, according to its author Louis-Ferdinand Céline (1894-   ), pseudonym for Destouches, a "voyage . . . entièrement imaginaire. . . . Tout le monde peut en faire autant. Il suffit de fermer les yeux" (*Préface*). This type of escape concerns Badamu, a French cavalryman who becomes a deserter and travels into the night of anguish and disgrace, the debased style of the author reflecting his degradation. Continuing his "journey" Badamu becomes a ruthless confidence man who gets mixed up with a big business enterprise in the French Congo, and ends as a doctor in the *banlieue* of Paris. The surprising thing about this book is that a kind of poetry results even from a moral quagmire and the abundant use of argot and profane language because there is also an atmosphere of striking images and picturesque anecdotes. Thus the cowardly hero of *Voyage au bout de la nuit* (p. 152) imagines his life in Paris as a veteran after victory:

> On entrerait au restaurant, on vous servirait sans payer. . . . On est des héros qu'on dirait au moment de la note. . . . On payerait avec des petits drapeaux français! . . . La caissière refuserait même l'argent des héros et même elle vous en donnerait avec des baisers quand on passerait devant sa caisse. Ça vaudrait la peine de vivre.

This adventurous escapism was previously found in a clumsier fashion in the fiction of two other authors, Pierre Benoit (1886-   ), and Victor Segalen (1878-1919). The first, juxtaposing with skill a primitive and a refined culture, shows in his *Atlantide* a modern lady who madly causes the death of her exotic lovers just to collect their embalmed bodies. The second in *René Leys* tells the story of a modern Belgian who lives a double life as a wandering European and the chief of the secret police in China.[4]

To have treated the exotic motif with irony at the expense of chauvinism is the originality of Amédée Guiard with his hero *Antone Ramon* mentioned earlier. This new Tartarin "s'exalte. . . . Il reprend Fachoda aux Anglais, soumet tout le continent noir, conquiert le Tchad, plante partout le drapeau français."[5] Fanciful irony becomes more satirical in Jules Romains' comedy *Donogoo-Tonka* (1920). Here a geographical mistake by Professor Le Trouhadec leads the daring adventurer Lamendin to rehabilitate the professor's reputation by founding this imaginary town and making a reality of it: "Si Donogoo-Tonka n'existe pas, il faut l'inventer." Georges Lemaître has very well seen why the modern travel books transform the world into a superreality.

> There is in distance, in remoteness, a magic . . .which transforms the most ordinary sights into something fascinating, ideal and poetic. The origin of this lure of things has not yet been clearly analyzed, though Morand mentions the strange optical illusion created by travel—a mirage of remoteness in space which . . . still awaits its Proust.[6]

This transfiguring superreality is due to that unprecedented speed of locomotion which works like intelligence and imagination by bringing together different, remote, contrasting "features of reality" in a "colorful meeting," "the foundation of all artistic enjoyment and creation."[7] The factor, however, which changed most the travel reality is the bird's-eye view of the airplane pilot, a view, as Saint-Exupéry explains, in which three orange trees, a little brook, a flock of sheep, a shepherdess and a farmer are more important than towns and streams: "Et peu à peu, l'Espagne . . . devenait . . . un pays de contes de fées" (*Terre des hommes,* p. 17).

The Far-Eastern backdrop of Malraux's great novels, particularly *La Voie royale* (1930), reveals an escape into harder, more absurd, unbearable conditions which challenge the adventurer's existential-heroic daring and brutality.[8] In *La Voie royale* the European explorers Vanner and Perken try to civilize the tribe of the Mois, but instead find themselves exposed to the inhuman and subhuman forces of the jungle. Victims of insects and snakes, they encounter their comrade Grabot as a slave of the Mois, blinded and harnessed to a treadmill, apathetic to any human stimulus.[9]

Modern French literature reflects to a large extent the newly found results of Gaultier in his study *L'Adolescent.* Youth, he concludes, is by principle romantic and "pendant cinq ou six ans le rêve va, littéralement, se substituer à la réalité."[10] The early masterpiece among many other minor novels of this kind is *Le Grand Meaulnes* (1913) by Alain Fournier (1886-1914). The hero of this novel escapes without leaving French soil into a romantic reality of his own:

> C'est la vie réelle avec ce lent paysage des rives du Cher, calme et recueilli . . , les fermes paysannes, la boutique pittoresque du vieux Nancy, le château indulgent et bizarre . . . mais avec cette légère intrusion de fantastique. . . . C'est l'existence réelle d'un coin de province aperçue à travers les yeux enchantés de l'enfance.[11]

Le grand Meaulnes forsakes school to discover wondrous worlds but he also forsakes his fairy-wife Yvonne de Gallais just after his wedding day for further romantic realizations.

The starting point for nineteen-year-old Alain Fournier's dream of escape materializing in Le Grand Meaulnes was, as one knows, "le jeudi de l'Ascension de l'annee 1905, devant l'escalier du Grand Palais," where he saw "une jeune fille, dont la grâce et la beauté resplendissante le frappèrent soudain."[12] Marcel Proust observes this aspect of youthful psychology which one may call the Beatrice-experience: "L'attrait d'une femme inconnue est une forme du désir d'évasion" (La Prisonnière, I, p. 193).[13]

In the case of Le Grand Meaulnes the transposition of a real experience into a novel is perfect. The friend of Augustin Meaulnes, François Seurel, the schoolteacher's son (Alain Fournier's other half), tells the story. In the country school of St. Agathe, Meaulnes is haunted by a spirit of adventure and wanderlust. Riding once in the little dog-cart, the boys discover a magic castle, Les Sablonnières, where a fancy dress ball is taking place; they are invited to take part and Meaulnes falls in love with the daughter of the estate Yvonne de Gallais, an ideal of beauty, purity and happiness. But Yvonne's brother Frantz, possessed also by an adventurous spirit, leaves the castle, and becomes a strolling player. Coming to St. Agathe, he persuades Meaulnes to meet him in Paris and to swear to follow him whenever he utters a certain cry. Having gone to Paris, Meaulnes discovers that Frantz lied to him when he said he would also find there his sister Yvonne. He falls in love with a seamstress, Valentine, who happens to be the abandoned fiancée of Frantz. Despite his obligation toward Frantz and Valentine who had become his own mistress, Meaulnes returns to Les Sablonnières. He dares to beg from Le Gallais the hand of his daughter. On the very wedding day, however, Frantz appears in the woods with his cry, and the grand Meaulnes in order to keep his promise leaves Yvonne after the wedding night. Having succeeded in reconciling Frantz and Valentine, he brings them back home, but finds there only his own infant child whose birth had cost the life of Yvonne. Seurel is afraid Meaulnes will disappear again some day.

The magic of this novel, aptly called *The Wanderer* in its English translation, comes from a mood of frustration and purity combined with a poetic exploitation of landscape and atmosphere, *intérieurs* of castles and schools and human relations. It is written in a simple "style of St. Matthew," and contains a kind of a melody of Debussy, discrete and musical. The simplicity with which are evoked different *états d'âme* is striking: "C'était un froid dimanche de novembre" (I, ch. 1); "Ce fut le matin le plus doux" (I, ch. 15); "Nous partîmes sur la neige, dans un silence absolu" (II, ch. 2). These evocations of nature are meant as preludes to human joys and sufferings. One often hears noises as "prémonitions auditives," a very profound type of suspense. The style of this excellent youthful novel responds to "notre soif de mythes."[14] Alain Fournier lives in two landscapes, a real and a symbolic one, both telescoped and inseparable: "D'un côté c'est la campagne du centre de la France . . . et de l'autre un paysage presque irréel, inexprimable, ou exprimable uniquement à l'aide de quelques symboles de pureté, tels que châteaux, villas, jardins, vieux domaines."[15] He finds his literary ideal realized when the wondrous has been deeply inserted into the real, not when it upsets or transcends reality.[16] Alain Fournier's youthful dream of a chaste love for an adored maiden remote and unattainable implies the symbol of the only attainable pure love, that of God, a viewpoint of Catholic critics such as Christian Dédéyan, Albert Léonard, H. Lelong, and Robert Claude, S.J.[17]

The main problem for modern escapism is to remain equally within the realm of poetry and possible reality. Although this goal was reached only in Alain Fournier's *Le Grand Meaulnes,* an attempt to do so was recently made by Julien Gracq (1909-   ) in *Le Rivage des Syrtes* (1951). Here tragedy springs from the romantic dream of a young officer. The quasi-peace or cold war between the Mediterranean ports of Orsenna and Farghestan is shaken after three hundred years. The young naval observer Aldo serving with the light flotilla of Captain Marino, while studying the maps in the chart room, is irresistibly attracted to the shores of Farghestan. A frivolous and adventurous woman, the beautiful Vanessa, succeeds in persuading him during a boating excursion to land on the island of Vezzano, close to Farghestan. During his next naval reconnaissance he navigates his warship *Le Redoutable* so close to the enemy's capital that he provokes the firing of three shots from Farghestan's coast artillery. Although the ambassador of Farghestan minimizes the incident, the young officers of Orsenna are very glad to have a reason for war, and refusing to tender the slight and formal apology demanded by Farghestan, they bring down upon themselves the destruction of their city. Here a modern situation—a constant threat of war whose outbreak is at the mercy of trigger-happy officers—disguised in the color and style of an undetermined Middle Ages, produces without any doubt a magic, operatic, but serious atmosphere where Destiny like the Greek *moira* is unpredictable. The style is very *précieux,* the sentences visibly labored and mannered but impresses the reader as brilliant.

Other novels are exclusively romantic youthful dreams where fanciful events occur only in the mind. In *Comme le temps passe* (1937) by Robert Brasillach (1909-1945), two cousins, René and Florence, live happily on Mallorca, a kind of wonderland for them. Nonetheless they are longing for "Alcudia . . . ville du pays des songes, . . . la cité des mirages" (p. 4). When they are united later in their honeymoon in Toledo, they both dream of their bygone children's paradise of Mallorca which is now their Alcudia. Children are poets within whom lives "ce désir de se dépasser, de rompre sa limite, de s'évader hors de soi."[18] Françoise, the heroine of *Méïpe* by André Maurois (1885-   ), finds escape in a similar manner after unhappy experiences with many of her nurses. Her Alcudia is called Méïpe, a non-existent but nonetheless real point at which heaven and earth meet.[19]

—Nous sortons ce soir, Françoise.
—Je veux aller avec vous.
—C'est impossible.
—Ah! Eh bien! tant pis, moi, je vais dîner a Méïpe . . .
—Mais où est Méïpe, Françoise, en France? . . .
—Méïpe! c'est même pas à un mètre.
Méïpe est dans notre jardin et il n'y est pas.[20]

The literature of childish escapism and dreams is rather rich today.[21] A particularly fine example with leanings towards the *Grand Meaulnes* is André D'Hôtel (1900-   ), *Le Pays où l'on n'arrive jamais* (Horay, 1955).

Certain objects and places, for instance a crowded highway, seem particularly to elicit youthful dreams. Young Francine in Jean-Jacques Bernard's play *Nationale 6* dreams "au bord de la route" of the prince who, because of engine trouble, will one day stop at her house and become her suitor. The disillusion comes when two drivers do indeed stop at her house, but alas, it is the old father Antoine and not the son Robert who falls in love with her.[22] Desire for fantastic adventure and juvenile lies sometimes cannot be distinguished from one another. This is the case in the mental world of Jean Cocteau's *Thomas l'imposteur* (1929), "trouvant déjà dans le mensonge une antichambre des aventures" (p. 307). The most poetic and chronologically first realization of a day-dreamer girl is *Marie Claire* (1910) by Marguerite Audoux (1863-1937). Marie Claire's dormitory door in the convent school must remain open, otherwise she sees green dragons with blazing mouths. She is punished for lying, after having seen the white cow in the shade of a tree and declared: "Tiens, on a changé la vache blanche sans doute parce qu'elle était méchante?" (p. 38, édition Charpentier, 1911). Locked in an old room as punishment, she feels that "une vieille armoire à ferrures rouillées devint l'entrée d'un palais magnifique, etc." (p. 39). As a shepherdess she has the "songe éveillé" that her beloved Soeur Marie-Aimeé comes to visit her and she hears "ses pas et le bruissement de sa robe sur l'herbe" (p. 108). When the wolf attacks the flock she sees wings on him and "n'aurait pas trouvé extraordinaire qu'il se fût envolé pardessus les arbres" (p. 133). "Où est la fantaisie? . . . Où est la vie? Où est le rêve? Pourquoi les séparer?" Marie Claire has a successor in the little heroine of *Orange bleue* (1940) by Yassu Gauclère (1908-   ).

The best example of youthful transformation of reality may be the short story collection of Valéry Larbaud called *Enfantines* (1918). Here Emile Raby has endless conversations with the imaginary friends Rose, Dembat and Arthur. Merely by singing a nursery rhyme "Dansez Bamboula" he transforms himself into Bamboula, screams like a savage and forgets his French.

Modern surrealism and escapism come necessarily to fairyland, not, however, as a fairy tale of the old romantic sort; they create a light ironic, relaxed fairy, gently scoffing at the humanities. In this kind of *fééries* things are wantonly turned topsy-turvy, but nonetheless fill life with poetry and poetry with life. The master of this kind of lively dream-associations is Jean Giraudoux (1882-1944). Magician-like, he makes us believe that "ses héroines . . . sont des marquises échappées d'une toile de Watteau."[23] He "creates an illusion, but smiles in the act of creation."[24] He makes new myths of electric streetcars pursuing one another and neglecting fair play by overrunning the stops.[25] He anachronizes old myths, giving them modern life.

Suzanne in *Suzanne et le Pacifique* (1921), the most unreal, anti-logical, fairy-like, paradoxical and beautiful female Robinson Crusoe one can imagine, is a young lady who in the desperate loneliness of a desert island thinks of her beauty care and Parisian love affairs, and writes letters to her friend Simon. Instead of mailing them she replies to them herself. What is much more important is that Suzanne's French culture enables her to make a paradise out of a desert and fill her loneliness with magic company. She gives names to all the hills, meadows and brooks, she identifies certain birds with members of the *Académie française*. The beautiful lines of the landscape would not exist without Suzanne's knowledge of classical harmony, measure and equilibrium. The details are fascinating: out for a swim to a nearby but similarly deserted island, Suzanne leaves a note like a concierge: "Je suis dans l'autre île, je reviens." (p. 131).

This is superior cultural criticism in the form of "a curious day dream in which fragments of reality . . . are surrounded by a sublime atmosphere."[26] But it is more than this. The whole method of Giraudoux is an effort, by the play of superficial fancies, to keep away from the dark depths of the soul where trouble, sin, crime and poison lurk. He leaves this whole domain to the psychoanalysts. Juliette Delavalle in *Juliette au pays des hommes* (1924) fully appreciates this wisdom to keep from introspection (p. 274). Giraudoux has thus contributed to a superficial but very poetic superreality made up only by the bewildering impressions of the modern world on the one hand and by everything he ever read in books on the other. With Giraudoux "On entre dans un ordre où sont changés les rapports ordinaires ... où tel monde logique revêt, en un moment, comme un serpent qui change de peau, une logique nouvelle."[27] Giraudoux's fairy tales are made up of an indiscriminate mixture of literally taken figures of speech, anticipations, preposterous statements about everyday realities, as appearing in dreams: "Le ruisseau soudain ne coulait plus . . . Les champs, où les glaneurs ont laissé une seul épi, avaient l'odeur du pain. Les barres de vigne où le raisin était encore vert sentaient le pressoir" (*Juliette au pays des hommes,* p. 9). But also like a fairy tale is the description of the First-of-May celebration in Paris which the author reads to Juliette as his *Prière sur la Tour Eiffel* (*ib.,* p. 169-192), a parody of Renan's insipid *Prière sur l'Acropole.* In this atmosphere she asks Professor Lemançon: "Qu'est-ce que la vie?" (*ib.,* p. 145). Juliette is seduced by Boris Selmalof in a dressing room of the Opera (*ib.,* p. 200). Then she returns to her fiancé, the herculean sportsman Gérard. But strangely, Juliette does not feel guilty. After her one-month tour through the centers of education in Paris she rather snubs Gérard. She simply does not find him sophisticated enough for her since he does not know anything about the place of the adjective in the Guarani language.

It is the ironical-practical characterization which makes Giraudoux's fairy heroines so charming. What he does with the college girls Suzanne and Juliette, he does with the married woman Alcmène. Of all Alcmènes in myth and literary history, the wife of *Amphitryon 38* (1929) is the most dignified because she is the shrewdest. She is filled with the psychology and sophistication of a modern wife who tries at the same time to act honestly and practically. A dreamer could take her simply for a model of chastity and faithfulness when in her practical *mesure* she offers

Jupiter a platonic friendship instead of love. The school teacher *Isabelle* seems fairy-like in view of the uplifting influence she exerts upon the little village where she is teaching school. But since a mere fairy-tale character is not possible in such surroundings, she marries the comptroller of weights and measures. A hobgoblin, a rare personality in French literature, is there to take part in the action of *Choix des Elues* (1926). Here the hobgoblin Abalstitiel haunts the heroine Edmée on her very happy thirty-third birthday. Without Abalstitiel she never would have passed a night in a hotel just for fun, thereby destroying her matrimonial happiness, because her husband Pierre, the architect, belongs to those "qui construisent, inventent les caves et les égouts, pensent par étages et par ascenseurs." Therefore he never can forgive his wife her taste for "la catégorie vagabonde." They live separated for years until Claudie, Edmée's daughter, starts her own romantic escapades and drives Edmée home to Pierre.

In his works for the stage, Giraudoux realizes the aspirations of Gaston Baty's (1885-1952) *Le Masque et l'encensoir*. He creates a theater of "such stuff as dreams are made on," in a plain understanding of the fact "que le théâtre n'avait plus aucun sens et aucun intérêt, s'il n'était tout d'abord et delibérément irréel."[28] There is superior irony in *La Guerre de Troie n'aura pas lieu* (1935) when the "League of Nations" actually would have prevented the outbreak of the Trojan war, had not a drunken Greek soldier, after the negotiations were already under way, shouted insults at the Trojans. The wise Hector tries to appease the Greeks to such a degree that he quenches the patriotism of his own Trojan poet laureate, Demokos, by killing him. But the patriotic poet dies with the lie on his lips that not Hector but the drunken Greek soldier slew him. No diplomat could do anything after the Trojans had torn the poor Greek soldier to pieces.

Giraudoux's more concrete dream of an eternal peace concerned rather his country and the neighboring Germany. Here novel and drama had to serve with *Siegfried et le Limousin* (1922), and *Siegfried* (1928), respectively, the idea that a French soldier captured by the Germans and losing his memory could become as good a German, under the name of Siegfried Kleist, as he was a Frenchman, until his fiancée, the French sculptor Geneviève, remakes him M. Forestier with all the French roots he had before. The Baron von Zelten, a minor figure of the play, makes a statement about Germany which might be applied also to the work of Giraudoux: "[Ce] n'est pas une entreprise sociale et humaine, c'est une conjuration poétique" (Act 1, sc. 2).

The ethereal and *précieux* Jean Giraudoux considers all women to be debased, excepting the young girls, who seem to come from a paradise of innocence, provided that they did not live with their mothers but grew up as orphans.[29] *Eglantine* (1927) tries to escape the general law of unhappiness, age, and death by choosing older men as partners and by keeping them always the same age. The later plays of Giraudoux have a bitter and blasphemous note. He handles biblical motifs unwisely and indelicately. Lia and Jean, Ruth and Jacques discover in *Sodome et Gomorrhe* (1943) that sex is the source of hate, change, infidelity, lies and death. Sex crime transcends death. Lia, the selected superhuman, wants the love of an angel; Ruth, the female, wants another man; Dalila, the cheat, makes Samson "happy." Irony interprets the Judith story in such a way that a woman who prostitutes herself may be declared a saint by the people. This is Giraudoux's infamous version of *Judith* (1932), a dramatized insolence. His own "Je m'en fichisme," and the "douceur de vivre" are recognized, however, by this highly intelligent author as identical with modern materialism and atheism. Therefore Holofernes declares: "Je suis l'ami des jardins à parterre, des maisons bien tenues, de la vaisselle éclatante sur les nappes, de l'esprit et du silence. Je suis le pire ennemi de Dieu" (*Judith*, acte II, sc. IV).[30]

The younger generation will not consider the playful Giraudoux as one of their own despite his insights into life. Rather he will be looked upon as an historical figure without existentialist importance.[31] His earlier *préciosité* will always be preferred to the inept cynicism which permeates his later works and also his posthumous drama *Pour Lucrèce* (Grasset, 1953), the story of the proud and "pure" wife of the *procureur impérial* Lionel

Blanchard, Lucile, who was told by her jealous friend Paola that while in a state of unconsciousness she, Lucile, was raped by the notorious Comte Marcellus. Finding out that the story was not true, Lucile kills herself to save face as a woman rather than avow to her husband the hoax played on her by Paola's lie.

Giraudoux's art has not been thoroughly studied, although some insights have been given. In his paradise of imagery it is difficult to separate symbolism from mere picturesqueness.[32] His *mots-clefs* reveal the tendency of toning down reality, namely *absence, innocence, écluse, tampon*.[33] A competent critic has interpreted his art as a penetration of higher metaphysical areas by the ironic magic of the words which hide something behind their beauty of Greek statues.[34] Giraudoux's unique gift was the elegant-ironical transformation.[35] Its outstanding features are the ternary rhythm, literary allusions, fanciful-contradictory descriptions, beautiful color shades.[36] Stress is laid on "substantifs somnambules et magnétiseurs" which appear in contrasting couples such as "minuscule:immense; nu:habillé; passager:eternel."[37] All this produces a "raillerie nuancée de tendresse."[38] Giraudoux's method is well described by the words of Georges Lemaître:

> Living things and inanimate objects are endowed with a peculiar, weird existence; as they are never directly portrayed, but are forcibly suggested to the mind, they almost partake of the nature of hallucinations; they are tremendously real and yet actually absent; and the phases both of their reality and their absence alternate according to a rhythm which confers on Giraudoux's creations a vibration all their own.[39]

This style is grasped more closely with the empathetic formula of Laurence LeSage, who praises Jean Giraudoux's conception of a fairy world as buttressed by "a pictorical thinking and an extraordinary mental agility," which dips the objects "in a golden bath," and which makes creatures appear under a "spring rainbow."[40]

In the manner of Giraudoux there are minor and accidental fairy story tellers with less variety and less poetry. Paul Morand creates sarcastic myths, wittily explaining certain institutions.

About Wall Street, for instance, he remarks that once there was a wall around New York, but "De ce mur il ne reste qu'un nom: Wall Street. Aujourd'hui le mur est démoli et les loups peuvent entrer" *(New York)*.[41] He attains a fairy effect by meaningless charming exaggerations and romantic lies in the style of *Gulliver's Travels*. The Siamese babies, Morand declares, who still take their mother's breast, are already passionate smokers: "Ils fument un cigarre et ne s'interrompent que pour téter" (*Rien que la terre,* p. 181). He praises in contradictory sarcasm an admired fairy, Great Britain, where "hypocrisy is respected according to its merit" (*Londres,* p. 332). He sees a modern liner in her beauty as a Greek temple (*Rien que la terre,* p. 235). He brings the fairy element into a comparison as in the following Hungarian landscape:

> Des bois de sapins se dévidèrent, gardant l'alignement malgré la pente, obscurs dès l'orée, placards, où étaient rangés des villages sommaires, autour d'un clocher bulbeux (*Ouvert la nuit,* p. 161).

The authors classified as "fantaisistes," besides their psychological truth, remain very close to art as such because "L'art commence à l'instant précis où naît la fantaisie."[42]

The style of the "fantaisistes" sometimes imitates the expressionistic painters. Their most realistic types are introduced in a surrealistic manner. We see them as though through a cubistic caricature: Morand's Isabelle in *La Nuit romaine:*

> Dès les épaules, elle se divisait instantanément en deux jambes maigres et pointues en forme de compas, s'avançant en piquant les pavés (*Ouvert la nuit,* p. 111).[43]

André Malraux, at the beginning of his career, when he tried to do in a moderate form what André Breton (1896-   ) had done in a new and exaggerated manner in his *Poisson soluble* (1924), created even a whole fanciful story of the *Lunes en papier* (1921), paper moons that become little men and go on a campaign to kill Death in his "royaume farfelu," moving through a wood where ropes turn into snakes feeding on hearts which grow on trees. But the grim humor of the story is that Death has already committed suicide and it is not necessary for the moon men to kill him. The kingdom of death in a later novel entitled *Royaume Farfelu* (1928), however, becomes a nightmarish Oriental town besieged by weird animals and shows the author's decisive direction towards a literature where Death is rather the victor.

Like a tragic version of *Lunes en papier* is Saint-Exupéry's short story of *Le Petit Prince* who miraculously comes from another planet and leaves the world after having taught the adults the great message of Love and Purity which are constantly endangered by his symbolic play with volcanoes, snakes, flowers and particularly roses, and his sadness about the fact that lambs still eat the roses.[44] Is there not at the bottom of this wonderful fairy tale the atmosphere of Arthur Rimbaud's *nostalgie d'enfance:* "O saisons, o châteaux, Quelle âme est sans défauts?"

Dreams of immoral behavior as the imagined happiness of the adult were an outcome of the famous *inquiétude* of teenagers' puberty as for instance in the reprinted (*Oeuvres complètes*, Grasset, 1951) novel of Raymond Radiguet (1903-1923), *Le Diable au corps* (1923). Here, without knowing exactly what he is doing, the schoolboy Raymond, during World War I, being without any paternal supervision, meets Marthe, the young wife of a soldier at the front. He gets involved in a love affair with her which becomes so scandalous in the small community that Marthe, pregnant, has to return to her mother's. Raymond meets her again in Paris, but after wandering together through Paris during a bad rain to find a hotel room, Marthe contracts a lung ailment from which she dies. Raymond faints at the news of her death and recognizes his jealousy and love for her as he acknowledges the fatherhood of her child which he defends against the soldier-husband. Here sad reality and bad reality still appear in a strange dream light because of the guilty "naiveté" of the teenage writer who wonders what life actually is.

The same kind of immature perversity is found today in Françoise Sagan's (pseudonym for Françoise Quoirez [1935-   ])

Bonjour tristesse, (1954). In this novel a young girl, Cécile, admiring the erotic adventures of her widowed father, becomes jealous when he intends to marry one of his mistresses, Anne, a forty-year-old friend of her late mother. Anne is serious enough to keep Cécile to her duties as a school girl and to a relatively decent life. Cécile induces her father's younger mistress, Elsa, to become involved with Cécile's own lover Cyril. Thus she succeeds in making her father feel like reconquering Elsa. This situation so upsets Anne emotionally that she leaves the father and dies in a deliberate automobile crash. After Anne's burial in Paris father and daughter continue their old frivolous life, he with a new, expensive mistress, she with Anne's cousin Philippe. Young Mademoiselle Sagan's remarks on the last page of her strange though extremely well-written short novel dispense us from a moralizing commentary: ". . . Nous ne croyions pas en Dieu . . . Quand nous nous retrouvons, mon père et moi, nous rions ensemble, nous parlons de nos conquêtes.—Il doit bien se douter que mes relations avec Philippe ne sont pas platoniques" (p. 187). Cécile is "happy" simply "to believe in fate" despite a recurrent remorse which she greets every morning with: "Bonjour tristesse." Françoise Sagan, the young college girl, was able to make a minor work of art out of a hedonistic story. The language itself is quite reserved given the lewd subject matter. The leitmotivistic evocation of sun, sea, bathing, sailing helps to create a fascinating world of modern "nature" where the moral laws actually appear suspended and a shade of true repentance in the souls would almost disfigure the beautiful sunburnt faces and bodies playing their dangerous game. François Mauriac is certainly correct in his remark that this story of likable criminals, which is so insinuating, could have been written by a devil.

Françoise Sagan's second miniature novel *Un certain sourire* (1956), if compared to her first, may be called a failure, since plot-originality is lacking, the love-making of Dominique without any reasonable psychology except a hunt for sensation, leans very much to the pornographic side; and the immature dreams of beautiful cars, movies, records and pajamas, cigarettes, opium, sunny beaches and spoiled boys and husbands reveal the young author's faulty education, as does her incapacity of handling the subjunctives and the *consecutio temporum* (see Jean Menard, "Françoise Sagan," *La Revue de l'Université Laval* XI [1956], 114-126). Her lack of cultural background became also fatal to the more ambitious plot of *Dans un mois, dans un an* (1957).

The fiction of Françoise Sagan is still sound compared to the novel by the Belgian teenager Françoise Mallet (1930-   ), *Le Rempart des Béguines* (1951), in which a daughter becomes the lesbian lover of her father's mistress. This monstrous plot is also couched in elegant language and shows stylistic skill. The same may be said about the fourth teenage writer Jean-Baptiste Rossi (1931-   ) who conceives a despicable but seriously treated plot, the love between a nineteen-year-old boy and a thirty-year-old religious sister in his novel *Les Malpartis* (1950).

There are also adult children who recreate a fanciful atmosphere according to the recipe of Henri Bosco (1888-   ) in his *Jardin d'Hyacinthe* where the young girl Félicienne exploring the house creates a weird atmosphere for its inhabitants:

> Tout à coup, dans le calme de la maison, un craquement près d'une chambre, une fuite dans le noir de l'escalier, un soupir sous les combles. Çà et là on notait aussi l'apparition d'objets inattendus, qui inquiétaient un peu . . . ; car ils dérangeaient l'ordre . . . (*Le Jardin d'Hyacinthe,* Gallimard, 1946, p. 202).

Using the forces of the past for hallucinatory purposes is the real strength of this Provençal writer from Luberon. Avoiding the *terre-à-terre* approach of Giono, Bosco offers only unbelievable stories, steeped in a dream-world atmosphere and couched in an oneiric style. Meyrel in *Un Rameau de la nuit* arrives at nightfall at a kind of enchanted castle:

> Arrivé à la porte, je tendis l'oreille. La maison et le bois se taisaient. J'ouvrais. Les gonds mal huilés gémirent un peu. Loselée apparut. D'elle même derrière moi se referma la porte. . . . Le loqueteau retombe. . . . Je ne reconnaissais ni la maison, ni l'eau ni le bois. L'hôte et l'ombre avaient disparu. Je venais d'entrer, peut-être en fantôme.[45]

Obsessed by the presence of a supernatural world, though not a very Christian one, Bosco has patterned his main heroes accordingly: Méjan in *Jardin d'Hyacinthe,* and Martial in *Malicroix* (1948). The latter is a story of uncanny happenings on a farm which the story teller inherited from his great uncle Cornelius de Malicroix.

In Bosco's master work *Le Mas Théotime* (1945) mystery is produced just by an abnormal kind of silence. The farmer Pascal without asking any questions receives his cousin Geneviève after her husband Jacques Lebreux has killed a neighbor. We do not know whether her husband was aware of Pascal's love for Geneviève, or whether the bullet was prepared for Pascal, who by some complication never explained even becomes the heir of the murdered man. Geneviève, torn between the love for her cousin and faithfulness to her murderer-husband, enters the convent of the Trinitarians in Marseille.

Bosco's art according to R. T. Sussex (*AUMLA* I, 1953, p. 36 ff.) consists in an almost dialogueless narration of an extremely slow motion full of uncanny symbols for anguish (empty house, lamp) and innocence (garden, dove, rose).

The problem of hallucination has a still more serious aspect, the psychotic's existence within a morally indifferent life. Thus madness as the only "happiness" is Henri Lenormand's suggestion in his prose story *Le Penseur et la crétine.* Jean, the hero of Jean Sarment's play *Le Pêcheur d'ombres* (1921), loses his mind because Nelly does not requite his love, and lives now in the delusion that he is a fisherman, catching not fish but knights. His mother's attempt to persuade Nelly to love him ends terribly because after a new disillusion he commits suicide. In Fernand Crommelynck's *Le Cocu magnifique* (1921), Bruno is obsessed by the possibility that his wife Stella might betray him. This gnawing doubt makes him so insane that he orders his wife to love other men because the certitude will cure him of the doubt. She does so and avows every adultery committed. So Bruno now is happy because he believes his beloved Stella is feigning everything in order to cure him of his jealousy. The catastrophe comes when, one day, Stella leaves the village with a herdsman and the fool's paradise is ended. In Pierre Molaine's (1906-) novel *Les Orgues de l'enfer* (1951), the drawn-out tragedy of an insane asylum is complicated by the plot of a love affair between a doctor and one of the nurses who happens to be the wife of one of the madmen and struggles to remain faithful to him.

Much more important than the topic of the fool in contemporary literature, of course, are the fool's mental associations. They are different from those of other people. Painters, such as Salvador Dali, have given us pictures seemingly sprung from a monomaniac mind: obsessions which are ridiculous and terrifying at the same time, such as *La Persistance de la mémoire*, where a wrist-watch appears under several aspects, e.g., as a saddle, a rug hanging over the branch of a tree, a kind of doily on a table. The official and radical surrealists have accomplished similar associations with humor. We may pass over their childish political program for revolutionizing the world that way and their ostentatious adherence to a white-collar and drawing-room communism. Their technical-poetic evasion was made into a literary program first by Dadaists of the 1920's like André Breton (1896-) Robert Desnos (1900-1945), Blaise Cendrars (1887-), Joseph Delteil (1894-), Ph. Soupault (1897-), Pierre MacOrlan (1882-) and the "avant-garde" of 1940, e.g. Julien Gracq, René Char, Henri Michaux, most of whom did not become *poètes engagés*. Their evasion comes close to the "poetic" associations of children, psychotics and aborigines. We treat here only the poetically interesting cases and merely mention the surrealistic theory. The childish scientific-philosophical propositions of surrealism, sufficiently refuted and rejected by Sartre, tend towards the finding of a new truth through poetry based on an automatic writing which on its part produces an imagery containing elements of myth. Telescoping objectivity and subjectivity, these elements reveal in the way of religion rather than in the way of science both a theory and a praxis, the "Weltanschauung" of the future.

The poetic tendency of surrealism is shared by first class writers who have nothing to do with the surrealistic program. Mental associations, uncontrolled by logic and criticism, whether they be in the domain of primitivism, infantilism, or madness, amazingly characterize true poetry as well. There is a relationship, because the child (and the madman as well) exists as a type who "takes no account of others and is untroubled by the need to conform himself to persons or circumstances."[46] So in Breton and Eluard, Apollinaire and Cocteau and many of the stream-of-consciousness writers, there is an actual tendency to insert something of mental alienation into literature. In others, such as Delteil, Soupault, Cendrars, Giraudoux, Morand, MacOrlan, even the Gide of the *Faux-monnayeurs* who makes an angel appear in the Luxembourg Gardens, there is a tendency to make a child mentality a literary form in which, as we have pointed out, "fact and fancy blend in perfect harmony."[47] Decisive in these tendencies is the understanding that "the child's way of representing things is symbolic by definition." "A running dog is a dog with a great number of legs painted."[48] Rolling a hoop is for Louis Bastide in Jules Romains' *Le 6 Octobre* the same as riding a horse, with all the details of pausing, exhaustion, hurrying, "avant d'être pris par la nuit," etc. André Breton even proposed the childish metaphor as a poetic myth. Both children and poets may say for "It is getting dark": "Le monde rentre dans un sac" or for "The brook is murmuring": "Dans le ruisseau, il y a une chanson qui coule."[49] Laurence LeSage has clearly pointed out that Giraudoux's bluff-metaphors have been worked out according to this pattern.[50]

This use of metaphor, however, is a two-dimensional art of arbitrary combinations, a sentimental anarchy, a wilful distortion and simplification just like the reduction of art forms to spheres, cylinders and cones, the indifference to verisimilitude, the refusal to grasp complicated ideas, depth of thought and artistically organic wholes.[51]

The extremist poets are in their program decidedly buttressed by certain medical authors, who maintain that children and psychotics may somehow grasp by their intuition more of the super-realities of life than do normal people. Often life itself offers surrealistic combinations. Jules Romains' hero Vorge gets inspiration for his dadaistic poems from suburban show windows where he finds queer arrangements like a waxen hand, a mirror, a children's trumpet, a little toy with silver, blue and red circles, and a black "pelote de laine" (*Vorge contre Quinette,* Anthol. Coindreau, p. 337).

There are also infantile types among serious authors. Francis Jammes (1868-1938) is one of the first known for a childish stammering in this style. Marcel Proust, far away from a stylistic infantilism, is psychologically a child-type because of his mother-bound and morally indifferent attitude.[52] It is indeed Proust who states that "La pensée empêche d'éprouver la réalité" (*Albertine disparue,* II, p. 76), and he insists with Lenormand several times on the neo-baroque conviction that our life is a dream (*La Prisonnière* I, p. 201; *Le Temps retrouve,* II, p. 159).

Other authors use infantile style to express their amazement before the paradoxes of life. Paul Claudel does so to such an extent as to exasperate the critic and classicist Pierre Lasserre (1867-1930). Claudel, for instance, says about the insufficiency of worldly wisdom:

> La raison des sages m'a instruit avec la sagesse du tambour; les livres sont ivres,

or about the other world:

> Voici donc ce pays qui est au-delà de l'eau! Comme une rivière quand on est de l'autre côté.

Lasserre, shocked by the lack of thought and the "illiterate" syntax, comments: "On dirait que Marthe fait le bébé"; his point seems well taken.[53] But there are excellent concrete examples of child-like surface-associations, of child-style in Claudel, a kind of "ellipsis" as to the thought,[54] when in one of his Odes he thus describes a summer evening:

> C'est le moment, où . . .
> quand les cerises sont rouges . . .
> que les enfants se baignent au dessous des moulins et
> mangent tout nus leur goûter,
> la moitié de la lune paraît blanche dans le ciel.

This childish way of concretizing things transposed into merely metaphorical language assumes features almost equally "real" and concrete in the following description of evening by the well known author of *La Poésie du hasard* (1934) and *L'Amour de trois oranges* (1947), Alexandre Arnoux (1884-   ): "La nuit toquait légèrement aux portes des logis, et parlait à voix basse, à travers les fenêtres, à ses amies les lampes, qui s'allumaient" (*Abbisag*, p. 11). This type of child-like talk was also the novelty Guillaume Apollinaire (1880-1918) had to offer during World War I: "Bergère, ô tour Eiffel, le troupeau des ponts bêle ce matin" (*Zone*), or "Nos coeurs pendent ensemble au même grenadier" (*Vers le Sud*), or "C'est la lune qui luit comme un oeuf sur le plat."

The ellipsis, the jumping over a thought, appears daring in Jules Romains: he suppresses the fact of the setting sun in the following evening picture:

> Deux hommes cheminent là-bas
> Dans la vallée où le coq chante;
> Tous les arbres sur les collines
> Sont maintenant rouges et noirs
> (*Ode I* du Livre II),

indeed an "image d'Epinal." Thus representatives of the first generation of the twentieth century, Claudel, Arnoux, Romains, practically choose only other forms of Breton's: "Le monde entre dans un sac," mentioned above. Paul Morand knows how to imitate the syntax of an infantile style: "Les chevaux grelottent sous un vieux sac à pommes de terre et fument des naseaux, les bouches des hommes fument aussi, et les maisons" (P. Morand, *Bucarest:* Plon, 1935, p. 120). Paul Claudel, however, remains the master of infantile style because he is intrinsically concerned with showing the stammering of God's children facing the over-whelming creation and the bewildering rôle of the "causae secundae":

Le théâtre. Vous ne savez pas ce que c'est. . . . Il y a la scène et la salle. Tout étant clos; les gens viennent là, le soir, et ils sont assis par rangées les uns derrière les autres, regardant. Ils regardent le rideau de la scène. Et ce qu'il y a derrière quand il est levé. Et il arrive quelque chose sur la scène comme si c'était vrai. . . . Et je les regarde aussi et je sais qu'il y a là le caissier qui sait que demain on vérifiera les livres, et la mère adultère dont l'enfant vient de tomber malade . . . (*L'Echange*, Acte I).

Henri Ghéon's (1875-1944) infantilism in his modernized miracle plays remains outside the realm of language and sometimes gives the impression of a mere "niaiserie," as when Saint Nicholas in *Le Dit de l'homme qui aurait vu Saint Nicholas* "informe M. Verdauchet que ses enfants, au Paradis, font des progrès rapides dans le choeur des anges."[55] Despite Ghéon's serious conversion, it is because of his childish confusion of faith with "la foi du charbonnier" that he is prevented from making a direct contribution to spirituality and consequently is not discussed in chapter six. In adapting medieval legends to his idea of a modern popular Christian theatre, he has underrated the critical powers of even the modern "people." One of his plays, however, his revamping of the story of St. Alexis in *Le Pauvre sous l'escalier* (1920), may be considered a contribution to the literature of spirituality.

CHAPTER V

EXISTENTIALIST "ENGAGEMENT"

In the early twenties two German philosophers, Karl Jaspers and Martin Heidegger, derived from the so-called phenomenology of Edmund Husserl a curious blend of philosophy and psychology which eliminated with one stroke the lingering idealistic concepts of Neo-Kantianism and returned to the ontology of the objectively existent. In this enterprise they had fellow travelers in Max Scheler and Peter Wust. But Jaspers and Heidegger went farther and considered as the main problem the conscious reaction of the whole human personality as a particular type of existent toward the other existents which alone can inform man about himself. According to them, speculation, let alone revelation, is inadmissible. And since objects reveal themselves in an entirely insufficient way or rather not at all, man is bound to consider himself as haphazardly projected into the world, to be threatened by death, fear, anguish, anxiety, and radical doubt. There is no being prior to existence which could give man any explanation, consolation or direction for his actions. Overcoming the fear of death and yielding to the sense of care for others, man both by choice and risk gradually brings himself from existence into a kind of moral and worthwhile essence. While Jaspers is impelled by this situation of an enigmatic immanence to appeal imperiously to a meaningful transcendence, Heidegger considers it rather a helpless absurdity with not much room for any transcendence, let alone God.

These ideas spread in the early thirties among French philosophers such as A. Koyré, H.-Ch. Puech and Jean Wahl who discussed them in the periodical *Recherches philosophiques*. Furthermore, a similar type of existentialism on a genuine theistic, even Christian basis, was developed rather independently by Gabriel Marcel. In his *Journal métaphysique* with entries dating from

1914, he distinguished philosophical problems from mysteries. Among the mysteries are human relations and death which overwhelm us with awe and hint at the supernatural. But the public at large was alerted to existentialism only during World War II by Jean-Paul Sartre (born 1905).[1]

Jean-Paul Sartre twisted existentialism into a brutal theory of activistic *engagement*. Daring decisions and courage are the proof of a free personality in an allegedly senseless and godless world. Man has the choice either of being a *lâche* acting out of a sense of imagined duty and a *salaud* believing in a divine redemption for himself, or of being free to act authentically and thus come really alive. Flirting with communism and nonetheless seeing the lack of intellectual dignity in it, this extremely superficial French existentialism of *engagement,* rejected by Heidegger as the creation of Sartre himself, looked for other predecessors. They seemed to be found in the Russian emigrés Berdiaeff and Chestov, remotely in the Dane Soeren Kierkegaard (1813-1855), even in Blaise Pascal, but mainly in Nietzsche with his slogans of "living dangerously" and "God is dead." Just as the Christian existentialist Gabriel Marcel cast his ideas not only into philosophical treatises but also into stageable dramas, (see chapter six) so the father of French atheistic existentialism, Jean-Paul Sartre, propagates his psychological-sociological philosophy not only in treatises like *L'Etre et le néant* (1943) but also in dramas, novels, even in short stories. In his first novel *La Nausée* (1938), the philosophical ideas are not as yet sufficiently fused with fiction. Sartre gives such a gloomy picture of human existence that whoever has read this novel will not believe his thesis: *L'Existentialisme est un humanisme* (1946). Anguish, absurdity, existence are defined as they occur in the pondering mind of the hero Roquentin who tells his own story:

> Exister, c'est *être là,* simplement; les existants apparaissent, se laissent *rencontrer,* mais on ne peut jamais les *déduire* ..., surmonter cette contingence en inventant un être nécessaire et cause de soi ... ; la contingence, c'est l'absolu, par conséquent la gratuité parfaite. ... Quand il arrive qu'on s'en rende compte, ça vous tourne le coeur ... : voilà la Nausée; voilà ce que les Salauds ... essaient de se cacher avec leur idée de droit (p. 167).

Antoine Roquentin, an intellectual "sans importance collective" and without any "pour-autrui," after much traveling around, works in the library of Bouville (Le Havre) on historical documents concerning the Marquess of Rollebon. Such an individualistic preoccupation away from friends and in practical seclusion makes him constantly deviate from his task. He starts meditating on his being *en-soi* and *pour-soi* in time and space (*Sein und Zeit* in Heideggerian terms). Such introspection leads him to a kind of physiological and psychological self-destruction of *angoisse* and despair culminating in nausea; the more so as a self-taught man, the other daily visitor to the library, reveals himself a pederast for whom scholarship only means flight, disguise and *mauvaise foi*. He is looking in the library for handsome young men. Small wonder that Roquentin, who is far as yet from finding the formula "action versus contemplation," is twice compelled to vomit out of disgust with an apparently senseless, sex-centered and perverted world, which left him only a more pleasant memory of his former Parisian love, Anny. He is constantly worried about the distasteful bourgeois of Bouville (symbolic *ville de boue*), city of dirt, slime and viscosity culminating in the obscene matter-of-factness of his landlady. The ancestors of this Bouville, whom one can see painted in the museum and who are admired by their sons and grandsons, provoke in Roquentin the same nausea as the living generation taking their silly Sunday walks. Roquentin, sitting drowsily in his landlady's café, feels that something like more real being seems hidden in the music of the popular song, "Some of these days," coming from the gramophone, a song which is certainly superior in value to the bluish suspenders of the waiter and reveals at least the power of creative composing and singing. But such thoughts are underlined as a parody of Proustian idealism since they came also to his mistress Anny in Paris who is satisfied with temporary solutions. Roquentin, stupidly philosophizing, is a *salaud* when it comes to action for he misses the only occasion to face danger by defending the "autodidact," caught by an employee of the library in an embarrassing situation. Disgust with his own precarious existence and the conviction of being simply one of the superfluous bourgeois is the result of Roquentin's philosophical-moral and Cartesian experiment: "I belch, therefore I am."[2] Roquentin's behavior is symbolic of any *homme non engagé.*

Sartre's second novel, *Les Chemins de la Liberté,* has greater range and is conceived as a tetralogy of contemporary history. The first volume, *L'Age de raison* (1945), is set in the atmosphere of the Spanish Civil War (1937); the second, *Le Sursis* (1945), in that of the Munich Compromise (1938); the third, *La Mort dans l'âme* (1949), deals with World War II and the defeat of France (1940); the fourth, *La Dernière chance,* has not yet been published. The unique work illustrates Sartre's philosophy through the main character, Mathieu Delarue, an intellectual whose behavior, at first selfish and ineffectual, finally reaches more sacrificial phases, growing in responsibility.

In the first volume Mathieu is mainly concerned with trying to secure in an abject and cowardly manner a secret abortion for his mistress Marcelle. Marcelle, however, prefers to give birth to the child and to cover the situation by a sham marriage with Mathieu's homosexual pupil Daniel. Mathieu commits a second act of cowardice when as a young communist he refuses to fight for Red Spain. In the second volume he joins all the cowards in preferring the Munich surrender to war. But in the third volume, Mathieu unpredictably fights from a tower against odds, mowing down everything with his machine gun, while the communist Brunet hides in the cellar with the excuse that he has to spare himself for the party. Within a slight framework of main action there is, however, much secondary action, descriptions and characterizations, all brutal, obscene, sub-human but psychologically interesting, partly disgusting, partly fascinating.

The hero Mathieu Delarue in *L'Age de raison* is presented as a professor of philosophy who attracts and fascinates his students, among whom is found the immature aristocratic Russian girl Ivich Serguine, unpredictable in her actions and addicted to drink. Her brother Boris, her protector and bad angel, and

Mathieu's uncritical admirer, has an affair with the nightclub singer Lola, so that all the plans of Mathieu and his Russian friends mature in the cabaret. It is from Lola that Mathieu steals the five thousand francs for the planned abortion when everybody else refuses to lend him the sum, even his brother Jacques who is ready to finance the marriage but not the abortion. It is in the nightclub that Ivich and Mathieu try to prove to one another that they are no *salauds* by piercing their hands with a knife, thus performing an *acte gratuit* which is supposed to "liberate" them. But Ivich succeeds no better than Marcelle in trapping the elusive Mathieu into marriage. Another milieu frequented by Mathieu is that of the communist party secretary Brunet, the Spanish revolutionary colonel Gomez and his Jewish wife Sarah. This milieu takes care of the historical moment, the time of the Spanish Civil War. Out of these groups Mathieu emerges at the age of thirty-four as a most despicable intellectual who instead of fighting with Gomez in Spain spares himself in Paris, seduces and abandons girls, steals, lives promiscuously with perverted friends, does not recoil from murder and tries to feel "liberated" when his bad conscience has refused to fulfill any serious obligation arising from situations he has willfully created. This first volume, *L'Age de raison,* actually ends with the question: "A quoi ça sert-il, la liberté, si ce n'est pas pour s'engager?" (p. 125).[3]

The second volume, *Le Sursis,* is mainly concerned with the *angoisse* caused by the fear of war in 1938, before the Munich appeasement. Using the technique of cinematographic profile, Sartre concentrates on showing all the countries in the throes of anguish, and is less interested in the petty problems of Mathieu who is on the verge of falling in love with his sister-in-law Odette. All the other persons try to cope with the political situation. The unbalanced Ivich gets married to a rich Frenchman but hates her new bourgeois milieu,[4] Boris is stupid enough to enroll in the French army for three years. Among the *salauds* feverishly waiting for the "good news" of a delay in the war are some new figures like the pacifist Philippe, son of general Lacaze, the mobilized shepherd from Prades, Gros-Louis, and the three members of a ladies' music band. But there are also people disgusted with Munich, those closely concerned, like the Czech couple Milan and Anna Hlinka, or the Jewish family Birnenschatz. Daladier and St. Leger as diplomats are full of contempt for the Parisians who receive them with flowers and applause at the airport on their return from Munich. There are the neutrals, too, the sick and the suffering who already, in the confusion of a general mobilization, have been evacuated from their comfortable hospitals and transported like cattle to other places. Among these sick people is the emotional cripple Charles who in his plight still craves for the love of one of the sick women, Catherine. Gomez, on leave from the Spanish Civil War, has been promoted to general and is wined and dined by Mathieu before he spends a part of his furlough with his wife Sarah. But Mathieu, having returned to Paris, meditates on the Pont Neuf about his irresponsible life and recognizes for the second time that he was and is a *salaud*.

Volume III, *La Mort dans l'âme,* gives a harrowing picture of *La France en déroute* after the outbreak of World War II, comparable to Zola's *Débâcle*. Among the people mixing with the beaten soldiers we find cowardly bourgeois fleeing to the south like Mathieu's moralizing brother Jacques, or Jews like Sarah with her little son depending on blackmailing taxi drivers. The safety-seeking communist Gomez even flees to New York and struggles with the humid heat. Boris, the aristocrat, goes to London. But Mathieu finally emerges during the German invasion as a kind of hero. He defends desperately the last French position in a village. There are some great scenes: Mathieu in the company of some *desperados* shooting with a machine gun from a tower at the approaching Germans until the last cartridge is fired and he is buried under the débris of the tower. In the second part of this volume Sartre dramatizes the horror scenes in a German prison camp in France. He focuses the interest on Brunet, the party secretary, who is made prisoner and becomes the self-imposed leader and nazi sympathizer. The enmity between the true French and the Alsatians, who are allowed to receive visitors, the Alsatian Schneider who is so important because he understands the language of the German guards, the desperate fight against hunger and vermin, and the organized gymnastics are aspects particularly stressed. Finally Sartre describes the transportation to Germany and attempts at escaping, the shooting of the boy who jumped from the train. There is no hope for the others either. "Demain viendront les oiseaux noirs." The only consolation for the prisoners is the answer which Brunet had given to Pinette, his ruthless friend: "Il faut attendre et garder la tête claire, se réserver pour une bonne occasion" (p. 154). However, as the fragments of the fourth volume of the novel, called *Drôle d'amitié* and published in *Les Temps Modernes,* have proved, the closing theme of the tetralogy will be the *Résistance.*

In the best of his dramatic works, Jean-Paul Sartre has the merit of having shown that the allegedly great problem haunting the century, the relation of individual versus collectivity (see chapter one) becomes false and absurd if the collectivity is a society without a sense of morality and engages the individual only in self-debasement and crime. While Charles Péguy envisioned this problem as political idealism betrayed by the pragmatic party, Sartre illustrates it by opposing in *Les Mains sales* (1948) the idealistic intellectual Hugo Barine to the fanatic party leader Hoederer who tells the idealist whose moral principles have kept him an individual: "Moi, j'ai les mains sales. Jusqu'aux coudes. Je les ai plongées dans la merde et dans le sang. . . . Est-ce que tu t'imagines qu'on peut gouverner innocemment?" Sartre would not be upset by the immorality of Louis who incites Hugo to assassinate Hoederer, but he resents Hoederer's abandoning any sound criticism in the blind service of his party. It is true that he is *engagé* but without any fresh decision or real *engagement*. So, the communistic problem turns out to be a challenge to the alternative of blind action or critical decision.[5] The action of *Les Mains sales* is based on events in a nazi-occupied country (Hungary?) during the last phase of the war. Hoederer, the party secretary, proposes an anti-German, national front together with bourgeois parties. Hugo and his friend Louis consider him a traitor of the proletariate. Hugo, the ex-bourgeois intellectual, has to prove his own reliability by assassinating Hoederer at the instigation of Louis. He does it in a fit of jealousy after many hesitations. He is imprisoned. When he is released, the party line has changed; it now conforms with Hoederer's vision. Hugo is liquidated, Louis now having turned against him.

To make a point for his atheism, Sartre restylized the tragedy of the Atrides in *Les Mouches* (1943). Jupiter has taken revenge on guilty Argos by sending against it a swarm of flies, modern Erinyes, for Aegisthus' murder of Agamemnon and quasi-adultery with Clythemnestra. Electra and Orestes, the new generation of "existence" versus the blind belief of Argos' older generation, abolish such divine tricks as superstitious tribal remorse "arranged" by Aegisthus who makes others atone for his crimes. Orestes' cure is simply to take the guilt complex *(Les Mouches)* away from Argos by another murder. He kills Aegisthus, but the new murder only turns the flies against him and Electra. While Electra's fear cannot take this and her repentance finally will spare her as fitting in with the superstitious community, the Promethean Orestes must flee from Argos since the inhabitants side with Jupiter and the Erinyes. This solution, not entirely unsound, means in Sartre's mind, of course, that the only engaged person (Orestes) becomes a victim of the *salauds*.

Sartre's reinterpretations of guilt and atonement concepts reveal themselves as typical secularizations of Christian values. They are not understandable without the Christian lore he fights (Guardini). Hell appears as "the others" with whom one has to live. Hell is the irrevocable being together with *salauds*. So Sartre invents his powerful *Huis clos* (1944), an after-death drawing room behind the closed door of which are bound to vegetate three persons: a coward and deserter, Garcin, an infanticide woman, Estelle, and a lesbian, Ines. While Ines tries desperately to excite the love of Estelle who hates her, Estelle desperately loves Garcin who rejects her. The two women in their rage constantly tease the coward for his desertion as a soldier. Driven to despair by the two hating and hated women he cries out: "Ouvrez, ouvrez donc! J'accepte tout: les brodequins, les tenailles, le plomb fondu, les pincettes, le garrot . . . , plutôt cent morsures, le fouet, le vitriol que cette souffrance . . ." (sc. V).

Sartre illustrates also the most brutal decisions he expects from the *non-salaud* by the example of the drama *Morts sans sépultures* (1946) where the partisans kill a young boy François out of fear he may betray names to the militia and thus cause their capture and torture. But later the murderers become *salauds* themselves, reveal their secrets and are shot nevertheless by the German militia.

Sartre takes American "hypocrisy" to task in *La Putain respectueuse* (1946). A white prostitute, Lizzie, first refuses to hide the crime of a senator's son who falsely accuses a negro of having raped her. Finally, however, for money and in order to be considered a decent white woman, she consents to deliver the innocent victim to the judge.

Sartre, to show off his atheism, even challenges God directly through Goetz, the hero of his sacrilegious drama *Le Diable et le Bon Dieu* (1951). Goetz, a Protestant leader in the Thirty Years War in Germany, prefers to decide for himself what is good or bad for mankind rather than to hope selfishly for some reward from a God who according to Sartre is impassive, silent and absent, i.e., non-existent. After having challenged God by doing evil, he challenges the Devil by doing good with the foundation of an ideal city, *La Cité du Soleil*. But with all his good intentions he only spreads the seeds of despair, murder and death. He decides to neutralize good and evil, therefore, by participating authentically in *la condition humaine* whose meaningfulness only depends on him, Goetz, devil and quasi-God himself. This reads like a new version of Orestes in *Les Mouches* but without a really new viewpoint, except the unveiled blasphemy.

In a gesture typical of atheists, Sartre has twice taken as a subject the afterlife in which he claims not to believe. The first time, as we have seen, he did so in his play *Huis clos,* the hell of the deserter Garcin, and the second time in his movie arrangement *Les Jeux sont faits,* where Pierre, the revolutionary worker, and Eve, the aristocratic wife of the chief of the regent's secret police, are on leave of absence from the other world after their death; but after having tried in vain to love one another, they are killed again, sent back to Hell where they are bound to their respective milieu from which nobody can escape without daring revolutionary acts.

The aspects of *angoisse,* projection, dereliction, and despair within the existentialist analysis of man have likewise been treated by Sartre in short stories. His obsession with *angoisse* comes best to the fore in his short story *Le Mur* (1939), published together with four other "situations": *La Chambre, Erostrate, Intimité, L'Enfance d'un chef.* In *Le Mur* we are not spared any of the horrors undergone by some communists made prisoners during the Spanish Civil War and scheduled to be shot the next morning. One of them gets his liberty for betraying against his will one of his comrades. In *La Chambre* we watch with his wife Eve-Agathe the gradual decay of the schizophrenic Pierre. *Erostrate* is the psychological story of a man who wants to commit unmotivated murder. After coldly preparing himself to kill six persons, he dares not act until he is provoked by a *salaud* into firing wildly at him. Fleeing to a restroom he surrenders to the police who are knocking at the door. *Intimité* is the ironic treatment of the lack of choice in a woman, Lullu, torn asunder between her impotent husband, her vulgar lover and her exacting girl friend. The most biting satire is *L'Enfance d'un chef,* description of the youth of Lucien Fleurier who is destined to become an industrial leader and to follow his father as director of a plant. His preparation for this task is bad company, indiscriminate sexual relations, normal and abnormal, and political associations which push him to intolerance, stubbornness and even unqualified murder. The presentation is of an unbearable vulgarity.

The Sartrian *engagement* itself seems to abolish the Christian conscience and its wholesome reaction to remorse, namely true repentance. This springs unequivocally from Sartre's entire work which knows only one value: courageous but ruthless daring.

The style of Sartre, forceful in his unrestrained sensations and comparisons, in his imagery moving between obscenity and poetry, not unlike that of Zola in moments of symbolic condensation, reaches clearcut forms of surrealistic heritage. Sartre, master of tripartite rhythm, imitates the unanimistic style of Romains and techniques of the American novelists. There is a whole rhapsody of *exister* and *existence* in *La Nausée* (p. 131-34). Sartre paradoxically is a naturalist with symbolic purposes. He creates characters who speak a passionate and unnecessarily profane language characterizing them as fence-sitters between the real and the literary cosmos.[6] Sartre is also a master of descriptive, forceful as well as colorful presentation ranging from prosaic matter of factness to poetic resonance in a climactic gradation as is the case with the chapter Dimanche in *La Nausée* (p. 60-76). He develops the theme of the boring provincial Sunday in the sense of Proustian re-evocation and makes it return again to prosaic banality. But as in his philosophical writings there is nothing uplifting, so in his fiction the triumphant symbols of fire and air are lacking. Earth and water, slime and viscosity symbolize Sartre's world of moral depravity.[7] And his cleverly used imagistic exemplification is disappointing because it misuses poetic means in order to debase human dignity. A human hand appears as *une éponge pétrifiée* (*Sursis,* p. 285), an embryo as *une petite marée vitreuse, une petite fraise de sang* (*L'Age de raison,* p. 73), an awakening in the morning as *se réinstaller dans son vieux corps pourri* (*La Mort dans l'âme,* p. 175).

When Chamberlain and Hitler discuss war and peace in the Hotel Dreesen, and the fear of war paralyzes every corner of the world and unifies it, Sartre dovetails unanimistically the different parts of the world:

> La folle guerre des blancs . . . , elle avait éclaté dans la chambre de Milan, elle s'échappait par toutes les fenêtres, elle se déversait avec fracas chez Marrakech, elle soufflait sur la mer, elle écrasait les bâtiments de la rue Royale, elle remplissait les narines de Maurice. . . , dans les champs, dans les étables, dans les cours de ferme, elle *n'existait pas,* elle se jouait à pile ou face (p. 59).

Sartre's variation of unanimism means according to Albérès the highest limitation of individual liberty: "Toute cette peinture collective et unanimiste montre que l'individu, si libre soit-il en lui-même, est visé par ce qui se passe dans le monde."[8] It means from the viewpoint of texture, that Sartre goes beyond the stream-of-consciousness technique and that of inserting letters, telegrams, diaries, and radio messages between blocks of narration. By unlinked but motivistically repeated actions and events reflecting the viewpoint of the heroes involved as well as Sartre's latent criticism of all these *salauds,* by a monotonous but clever fusion of objectivity, empathy and irony, paralleling the technique of "fondus enchaînés," he actually achieves his program exposed in *Situations* II (p. 327-53): "la pluridimensionnalité de l'événement," "le réalisme de la temporalité" and "la relativité généralisée." Sartre pushes this technique to disagreeable forms of virtuosity as when he telescopes three and more different actions, changing in the very same paragraph, even from one sentence to another without, however, reaching the Joycean amalgamation of action, discourse and thought.

As far as plausibility of character is concerned, one may admit that in the selection of borderline existences of a lawless humanity his analyses look acceptable. He entirely leaves out, however, the more precious aspects of mankind which exist despite his intentional exclusion of them from the dark picture he wants to paint. The communist critic Roger Garaudy, therefore, has condemned Sartre's view of man in the following reprimand: "It is possible that men are like that where you go to observe them . . . at the Café de Flore, in the night clubs of Montparnasse or Montmartre. Such places may be filled with these dead souls, these aimless existences, these débauchés who can only brood over their impotence and their frustration."[9] Sartre could still say that some of his critics do not brood at all and that this may be worse.

Theophil Spoerri has well seen that there are passages in Sartre's work where one is aware that Sartre is truly haunted by the God whose death he tries to proclaim, that he proves that he sometimes has his head outside and above the mud and slime into which he lures his readers. The answer given by Hoederer to Hugo in *Les Main sales,* that it is the value of every man that counts and not an anti-human ideology, seems to Spoerri the only way to counter existentialism and communism, for it is at the same time an affirmation of the essential God whom all existences have to obey in love.[10]

Existentialism crossed with American behaviorism, and not distinguishable from it, or, as Sartre puts it: "Du Kafka écrit par Hemingway" comes to the fore in the novel *L'Etranger* (1942) by Albert Camus (1903-   ). This is the story of the naively alleged absurdity of human existence. Exterior events in themselves do not lead to any explanation, of course, but Camus is not at ease with Sartre's *passion inutile.* He tries to overcome the absurd by the life story of Meursault. Meursault buries his mother, takes a mistress, commits a crime and is executed. He was a stranger on an absurd earth. He simply revolts against the usual. This is illustrated by Camus' theoretical exposé of the *Mythe de Sisyphe* (1942). Camus technically gives some loosely connected events which make a story in the sense of Voltaire's propaganda novel.

L'Etranger, written in short sentences with a *phrases hachées* technique, is reminiscent of Hemingway's *Death in the Afternoon,* but with a definite propensity to poetic prose.[11] There is, however, much more in this classical novel. The heart of the problem is that the judge in Algiers who condemned Meursault changed his mind absurdly. He first is favorable to Meursault's case and never would have condemned this commercial clerk for a first degree murder. That he killed an Arab, who hated and who waylaid him, in a mood of intoxication from sun, heat, and danger was thoroughly explainable. But the "witnesses," the concierge and others, found it shocking and typical of a criminal that Meursault did not behave decently in the home for the aged, when at the wake of his mother he drank coffee in the presence of the corpse and did not shed a tear. Then after the burial he went to the beach where he started amorous relations with a girl, Marie, and took her to a humorous movie. Such "monstrosities" influenced the jury in the belief that Meursault was a born criminal. Consequently the absurdity of a traditional bourgeois concept of conventions, falsifying the meaning of behavior and events, is Meursault's undoing. It confirms him in his own robot reactions as reflected in those of his surroundings. Condemned to be beheaded, he rages against the chaplain who tries to reconcile him with God. Here Camus outdoes Kafka because Kafka's abstract construction of the wrongly accused and condemned has here been made palpable, experimental, plausible, and *terre-à terre*. We may agree with Boisdeffre that the story is outstanding and extremely well written, an I-story, about a man who becomes a stranger to his surroundings and to himself when giving up social conventions. The story is told with lucid objectivity[12] in a classical style (Charles Bruneau).[13]

Camus stands halfway between Sartre and a humanism as earlier proposed by Duhamel. Therefore in his second novel *La Peste* (1947) the crucial question is formulated by the Gandhi-like pacifist Tarrou: "Peut-on être un saint sans Dieu, c'est le seul problème concret que je connaisse aujourd'hui." He will become a victim of the plague. The moral substance of the apostate Christian is still strong enough in such types to lead to the decision to abandon the animalistic drift of egoistic "happiness" and accept self-sacrifice for the millions who suffer.[14] But in Oran, under the spell of the plague, this message has no appeal. The people of that city recur to fear and debauchery if they do not recur to prayer. Only the poised ones face the facts and try to do something, as Father Paneloux proposed in his first sermon. His second sermon, however, seems desperate as a poignant replica of Kafka, justifying from the Christian viewpoint the absurd condemnation of a guiltless prisoner, as it was the case in *L'Etranger*: "Ils étaient condamnés, pour un crime inconnu, à un emprisonnement inimaginable" (*La Peste*, p. 117). There seems only one way out, the naturalistic, behavioristic, practical, technical way, to get the situation under control. This is the contribution of Bernard Rieux, the doctor, who, as we learn from his fictional diary of the plague, binds himself to duty, hope, organization in fighting epidemic and death in order to make mankind happier. He believes absurdly enough in another ideal: *la tendresse humaine*. Nonetheless this romanticism makes Camus more sympathetic than Sartre. Love links Dr. Rieux to his mother, to his suffering and doomed wife; friendship links him to the writer Tarrou who at least has the vague desire for peace, for perfection and goodness, but always, paradoxically, a peace without God, one comparable to the utopia of Duhamel's Salavin. The only man who has *ex officio* a metaphysical message for this Kantian-Stalinist world of organized duty is Father Paneloux. He is, however, a purposely misrepresented priest whose hobby is archeology. In one of his sermons, as a half-believer, he tries in vain to recover from his own shock at the terrible agony and death of the innocent little boy, the son of the judge. Father Paneloux' bitterness and pseudo resignation at his own death show Camus' shortcoming in judging the spiritual side of life because with the type of priest he selected, he excludes spirituality precisely there where it normally works. Therefore even the journalist and lover Rambert, the criminal Cottard, who enjoys the plague because it stopped his prosecution, and the municipal employee and amateur writer Grand, who believes at least in literary style, all turn out more real than the Jesuit Paneloux.

Camus' *Peste* was meant and read as a symbol of the German occupation of France. Doctor Rieux, organizer of a "résistance," encouraged the French in their catastrophe. The uniting quality of such a catastrophe is classically worked out. From the moment the city of Oran is sealed off from the exterior world, the citizens exposed to the same danger bury their individualism and form a collectivity of emergency "dans une situation sans compromis [où] les mots 'transiger,' 'faveur,' 'exception' n'avaient plus de sens" (Ed. NRF, 1947, p. 82). Even the municipal prison, where inmates and employees are as a crowded group particularly exposed to the danger of contagion and death, forms a grotesque unity:

> Du point de vue supérieur de la peste, tout le monde, depuis le directeur jusqu'au dernier détenu, etait condamné et, pour la première fois peut-être, il régnait dans la prison une justice absolue (*Ib.,* p. 190).

But curiously enough the monasteries distributed their monks among the houses of pious families and the garrison dispersed its soldiers into the empty schools. "Cela faisait du désarroi" (p. 191).

Camus' half-existentialism, half-humanism stressing man's capacity for sincerity, liberty and justice again is a Christian echo. There is the liberal tendency to secularize mysticism, making out of a pessimistic despair something like a dark night of the soul. Therefore he writes:

> L'homme . . . , s'il doit rencontrer une nuit, que ce soit plutôt celle du désespoir qui reste lucide, nuit polaire, veille de l'esprit, d'où se lèvera peut-être cette clarté blanche et intacte qui dessine chaque objet dans la lumière de l'intelligence (*Le Mythe de Sisyphe*, p. 90).

The acceptance of death, political murder and capital punishment with a feeling of satisfaction, by Dora in the drama *Les Justes* (1950) is a travesty of Christian sacrifice leading to "peace" by identifying Russian terrorism and its boomeranging consequence with martyrdom. Dora receives from the execution of Kaliayev the impulses to new murders. This is the peace of terror.

All this romanticism taken into account and theoretically made plausible by Camus' essay *L'Homme révolté* (1951) provoked the antagonism of Sartre (*Temps Modernes,* May and August 1952), but Camus came out of the discussion with a more consistent humanism than that of Sartre which is highly vulgar, political and unconvincing. Camus discovered the ugliness of self-love and sin in *La Chute* (1956). He even looks for Christ symbols befitting our time (see Carl A. Vigiani, *PMLA* 71 [1956], 865 ff.)

About Camus' style one would say with Germaine Brée[15] that with all its terseness, laconic objectivity and clear landscape drawing, conversations and situations, it reveals great visionary power, dramatic rhythm, and a captivating symbolism of death, threat and suffocation linked to the evocation of relentless light and breathless air. Camus' powerful originality is also praised by Charles Bruneau who points out that Meursault's sun-intoxication which impells him to the murder of the Arab is expressed by a gradation of impressive imagery:

à moitié endormi par tout ce soleil sur sa tête nue;
immobile sous la pluie aveuglante [du soleil];
il sentait son front se gonfler sous le soleil;
le soleil lui déversait cette ivresse opaque;

Thus in short and intentionally simple clauses Camus gathers precise notations[16] which finally explode into a catastrophe.

The sun and the sea combined as symbols of existentialist freedom have been elucidated in a special study by S. John.[17] The sea under the sun appears as *la mer cuirassée d'argent,* but also sea and landscape under the sun are felt like skyscapes with "la lumière à gros bouillons dans les amas de pierre," "d'immenses cuves où l'air bouillonne," and "un bain violent de soleil." Few people know that the imagery of Camus is largely derived from that of Giono though modified in degree, function and meaning.[18]

John Cruickshank in his study "Camus and Language," *Lettera-ture Moderne* IV (1956), p. 197-202, has shown that in Camus' "verbal puritanism," imagery and personification appear in purple patches only for structural reasons, while during the ordinary flow of narration the imagination of the reader is constantly called upon to supply the lacking connectives and bestow on the ambiguously used simple past in turns the meaning of a con-tinuing possibility, a prolongation of the past into the present, or an emphasis on the gratuitous, indefinite, nay absurd nature of experience.

Simone de Beauvoir (1908-   ) who, curiously enough, knew at the Sorbonne the other Simone, Simone Weil, is a cooperator and competitor of Jean-Paul Sartre. She puts, however, a little more of Jaspers' ingredients into the Sartrian type of Heideg-gerism. She admits at least a kind of transcendence consisting in the prolongation or radiation of one's self into others. This attempt, of course, requires reciprocation on the part of the partner (Jaspers' "Communication"); otherwise there may arise a situation which demands a *choix,* namely that of the other or that of one's self, implying necessarily the elimination of one of the two. This particular case of existentialism is illustrated by her first and best novel *L'Invitée* (1943). The invited one is a rebellious, badly educated girl, drama student from Rouen, Xavière Pagès; the invitors are the Parisian theatre director Pierre Labrousse and his mistress, the novelist Françoise Miquel. Each of them loves the girl in a particular way, Pierre as a friend, Françoise as a mother. Both try to make the situation harmless by including Xavière, the object of their common protection, in a kind of triangle where Pierre would even have the liberty of intimate relations with Xavière under the assumed condition that he never would prefer her to Françoise. But when Françoise hears from Gerbert, both her lover and Xavière's, that Pierre prefers Xavière to her, she nevertheless finally "chooses herself" by killing the girl instead of effacing herself. She does it so secretly by opening the gas in the room where the girl is sleeping that nobody will ever discover this act of self-liberation, except that the equally liberated Pierre perhaps will learn it from her at a later date when he returns from World War II. To use the language of one of Mme de Beauvoir's theoretical works, hers is the fight *Pour une morale de l'ambiguité* (1947).

Of course, nobody will take very seriously the existential language "to choose oneself" of this clever triangle story. It remains a well-told story of jealousy with and without the existentialist interpretation. This is different with the resistance novel *Le Sang des autres,* where Jean Blomart makes quite another decision. To avoid endangering the future of the organized sabotage directed by him, he chooses not to surrender himself as a saboteur to the nazis, but rather to cause the death of innumerable hostages. This is done at the price of remorse and relentless anguish. In this case the *choix* makes more sense, a tragic sense, directed toward a kind of common good.

The same demonstration of an ethics derived from exceptional situations comes from Mme de Beauvoir's drama *Les Bouches inutiles* (1945). Here the men of the besieged Flemish fortress of Vaucelles (in the fourteenth century) have to make a great decision: impelled by dwindling food supplies, will they sacrifice women and children and build up new families after a possible victorious defense or will they defend instead their present families in order not to make the war which they are waging entirely absurd? The compromise is a daring sortie which may bring victory, slavery, or death to all.

With her last self-debasing novel *Les Mandarins* (Gallimard, 1954), it seems as though Mme de Beauvoir had anticipated the fourth volume of Sartre's *Les Chemins de la liberté,* since the action takes place during the years immediately after World War II. The Résistance is revenging itself upon the former collaborationists with the Germans. The journalists are busy founding new periodicals and the politicians new parties, a wonderful time for the *salauds.* It is in this atmosphere—as Anne Dubreuilh (another name for Simone de Beauvoir?) reports—that Henry Perron (another name for Camus) deserts his mistress Paule Mareuil for Anne's degenerate daughter Nadine, and is willing to commit perjury in order to save the young actress Josette and her mother Lucie Belhomme who had intimate relations with German officers. Anne Dubreuilh, as wife of Henri's best friend Robert Dubreuilh (another name for Sartre) and mother of Nadine, still finds it compatible with her existentialist liberty to fornicate with the writer Scriassine and the American millionaire Lewis whom she met during a trip to Chicago. Bored by her own unfaithfulness and the visible aging of her husband Robert, this *femme de quarante ans* finally comes to the point of poisoning herself. Only the thought that Nadine and Robert would discover her esthetically ugly suicide makes her again "choose herself" in the hope of another adventure of "happiness." Confronted with these female existential heroines, it is extremely difficult, as was the case with Sartre's male hero-criminals Roquentin and Mathieu, to decide which ones are the *salauds* and which the *non-salauds.* Their crude concepts of life and their salacious behavior, at least, are described in a language less crude than that of the Sartrian novels, although Mme de Beauvoir can also handle this latter style as proved by her book *Le Deuxième sexe* (1949). Some source material of the plot of the *Mandarins* which is awkward also draws from *L'Amérique au jour le jour* (1948).

The constant allusions to living persons, the abundance of the most compromising political and erotic situations produce a bad, nay repellent, impression which is intensified by indiscrete detailed comparisons like the following: "Elle était habillée avec une perfection qui eût donné des complexes d'infériorité à la duchesse de Windsor" (p. 342). Let us for the sake of understanding accept provisionally the unacceptable immoralism of Mme de Beauvoir. She wants to offer a morality of ambiguity. She wants to give a meaning to the allegedly fundamental liberty of accepting or rejecting any human relation which may occur in a concrete situation. There is involved however also the liberty of fighting for the social and political freedom of man or of submitting to any dictatorial infringement on human rights for reasons of a temporary materialistic advantage. These two points of decision of a quite different value explain also the apparently monotonous wave movement between sex and communism. No one can doubt that Mme de Beauvoir, with all her lack of decency, restraint, and taste, and despite all her philosophical and human errors, has penetrated to the heart of the evils of our times in which actually the Parisian literary *mandarins* are deeply interested.

In her very scholarly defense of modern women, Mme de Beauvoir surprisingly rejects the merely biological, psychoanalytical and materialistic viewpoint in judging the second sex, because all these approaches exclude *choix* and *valeur*. Her *choix* and *valeur,* often not different from sin and crime, re-echo the old immoralism of Nietzsche, but would admit also of a reversed, i.e., Christian interpretation of human actions not envisioned *sub specie aeternitatis* as cowardly egoism: "Puisqu'il faut ou mourir innocents ou vivre en criminels, nous choisissons le crime parce que nous choisissons la vie" (Louis in *Les Bouches inutiles,* 4° tableau, Ed. Gallimard, p. 8).

Stylistically, Mme de Beauvoir goes in *medias res* and suggests things rather than describes them. Her coinages of unique word groups such as "fatigue douillette," "solitude désolée" are striking. The remote possibility of a love affair is hinted at by almost imperceptible motives. Indications of place, time, age appear poeticized. There is an elliptic condensation everywhere and a short sentence like "Elle tourna une page" evokes a previously mentioned manuscript and excludes the idea of a book only to the closely attentive reader. The persons always speak in character. She herself uses very ordinary language, says *couper* for *interrompre, sur une grande échelle* for *à une grande échelle, s'avérer* for *se révéler, se vouloir* for *désirer être*. She adds "non?" to any kind of question, and says *qu'est-ce que* for *eh bien!* She coins hyphenated compounds (as Americans do in such expressions as "pay-as-you-go method") and would say "ce spécimen écrivain-de-gauche-qui-s'est-fait-lui-même." Everything is introduced as known or half-known with the definite article and reveals itself slowly in its particularity. Her conciseness of style is paralleled somewhat oddly by rather a prolixity of action. Mme de Beauvoir, were she not so unrestrained, would be able to tell a story at least as well as she handles colorful description with keen metaphors: "Au milieu des agaves bleues qui poignardaient la terre rouge . . . une maison blanche." As to the French language on the whole: "elle apparaît . . . savoir user en virtuose d'un instrument délicat et puissant."[19] But no aesthetics can excuse her treason to feminine dignity, visible also in the lowest vocabulary: dégueulasse, merde, etc.

Jean Anouilh (Bordeaux, 1910-   ) with his *Pièces noires* (much superior to his *Pièces roses*), e.g., *La Sauvage* (1934), *Eurydice* (1941), *Antigone* (1942), *Roméo et Jeannette* (1946), *Médée* (1946), at first glance seems to bring his whole theatre into the service of the absolute as opposed to the vulgar search for an impossible earthly happiness. In good classical tradition his defense of the absolute always is bound to end in struggle and death.[20] But Anouilh's absolute is nothing else but an individual revolt against social corruption. This is particularly true of the heroine in *Antigone* who, unreasonably distraught, fatally runs to her death by opposing Creon's despotic order forbidding the burial of her brother Polynikes. Despite all the efforts of Creon to avoid the catastrophe by compromises, Antigone, rather than acknowledge the immoral law established by Creon, feels that she belongs existentially to the group of offended, disinherited and down-trodden creatures who cannot simply be spared in the atmosphere of general injustice. But all this is only vaguely felt in the fashion of Kafka. Anouilh knows that her death is gratuitous and absurd since he has taken out of the tragedy the religious implication so strong in Sophocles.[21] Equally absurd is the behavior of Frantz in *L'Hermine*. Out of a desire to have Poverty triumph against Wealth or dignified Pain against capitalistic Corruption, Frantz kills the rich duchess of Granat in order to obtain the necessary money to live with her heiress Monime, since the duchess refused her consent to Monime's marriage to him, a poor man; he thus destroys the love of Monime and surrenders to the police; without, however, the slightest remorse.

In *L'Invitation au Château,* the rich banker with all his money cannot "buy" the dancer Isabelle. Thérèse Tarde in *La Sauvage* rejects her rich lover Florent France because she belongs to the world of the suffering dogs rather than to him. She simply chooses herself by an existential gratuitousness. So, Anouilh, too, joins the choir of the absurdly *révoltés,* not seeing that the true redeeming light would do away with any absurdity. Since he does not understand the value of suffering, suicide, even planned suicide, seems a greater guarantee of happiness. Therefore in his *Eurydice,* a fifth-rate actress kills herself to escape the lust of her manager and beckons Orphée, her lover, a poor musician, from beyond the grave to the happiness of nothingness.[22] Anouilh's concept of man, combined with brilliant dialogue and heroes who are at the same time individuals and types, can reach tragic proportions (but not real tragedy which supposes sin and atonement under a Supreme Being) and does so for instance in *Médée* where the heroine is made despicable in her hatred and Jason comes out as a man with common sense and the ability to cope with life since he has done away with demons and with gods. Before she commits her revengeful murder, Medea recites a monologue which reveals among other things the pessimistic turn of literary *naturism* within half a century:

> Et, toi, nuit, nuit pesante, nuit bruissante de cris étouffés et de luttes, nuit grouillante de bonds de toutes les bêtes qui se pourchassent, qui se prennent, qui se tuent, attends encore un peu. . . . Un même sang bat dans nos veines. Bêtes de la nuit, étrangleuses, mes soeurs! Médée est une bête comme vous! . . . Je pousse avec vous votre cri obscur. . . . Bêtes, je suis vous! Tout ce qui chasse et tue cette nuit est Médée (Anouilh, *Médée*, pp. 397-98).

Sensuous pantheism (see chapter two) has also turned into something negative and terrible in Louis Ferdinand Céline as when the love life of the animals in the jungle is described with all its horrors:

> Et la nuit avec tous ses monstres entrait alors dans la danse parmi ses mille et mille bruits de gueules de crapauds. La forêt n'attend que leur signal pour se mettre à trembler, siffler, mugir de toutes ses profondeurs. Une énorme gare amoureuse et sans lumière, pleine à craquer. Des arbres entiers bouffis de gueuletons vivants, d'érections mutilées, d'horreur (*Voyage au bout de la nuit, NRF,* 7th ed., 1952, p. 155).

Contemporary existentialist man does not identify himself any longer with the animal world but—worse—with the world of things existent. This dehumanizing turn reflects the complete depersonalization and dependence on objects. Man is simply an item in the inventory of things, as is the case in the "poem" of Jacques Prévert (1900-   ):

> Une pierre
> deux maisons
> trois ruines
> quatre fossoyeurs
> un jardin
> des fleurs
> un raton laveur
>   (*Inventaire*).

This is the graveyard climate and the end of the alleged *littérature engagée,* the Promethean revolt, the "acceptance" of the absurd, a dead end, which seems not to admit of any *Sursum corda.*

CHAPTER VI

SPIRITUALITY

DESPITE ALL the new literary worlds discovered by writers who, disgusted with crude realism, are fleeing from everyday banality, there was only one refuge which satisfied human dignity rather than human curiosity—the realm of Spirituality. Its discovery is mainly a consequence of the new understanding of mysticism as revealed by the theologian Reginald Garrigou-Lagrange, O.P., and Abbé Henri Bremond. It is significant that of the whole so-called *Renouveau Catholique* only those authors have survived who are somehow linked to mysticism. We might single out, for example, Charles Péguy, Emile Baumann, Paul Claudel, Georges Bernanos, Joseph Malègue, Gabriel Marcel, and Simone Weil. Representatives of the younger generation such as Luc Estang, Béatrice Beck, Pierre Emmanuel, Patrice de La Tour du Pin, Jean Cayrol do not have the stature one would expect from successors of the genuinely great older generation or have no genuine spirituality.

If Joris-Karl Huysmans (1848-1907) rediscovered the beauty of the liturgy, and Léon Bloy (1846-1917) the spirit of poverty, Charles Péguy (1873-1914) discovered the spirit of the *com-unio,* the spirit of solidarity and interdependence of the members of that Mystical Body headed by Christ who imparts His charity to its members. This was the reason why Charles Péguy startled his contemporaries in 1906 when he published *Le Mystère de la charité de Jeanne D'Arc.* Péguy is not easily satisfied with the Church as he sees it. Saint Joan of Arc's problem in her discussions with the little girl Hauviette and the old, poised, and saintly Madame Gervaise does not concern art and taste, but turns around the central problem whether salvation is for a few or for many. In view of a mankind that does not meditate on the passion of Christ, St. Joan observes that some may seem to be lost in spite of Christ's blood shed for all. This point disturbs Péguy but he is disturbed even more by another thought, namely that modern socialism seems to come nearer to the spirit of brotherhood than the Church of the twentieth century, which in spite of her tradition and spirit of poverty seems linked to a capitalistic world. Péguy ponders and ponders over the greater values present in the French peasant and worker and all poor little families, real pictures of the Holy Family, as he believes. From the natural he wants to get a logical access to the supernatural. He intimates that the natural, in the sense of the forces of blood and soil, clan and nation, was not neglected by Christ Himself. Therefore he makes Him say:

> Les pleurs que j'ai versés sur un mont solitaire,
> Les pleurs que j'ai pleurés quand j'ai pleuré sur eux,
> C'étaient les mêmes pleurs et de la même terre
> Et de la même race et des mêmes Hébreux.

The Universal Church makes sense to Péguy only if it is first of all rooted in the French soil. Was there a more pious woman than his mother, the caner of old chairs in the Cathedral of Orleans? She was the ideal Catholic woman. She educated him in the Catholic peasant way for which body and soul, earth and heaven, flesh and spirit, France and God are inseparable. For him, therefore, the spiritual begins with the earthly, the supernatural with the natural: "Car le surnaturel est lui-même charnel" (Eve). One must first foster all the natural virtues, reliability, patriotism, unselfishness, and develop a natural practical spirit of sacrifice, otherwise the socialists will take over the rôle of the Saints of the Church whose charity was practical altruism, whereas the modern Catholic serves Mammon and talks about the infused virtues.

With all his faithfulness to the soil, with all his atavism and his sincerity, with all the stubbornness of a peasant, Péguy is a devout servant of the Blessed Virgin into whose arms at Chartres he puts his sick child, to whose care he recommends his family, whose statue he decorates the night before his death in the forest of Saint-Witz. But he never practices his religion, he never approaches the sacraments because he wants the solidarity in the *com-unio* of his still unbelieving wife which he feels he cannot get. Blasphemously but with unbounded charity he dares to offer God his damnation:

> Et s'il faut, pour sauver de l'absence éternelle
> Les âmes des damnés s'affolant de l'absence,
> Abandonne mon âme à l'absence éternelle,
> Que mon âme s'en aille en l'absence éternelle
> *(Le Mystère de la charité de Jeanne d'Arc).*

With the same peasant stubbornness in a style of endless permutations and repetitions, at the same time elementary and sublime,[1] in heroic monotony, he reiterates to his readers that all the saints had something of the traditional French peasant and worker in them, not only Joan of Arc but also Saint Joseph and even Our Lord Himself who was truly great when He worked as a carpenter, even, as Péguy surprisingly intimates, as a *tekton* in his foster-father's shop:

> Il travaillait, il était dans la charpente,
> Dans la charpenterie.
> Il avait même été un bon ouvrier
> Comme il avait été un bon tout.
> . . . .
> Il était fait pour ce métier-là.
> Sûrement
> Le métier des berceaux et des cercueils,
> Qui se ressemblent tant.
> Des tables et des lits.
> . . . .
> Le métier des buffets, des armoires, des commodes,
> Des mées,
> Pour mettre le pain.
> Des escabeaux,
> Et le monde n'est que l'escabeau de vos pieds
> Car dans ce temps-là les menuisiers n'étaient pas encore
> Séparés des charpentiers.
> *(Jeanne d'Arc).*

The social program turns into prayer, the idea of social solidarity into charity. Péguy has a vague idea of something like a

Christian communism. Of course, Péguy was attacked for his ideas, but he answered that today the only imitator of Christ is the worker. He declared bitingly that:

> L'homme aujourd'hui qui travaille est un homme qui fait comme Jésus, qui imite Jésus. . . . Des milliers d'ateliers obscurs . . . sont les reflets parmi nous, reflètent, répètent, parmi nous, l'atelier obscur, l'humble atelier de Nazareth. Et ceci est le tissu même et la moelle du monde chrétien. . . . Et celui qui n'a quitté l'établi et la varlope que pour se coucher mourir est celui qui est le plus agréable à Dieu.
>
> M. Laudet est . . . un chrétien pour paroisses riches (c.a.d. isolé!). Toute famille chrétienne a les yeux fixés sur la famille de Nazareth. Des milliers de familles . . . ont gagné le ciel, ensemble, en famille, les yeux uniquement fixés sur la famille de Nazareth. ("Un nouveau théologien, Monsieur Laudet," *Nouvelle Revue Française,* 1936, pp. 30-31.)

Péguy, though he died a hero, did not see that the supernatural Catholic spirit of sacrifice, formed certainly by the life of Christ, is still more formed by His sacrificial passion and death than by His "workman's" life. To have used this fundamental Catholic value of Christian sacrifice and vicarious suffering for his novels is the merit of Emile Baumann (1868-1941).[2] He published in 1908 a novel called *L'Immolé.* It was followed by many others, among them *Le Baptême de Pauline Ardel* (1913), *Job le prédestiné* (1922) and *Le Signe sur les mains* (1926). Baumann unfortunately does not start from the observation of life but from the study of the Scriptures and St. Thomas. He thus interprets, nay constructs, life in the light of his theology. Therefore there is no enigma for him. He has the courage or perhaps the temerity to apply to everyday life the most difficult teachings, as for instance St. Paul's that we have to make up for what is still lacking in the suffering of Christ, or the doctrine of vicarious merit. He then constructs cases of hardly possible sacrificial lives in the setting of contemporary France to prove that these doctrines actually do materialize in the Church. He implies that cases of grace are verifiable for every Catholic and not only for the few who have the discernment of spirits as a charism. He does not hesitate to give the reader direct explanations for everything so that no interpretation is possible except that of the author.

Daniel Rovère, *L'Immolé,* and his mother, advised by a priest, offer their lives in atonement for their father's and husband's guilt. Daniel, in a fight with anti-clericals, is actually nailed to the church door, while his mother renounces a cure for her malady.

In *Le Baptême de Pauline Ardel,* the voluntary victim is the girl's lover, who failing to bring the unbaptized girl into the Church by natural means attains this end by offering his young life as a sacrifice which is accepted, as is revealed from the diary left by the boy after his death.

Job le prédestiné is a modern henpecked husband, Bernard Dieuzède, a bookseller who experiences every imaginable degradation and sorrow as a conscious victim: bankruptcy, the unfaithfulness of his wife, abandonment by his daughter, and starvation and blindness.

The victim of *Le Signe sur les mains* is Jérôme Cormier. He is summoned by his friend who is going to be killed during an attack in World War I, to become a priest in his place, although he is without any vocation and entangled in a serious love affair. The half-promise weighing on his conscience and the encouragement of his confessor make Jérôme accept the priesthood as a consenting, happy and triumphant "victim."

In spite of, or better, with his constructed and doubtful cases, Baumann made the Catholic reading public restless. Although he erroneously lowered the cases of higher spirituality to a banal level, he showed for the first time almost against his will that serious problems in spirituality cannot get a wholesale and easy-going solution. Accordingly, his stylistic expression is not sure of itself; it is characterized by slow movement, the use of heavy sentences with many anticipated adverbial circumstances, and very detailed descriptions of sinful situations. Dealing with complicated cases, he necessarily has to resort to the use of many parenthetical elements. Trying to create a Catholic atmosphere, he endlessly expounds spiritual history, literature, and art. His strength consists in his stirring and passionate dialogues. When the modern Job tries to win over his wife, she answers: "Trop songer à Dieu est au-dessus de mes forces," a laconic remark which will destroy the marriage of the pious man. Pauline Ardel's father prevents her from joining the Church with the remark: "The only true paradise is the paradise of labor and thought" to which Pauline Ardel's suffering fiancé gives the overwhelming answer. Baumann's apologetical novels found a continuation in those of Daniel-Rops (1901-), e.g. *Mort, où est ta victoire?* (1934).

Baumann's failure to distinguish between genuine higher and lower spiritual levels becomes apparent when compared to the sure grasp on spiritual problems of Paul Claudel (1868-1955) since he published in 1910 his *Cinq grandes odes.* With this work he, a converted witness, made his Christ-centered love the key to all individual, collective and cultural problems. The inseparability of love from sacrifice (on which we have already touched, in chapter three) is one of Claudel's favorite themes. He treats it on many levels and always in a convincing manner. The great odes contain his dramas *in nuce.* In the first ode called *Les Muses* and in an early play, *Le Repos du septième jour* (1901), Claudel expresses the idea that the pagans may have had some awareness of Christian truth and that certain persons among them may have been granted the extraordinary grace of a private revelation. In *Magnificat,* the second ode, we read his jubilation on being freed from darkness and led to faith by Christ's Redemption which brings to the individual a truth opposed to the idols of antiquity or of modern non-Christian civilizations. These idols were first encountered when Claudel translated the Greek tragedies of Aeschylus, and were exposed by him in his play *La Ville,* where he took to task the idol of a lay state, and in *L'échange,* where he stigmatized the idol of capitalism.

In *Le Soulier de satin* (1929), the *Magnificat* has still greater echo. There he wants to stress that at the very time when the idols of the Renaissance and Reformation were ravaging Europe,

Christ redeemed the Negroes and Indians of the continents of Africa and America through the work of Spanish and Portuguese missionaries. A third great ode is *La Muse qui est la grâce.* This Christian Muse is not so easy to follow: wooing the Christian, she offers him sacrifice, self-surrender, detachment, in short the "folly of the cross." This theme also has its variations in the great dramas. In *L'Annonce faite à Marie,* Violaine accepts this Muse, and is led to a superhuman charity which makes her embrace a leper and contract his terrible disease herself. Rejected by her love, Jacques Hury, who suspects that her contagion is the result of infidelity and impurity, she is forced to withdraw to the woods where the other lepers are living. She becomes blind and finally is fatally wounded by her jealous and revengeful sister, Mara. The grace she gets is two-fold: first, to approach the love of Christ by giving up her earthly love under unimaginable suffering, and second, to use the charism of raising the dead to the advantage of her sister's child who for this service of a supernatural order only hates her the more.

Doña Prouhèze, heroine of the above mentioned *Soulier de satin,* is another saint in the making because she, too, accepts the "Muse that is Grace." Married without love to an older man, the nobleman Don Pelagio, she falls in love with young Don Rodrigo. When she sets out to meet Don Rodrigo, her Catholic instinct tells her to put her satin slipper in the hands of a statue of Our Lady at the Gate, so that if she runs into temptation she may run with a halting foot. But Rodrigo is appointed viceroy in America and she herself at the strange wish of her husband is appointed ambassador to Mogador. There she is exposed to the will of the unattractive commander Camillo. Doña Prouhèze has to marry him after her husband's death to prevent Camillo's apostasy to Mohammedanism, although her love for Don Rodrigo, whom she would have been free to marry now, tortures her night and day. Rodrigo after a fatal delay comes as a general to take Camillo to task and to set Prouhèze free. She has the strength by grace to surrender only her little daughter, remaining herself in the fortress together with her legitimate husband to be blown up by her lover's naval artillery. But she fulfills a mission by her heroism: she makes a saint; after he is disgraced by the king Rodrigo dies rejoicing in the utmost poverty.

Saying yes to sacrifice, to heroic sacrifice, is the *Fiat* to sanctity and to fullness of life in the Catholic sense. Small wonder then that the drama of Claudel "almost bleeds from the wounds of Christ" because the Claudelian hero walks the hardest and at the same time the most loving way in order to find his supreme expression. The Claudelian hero moves towards Christ's cross, to what for Voltaire would be the peak of folly. He knows that he is on earth not to shape the cross for others but to mount it himself and to mount it joyously.

It was an idea cherished by the seventeenth century that in spiritual guidance the director has to be, or rather to remain, the priest offering a sacrifice. The guided penitent has to be the victim and the host. Claudel exemplifies this idea in the best of his minor dramas, *L'Otage*. Here he frames a plot according to which a French aristocratic lady, Sygne de Coufontaine, is willing to marry a revolutionary, her erstwhile servant and the murderer of her parents, in order to save the pope from imprisonment by Napoleon. She tries to make the superhuman sacrifice although she is not really capable of it for she hates her husband Turelure to the end of her life. Only her last gesture is a gesture of forgiveness. Here is one of the breathtaking dialogues between Father Badilon and Sygne de Coufontaine before her consent:

> Badilon: Mon enfant, sondez votre coeur.
> Sygne: Mon Dieu! Cependant vous voyez que je vous aime.
> Badilon: Mais non point jusqu'aux crachats, à l'arrache-
>   ment des habits et à la croix.

All the Christ-centered souls in Claudel's dramas understand that earthly love can never be fulfilled and that it is only a way, a means of reaching the starting point from which the search for the real Spouse begins. This is stated most explicitly in *La Cantate à trois voix* (1933). Three beautiful young women in a festive mood sing about love during a balmy summer night. The unmarried brunette Laeta, unaware of love's bitterness and thinking only of her personal happiness in hope and desire, is jubilant about her youthful body ready to be conquered by a daring suitor, violent like the Rhone river, and whose arms never would appear too strong to her. She recognizes in love "the force which fastens the stone to its base." The blonde Fausta, full of regret and remembrance, but full also of strength and faith, has learned through a necessary temporary separation from her husband that concern for the beloved one in danger and forgetfulness of self have become the decisive elements in her love and that the gold of love is a kind of renunciation. She has understood that she has to be for her husband not a prison but a harbor, an arsenal, a tower. The young widow Beata, mild and charitable, has been taught by experience that love must be renunciation, even radical renunciation, and she praises her husband's death which has made her free for the invasion of God. Beata has learned that the word has to expire so that the sentence may exist and the meaning may prevail, that the face of the beloved man which hinders the Vision of the True Face has to disappear like the froth on a glass of wine.

Because of Claudel's missionary zeal and outrage at the secularized world, it is not always easy for him to hate the sin, but love the sinner. We are shocked to hear him call Goethe "the solemn old ass," to see him consider Darwin absurd and Bergson queer and mediocre, to have him represent hatred by Calvin, Robespierre and Lenin on the same level, and human stupidity by Voltaire, Renan and Marx. We will scarcely feel like joining him in his prayer:

> Ne me perdez point avec les Voltaire, et les Renan, et les Michelet, et les Hugo, et tous les autres infâmes!
> Leur âme est avec les chiens morts, leurs livres sont joints au fumier (Magnificat).

Of course, in life he acted differently. He was convinced of the good faith of his friend Romain Rolland; at the grave of the man who was his chief in the diplomatic service, an agnostic, he says: "I give you with confidence into the hands of that God you did not know." This attitude honors Claudel the man, and reveals at the same time the strength of the sentimental element in him.

Often Claudel expresses himself with an ironical contempt for the simple reader who is puzzled by the crude comparisons, the wishful interpretation of biblical passages, the mixing-up of climates and continents, reality and dream, street gossip and liturgical solemnity, and the insolent remarks which in their triumphant faith seem blasphemous to the spiritual weakling. Claudel's stylistic tool is the paradox: "Dans mon néant j'existe." Daring wordplay is used even in the most sacred statements: "Il faut subir . . . Quelqu'un qui soit en moi plus moi-même que moi." The fine balancing between the abstract and the concrete makes this linguistic revolutionary a real classic. His unique rhythms move between awe and tenderness, solemnity and familiarity with God, mystical outcries and down-to-earth statements: "Son cri intarissable en moi comme une eau qui fuse et qui déferle." Claudel's style is truly obscure, but it is the expression of the darkness of the Faith, more luminous than any discursive clarity. It is the way of "sensing" the spiritual: "Nous sommes avec ces deux mains partout du potier spirituel" *(Un Poète regarde la croix)*. The uniqueness of Claudel's symbolism lies in its liturgical quality, which informs the poet's modern and poetical manner, and makes it vibrant and profound. The keenness of Claudel's imagination may best be demonstrated by one of his meditations, that on Christ's words *(Luke XXIII, 43)*: "This day thou shalt be with me in paradise." In a second, as Claudel points out, the good thief is absolved and sanctified. On this infamous cross no longer dies a criminal but a martyr, a burning host. And he goes straight to heaven, a vast locality where he is quite alone. In front of the Holy Trinity and the innumerable angels he is lost, insignificant. The throne of the Immaculate is still empty. There is no Peter, no John, no Paul, no Gregory, no Benedict, no Francis, no Dominic, no Thomas, no Ignatius, no Teresa. He feels like someone alone in a cathedral when the clergy and faithful have gone out in procession. The candles are burning, the altar is decorated, a graceful canopy above the armchair in cardinal's red is there, too; but—around the lonely man only empty chairs, endless empty chairs. And suddenly, above him, high in the steeple a tremendous thundering. The great bell begins to ring.

Understanding Claudel is tantamount to understanding his spirituality through his symbolism,[3] his mystical allusions through his stylistic ellipses,[4] his own permeation by the Scriptures through his many sacred metaphors from it,[5] his militant Catholicism through his somewhat pietistic exaggerations which expose his style to easy *pastiche*,[6] his fundamental concern through his archetypical patterns, especially the tree[7] standing for life and the water[8] for death, and his sensuous paganism mitigated by his theology, as results from the wave movement of his style.[9]

Alexandre Maurocordato (*L'Ode de Paul Claudel*, Genève: Droz, 1955) has said the decisive word about the lyrical style of Claudel and the musical treatment of his themes. There are always effects of counterpoints (e.g., exclamations taken up by interrogations) as well as diverting counter-themes. His biblical versets have a chosen dominant in harmonious relation to the final cadence of the sentence. He crosses the ordinary syntax by a highly psychological word-order where the subject-theme and the predicate-proposition have a place in the sentence other than the grammarian would expect. Segmentation of the sentence, syllepsis, anacoluthon, complex *reprises,* syncopes, daring insertions of suspense, parenthesis, appendices, retardations make the sense obscure but are never detrimental to the balance of the period. This consists of challenging, pregnant and metaphorical nouns or verbs with enormous magnetic fields. Within these fields there is room for striking imagery where, e.g., the starred sky at night appears as "l'immense clergé de la nuit avec ses Evêques et ses Patriarches" or as "un grand butin de poissons à demi sorti de la mer, dont les écailles vivent à la lueur de la torche." But these images are full of an enigmatic symbolism which seems an invitation to the enjoyment of the world but is only an extraversion directed to the interior. Therefore each ode asks: "Que m'importe?" namely science, love, cosmos, poetry, family, if they do not free the soul from any attraction that is not God.

Where Claudel's poetry is genuine,[9] his overwhelming and triumphant faith expresses itself in vibrating apostrophes of beauty deriving from a doctrine which assumed life and love in the poet himself:

> Salut, grande Nuit de la Foi, infaillible Cité astronomique!
> C'est la nuit, et non pas le brouillard qui est la patrie d'un catholique.
> ("Chant de l'Epiphanie" in *Corona benignitatis*.)

Claudel's enthusiastic faith bridges poetically the historical event and the liturgical implication when at the piercing of the heart of our Lord on the Cross he exclaims:

> L'Eglise entre ses bras à jamais prend charge de son bien
> aimé. Elle est le prêtre et l'autel et le vase et le Cenacle. Ici finit
> la Croix et commence le Tabernacle. ("Chemin de la Croix," *ib.*)

This solemnity is replaced by a shocking realism whenever he tries to analyze what the psychology of the faithful ought to be. The soul unworthy by principle to receive the Eucharist behaves like a once beautiful woman who on her hospital bed hides from her love the side of her face destroyed by lupus (*Communion* in *La Messe là-bas*).

The two poles of a well-placed solemnity of awe and a sometimes misplaced realism are the extremes between which Claudel, the apostle, and Claudel, the *gamin*, move. It is difficult to assess his greatness throughout the bulk of his works which cannot even be enumerated here. But the poet of apostolic zeal, sacrifice and charity deserves a high place in the history of poeticized spirituality. The short time elapsed since Claudel's death does not permit a final judgment on his poetic qualities. These, however, seem definitely more of a lyrical than of a truly dramatic kind. While many of his dramas like *L'Otage, Le Pain dur, Le Père humilié* may soon appear strained, contrived and unconvincing in their plots, his *Odes* and his *Cantate à trois voix* will remain priceless as the most dignified lyrical receptacles for the highest message of Christianity—charity.

The second great representative of Catholic spirituality after Paul Claudel is Georges Bernanos (1888-1948).[10] He inherited Spanish blood from his father's ancestors which may account for his being primarily mystic in his interests, while his mother's family belongs to the French province of Berry, which may explain his critical and sociological capacities as a *moraliste*. Both gifts together made him a wholehearted advocate of spiritual reality and moral standards as against all kinds of psycho-analytical escapism, "l'étrange érudition de Siegmund Freud" or existentialist evasion, "certaines conjonctures où l'homme ne sent plus Dieu que comme un obstacle." Educated by the Jesuits in the Collège de Vaugirard, he got from his training a natural love for and closeness to the Church as well as a mistrust for any sort of "clerical" policy which compromises with the world because it takes no spiritual risks.

The central and logical theme of Bernanos' four classical novels is sanctity in a world of sin. They are revolutionary in presenting the vital issue of Catholicism as a challenge to the modern world. Six years before Henri Bergson,[11] Bernanos understood that the existence of the saint with his moral perfection, his absolutely sound constitution and nonetheless his claim to be in a mystical contact with the Divine, remains a disturbing fact for the rationalist and involves an appalling and terrifying call for the Catholic.

One year earlier than Gabriel Marcel,[12] Bernanos with his artistic intuition recognized that suffering and injustice, love and hatred, virtue and sin, purity and guilt, God and immortality are not problems but mysteries, because the creature pondering them has not the liberty of putting himself at a "scientific" distance from them. Man is rather involved in them, being *embarqué*, to use the Pascalian term. Finally Bernanos must be linked to Claudel. It is with Claudel that Bernanos shares the fundamental idea that all the sinful, proud, egocentric forms of love can only be barriers, or, at best, detours to the theocentric, sacrificial and redeeming charity. To substitute anything whatsoever for the Love of God is the fundamental madness which spurns the Redemption: "Nous ressemblons à des fous qui tendent les bras vers le reflet de la lune dans l'eau."

The most original contribution to French literature from Bernanos' creative genius is the priest as hero, the secular priest not as a minor character for local color but in his relation to God, to the contemplative monks, to the hierarchy, to his confrères, to the *société dévote*, to the "tepid" members of the flock and to the liberal world. What is more astonishing still is that Bernanos created four of these priest types without actually repeating himself. Among these priests are three outspoken mystics, Abbé Donissan *(Sous le soleil de satan-S)*, the Curé d'Ambricourt *(Journal d'un curé de campagne-JC)*, and the ideal humble priest, "miracle de douceur et abandon," called Abbé Chevance *(L'Imposture-I, La Joie-J)*, as well as one renegade and rationalist, Abbé Cénabre *(I, J)*. The critics who have complained about the "extreme" characterization of these priest heroes forget that average commonplace and mediocre priests surround the central figures like satellites. There is the unctuous, cowardly, political compromiser, Monseigneur Espelette, who fears "L'importance des positions prises par la critique rationaliste" *(I, 112)*, the practical, shrewd, feudal *routinier,* Monsieur le Chanoine De La Motte-Beuvron *(JC),* the humanly sympathetic gentleman-priest Menou-Segrais who lacks only one thing and knows it very well—spirituality *(S)*, the lovable, sound, rich, good-natured parochial dictator, the pastor of Torcy *(JC)* who is afraid of miracles and "unhealthy saints," and "des mystiques poitrinaires" *(JC 18)*, the intellectual professor of chemistry, Abbé Sabirous *(S)*, who thinks that, after all, a priest is just an organizer of morality among mankind; and there are still many other priestly background figures like "le doyen de Blangermont," who finds the commercial exploiters tolerable for the Church because "s'ils nous volent, ils nous respectent" *(JC 88)*.

In spite of his ironical treatment, Bernanos shows by his literary art of analyzing priests' souls the same interest which the Church has in practice—to create priests who, though living in the world, would be rocks of prayer and self-sanctification, able to become not only the institutional, doctrinal and sacramental leaders, but also the heroic, exemplary and apostolic shepherds of the flock. This problem seen from the viewpoint of the serious priest himself—and this is precisely the viewpoint of the layman Bernanos in unison with modern French priest-poets such as Louis Le Cardonnel (1862-1936) or René Fernandat (1884-   )—means a true and tremendous drama in which Heaven, Earth and Hell are engaged. In arid isolation those priests are struggling with the Lord as Jacob did with the Angel.

The lifelong temptation to despair which Abbé Donissan undergoes, owing to his mystical insight into the unyielding pride of souls that resist grace, assumes the character of a purifying diabolical possession in the novel *Sous le soleil de Satan* (1926). It is conditioned by his flock's sheer pleasure in being untrue, impertinent, proud in preferring one's ridiculous "divine" egotism to one's condition as a creature. All this falsehood and pride coalesce in the lust-haunted girl Mouchette and drive her to murder and suicide, although the saintly priest is willing to put the blame on heredity and education. For her "hysterical obstinacy," as the modern world would say, the old Christian designation of diabolical possession seems to Bernanos the only true one. Now, Abbé Donissan, with an immense love for those confided to him, even wants to break this satanic resistance, the sin against the Holy Spirit, and therefore offers his own reputation, will, joy, peace and even eternal bliss, if possible, to snatch such prey from Satan. By making such an offer, however, and such a vow, he invites his own atoning, purifying and vicarious possession, that is, in practice a lifelong desperate fight with Satan, the logical appalling reverse side of the radical love of God, boundless, unconditioned, the *pur amour* which Fénelon and Bossuet have so much discussed.

Bernanos, dealing with another question of spirituality at the same time, namely the relation of asceticism and mysticism, makes of Abbé Donissan a stubborn, awkward peasant character whose goal is ascetical suffering and who fights any mystical consolation and illumination as something easygoing and lenient. He does not understand that asceticism is an active preparation for the passive grace of mysticism. Never expecting God's embrace, he lacks hope in spite of his burning faith and charity and almost forgets God in his constant frontal attack on the devil. Therefore Satan actually leads him around in a vicious circle, as is symbolically described in the chapter on the nocturnal encounter with the horsedealer. Donissan's charismatic gift of seeing into the very depths of his own and other people's souls keeps the ugliness of sin before him. Consequently he is bound to mistrust at every step the diabolical force behind sin. Seeing the snares of the devil also in apparently good and holy things, he thinks even of his gift of miracles as a satanic trap. Therefore, not daring to call to life a dead child in the name of God, he almost renounces the gift. Again, for lack of hope he becomes a broken man. Nonetheless, out of duty, he returns to his always besieged confessional and there he is found struck down by a heart attack "telle une sentinelle, tuée d'une balle dans sa guérite" (*S* 360).

Thus, Bernanos tried with refined methods to reveal the psychology of a saint in the making, very different from what the superficial believer, thinking of plaster saints, would imagine one to be.

If hope blacked out by a boundless charity produces Donissan's purifying possession in *Sous le soleil de Satan,* charity blacked out by critical knowledge without faith produces as a consequence of guilt the real possession of the apostate priest-scholar, Monsignor Cénabre, in *L'Imposture.* Cénabre belongs to the family of such Catholic ecclesiastical scholars as Renan, Loisy, Tyrrell, Schnitzer, who because of their historical-critical studies in religious matters run into difficulties with their faith. According to Bernanos' analysis, by yielding to curiosity and self-realization, such priests are guilty of dismissing too easily their instinct of faith. Thus, Abbé Cénabre, knowing that he reverses the order of values, subordinates the realm of charity to the realm of geometry in Pascal's sense, the divine paradox of faith to human planning, the inseparable unit of the supernatural and the ascetical to a natural pseudo-morality of an alleged higher sincerity. Cénabre can never escape his bad conscience any more than Renan could; both betray themselves by a "serenity" which is in reality a disgraceful affectation. Cénabre's case is particularly grave because as author of the *Mystiques florentins* and writer of *La Vie de Tauler,* he was always aware of the irrefutable and obligating message which came from the mystics. But he refused to surrender, and instead ridiculed their alleged pathological hallucinations with skeptical criticism, never saying too much, however, in his "scholarly" irony, so that, barely escaping ecclesiastical censorship, he became the idol of the intelligentsia and the lion of the *salons bien pensants.* Cénabre, however, knows his dangerous spiritual situation better. Finally it happens: "Lentement désagrégée par la délectation du doute volontaire, par le sacrilège d'une curiosité sans amour, la croyance s'était évanouie" (*I* 36). One night, a night of real, hellish, suicidal despair, he is fully aware of this fact and calls for a simple priest, Abbé Chevance, to help him. But because this lucid priest pierces his treacherous, proud, loveless, apostate soul, Cénabre falls into a satanic rage "comme un homme qui crie au bord de la mer" (*I* 53). He will be marked by a dire habitual *ricanement,* the expression of a stage of a desperate *angoisse,* "forme hideuse et corporelle du remords" (*I* 29), without any consolation. It is the very same *angoisse* about which Heidegger and Sartre have said so much, denying like Cénabre its fundamental character of despair, and recommending it as a philosophy of life to a godless world.

In Cénabre's case there still seems to be a way out. Abbé Chevance offers his own soul for atonement and actually dies himself with all the signs of an apparent satanic possession and despair as a self-chosen and mystically granted vicarious suffering —a bewildering experience but one well known in the history of the Church. Cénabre's possession seems indeed somewhat relieved after Chevance's death, a relief which Cénabre ascribes to a psychological torture which he himself applied with indescribable sadism to a poor epileptic beggar as though he were his double. Thus he foolishly believes that he has performed a self-liberation. Yet he does not know, any more than did Freud, Jung and Adler, that only Love can liberate. This is the secret of Abbé Chevance's holocaust.

Chantal de Clergerie, heroine of the next novel, *La Joie,* was the only person who watched Abbé Chevance's horrible agony with but a vague awareness of what it meant. She is in the mystical state of *quietude* and joy when Abbé Chevance dies (*J* 44). Even her father, the famous Catholic historian with liberal leanings—and therefore under treatment for his nervousness by the Freudian Dr. La Pérouse—says sometimes: "Tu n'as jamais été si gaie" (*J* 44). Everybody admires in her "le bons sens, la raison" (*J* 24), "sa jeune sagesse" (*J* 57), "ses yeux tranquilles" (*J* 21), "sa petite main toujours calme" (*J* 22), "l'espéce d'indifférence heureuse" (*J* 34), "l'humble allégresse" (*J* 35), "le rayonnant esprit de confiance et abandon" (*J* 36), "son regard lumineux" (*J* 21), "aussi ferme et aussi sûr dans son implacable pureté que celui d'un homme intrépide" (*J* 47). Often she is enraptured in contemplation: "Elle glissait dans l'oraison comme dans un sommeil enchanté" (*J* 45), "elle tombait en Dieu" (*J* 40). The Russian chauffeur Fiodor has spied on her ecstasies and bluntly calls her a "sainte en extase" (*J* 25). She answers naively: "Ma pauvre maman souffrait de ces crises nerveuses" (*J* 25).

Now it is a masterstroke of Bernanos that the further development of Chantal's mysticism out of the stage of *quiet* is dependent on her intuitive and comprehensive penetration of the sinful world concentrated in this little country house of her father's, from whose spell of lies and hypocrisy some guests have already escaped. Only the drunkard Fiodor, the atheistic psychiatrist La Pérouse, Chantal's grandmother who is pride incarnate, Abbé Cénabre, and some kitchen employees are the last Strindbergian inmates. Chantal is in a kind of *attente* (*J* 34), an expression typical of the seventeenth century French mystic Marie de l'Incarnation, which Bernanos probably learned from Bremond and uses to the point. What Chantal intuitively expects is the yet unknown form of her *sacrifice total* (*J* 64). She has the mysterious death of Abbé Chevance always before her interior eyes;

she ponders on the name of Cénabre which the dying Abbé mentioned so often; she hears Abbé Cénabre ask her nervously about the death of Chevance; she sees the puppets, the *insectes* (*J* 17) in her father's house ranged in one line with Cénabre, and she understands, with "cette sorte de pitié qu'on ne voit qu'aux yeux des mères" (*J* 101), that as a force in God's economy of salvation she has now to take "la courbe immense de son vol, le vide peu a peu creux sous ses ailes" (*J* 44) in helping to save their souls.

Thus consciously she enters the dark night of the spirit: "En une seconde elle reconnut la solitude effrayante, fondamentale, la solitude des enfants de Dieu (*J* 120) . . . , le délaissement sacré, seuil et porche de toute sainteté" (*J* 121). And when she has had the vision of Christ's agony, "elle la recueillit dans son âme ainsi qu'un plongeur remplit d'air sa poitrine" (*J* 247). In this state she learns the secret of Cénabre, who surprises her in her ecstasy. The scholar of mysticism tries this time in vain to escape Truth. In the very same night of her Gethsemani Chantal is killed by the drunken, sacrilegious Fiodor. The atonement seems to reach Cénabre, "percé à jour, incapable de retenir aucun mensonge, livré sans défense" (*J* 308). He finds Chantal's body beside that of her suicidal murderer and, thunderstruck, has just time to say *Pater noster,* "d'une voix surhumaine" (*J* 317), probably in "parfaite dépossession" (*J* 304), before he falls into madness from which he never recovers. Thus Bernanos has again played his Pascalian trump—that even in the lives of the "lovely" saints, because they are imitators of Christ, "le dernier acte est sanglant," even if the saint is a "little flower" or "une alouette . . . , une touffe de plumes avec une chanson dedans" (*J* 211).

Chantal's masculine counterpart, the young Curé d'Ambricourt, starts on a still higher mystical plain (*JC* 35). The description of his mystical stages is intermingled with the account of his priestly activity in his *Journal d'un curé de campagne.* The spiritual advance is paralleled, on the other hand, with the development of a stomach cancer which brings the young pastor of thirty to an early death just when he was becoming acquainted with his first parish consisting of greedy grocers, sinful girls, a local count who maintains illicit relations with his fiendish daughter's governess, and many avaricious peasants far removed from God.

The pastor, whose sanctity emanates from him as a force, is the hated object of awe for this sinful parish. An object of God's loving election from his earliest youth (*JC* 64, 75), he is too modest to admit his habitual state of mystical union, explaining it as "une voix qui parle, ne se tait ni jour ni nuit" (*JC* 134), or as "une présence invisible qui n'est sûrement pas celle de Dieu —plutôt d'un ami fait à mon image" (*JC* 30), or as "cette paix intérieure où les événements se reflétaient comme dans . . . une nappe d'eau limpide" (*JC* 160). Exploring his conscience "avec une rigueur inflexible" (*JC* 9) he finds his judgments straightforward and mitigated only by charity, because he looks upon his parish as one crucified for it (*JC* 49), with the loving and pitiful eyes of Christ on the Cross (*JC* 35). Living only on bread and red wine, because of his stomach ailment, he is considered a drunkard (*JC* 261), but he is willing to "souffrir *par* les âmes" as are the monks to "souffrir *pour* les âmes" (*JC* 49). He is in constant prayer; even his diary is "un prolongement de la prière" (*JC* 29). Aware (*JC* 242) of his fast-approaching death and convinced of the necessity of the fullest spiritual detachment in spite of his natural plight, he sees that without heroism there is no spiritual life possible (*JC* 135). In long nights of spiritual abandonment, he reaches stages of apparent revolt (181), but actually becomes more detached (221). He is very reticent about this with his confrères who do not understand him. But his heroic virtue is discovered by a daring officer of the *Légion étrangère* who "canonizes" him in his own language: "Vous êtes un chic garcon. Je ne voudrais pas un autre curé que vous à mon lit de mort" (*JC* 304). He lives and preaches an "acceptation joyeuse" (*JC* 332) of life with all its suffering. As opposed to Cénabre, his faith is so strong that it cannot be lost, and his suspected *peur de la mort* turns out to be *la crainte de la mort,* that is, the trembling awe of appearing before the Eternal Judge. This *crainte* still seems to him an imperfection, although he cannot help having the conviction that he possesses the spirit of poverty and childlikeness, and that there is no self-love in him whatever. Anguish and fear to him are signs of mystical impurity, his mystical experiences having revealed to him the inseparability of purity and faith as present in a perfect Christian life:

> La pureté . . . est une des conditions mystérieuses, mais évidentes—l'expérience l'atteste—de cette connaissance surnaturelle de soi-même, de soi-même en Dieu, qui s'appelle la foi. L'impureté ne détruit pas cette connaissance, elle en anéantit le besoin (*JC* 157).

His visions are chiefly concerned with Christ's agony, but once when the Curé de Torcy has become poetically enthusiastic about the childlike purity of the Blessed Virgin, he has the true vision of it after a severe hemorrhage and he tries in vain to ascribe it modestly to a mere dream based on those reminiscences. He considers himself weak for flinching at the moment when the doctor tells him that his death is imminent. He is humiliated by having to pass his last hours in the home of an ex-priest and his mistress, but the truth concerning his interior state was confided previously to his diary: "Je déborde de confiance et de paix" (307).

Bernanos' stylistic greatness[13] is of the same kind as that of Dante or Pascal. He explains the supernatural with everyday analogies as though he had experienced it himself. He even harmonizes these analogies with the mentality of the heroes so that the symbols perfectly fit the characters. Moreover, he challenges the real mystics who invented the most subtle comparisons for their experiences, and, finally, he discovers poetical analogies that are true symbols, the kind called by Flaubert *rapports fatals* and by Baudelaire *correspondances*.

The old analogical patterns of mysticism, music, nature, military strategy, swimming, diving are changed into very modern ones, among which are the motorcycle and the artificial lung. The soul invaded unawares by the mystical grace of illumination in her ordinary life is compared to the conductor of the orchestra who "dans le déchaînement de l'orchestre . . . perçoit la première et l'imperceptible vibration de la note fausse, mais trop tard pour en arrêter l'explosion" (*S* 126). While this comparison was chosen for the case of the pessimistic Abbé Donissan who almost fears bliss, little Chantal surrenders to God's exacting grace playfully, just as her little dog does to her: "Voyez mon chien Tabalo: que je fasse mine de courir dessus, il se sauve. Que je le poursuive réellement, il se met tout de suite sur le dos, les pattes en l'air. Voilà. Je ne me défends pas" (*J* 274). When this courageous girl is really disposed to face the dark nights of the soul of whose specific character she has no idea as yet, she has acquired the stature of a military leader owing to "Son admirable effort . . . d'engager à la fois, ainsi qu'un chef de guerre, ses régiments contre un ennemi dont il ignore la position et les desseins, toutes les forces de son coeur" (*J* 47). Her strength comes from her absolute confidence in God, who will not act differently from her swimming teacher in Trouville who taught her how to act whenever she faced the big waves:

> J'aurai toujours assez d'esprit pour ne pas me débattre, me faire la plus légère possible comme à Trouville, quoi! au bras du maître nageur. . . . Les petites vagues vous amusent. Et qu'importe une vague de fond? Elle ne nous lèvera que plus haut (*J* 91).

The Curé de Torcy has discerned that the Curé d'Ambricourt is a chosen mystic with all the consequences of solitude and isolation, and in his own way he tries to deter him: "Tu tiens ta petite partie dans le concert, tu joues ton triangle et violà qu'on te prie de monter sur l'estrade, on te donne un Stradivarius et on te dit: 'Allez, mon garçon, je vous écoute': Brr" (*JC* 17). But the Curé d'Ambricourt knows better. He can compare from experience the poor theoretical faith with the mystically illustrated vital Faith, the ordinary practice of prayer with granted contemplation:

> On ne saurait donner le nom de foi à un signe abstrait qui ne ressemble pas plus à la foi, pour reprendre une comparaison célèbre, que la constellation du Cygne à un cygne (*JC* 152) . . . Une malheureuse bête, sous la cloche pneumatique peut faire tous les mouvements de la respiration, qu'importe! Et voilà que soudain l'air siffle . . . dans ses bronches, délie un à un les délicats tissus pulmonaires . . . , les artères tremblent au premier coup de bélier du sang rouge, l'être entier est comme un navire à la détonation des voiles qui se gonflent (*JC* 207).

Let us close with a comparison according to which the mystic after all his purifying trials sees and enjoys nature with eyes so pure that he almost sees God in and through nature. This is the meaning of Saint Francis of Assisi's *Cantico del Sole*. The Curé d'Ambricourt sings his mystical hymn to the sun in a technical age, in a most daring and modern fashion on the back seat of a motorcycle, when he rides over hills and through valleys as though in an unearthly flight which encompasses the spiritual reality:

> La haute voix du moteur . . . était comme le chant de la lumière, elle était la lumière même, et je croyais la suivre des yeux dans sa courbe immense, sa prodigieuse ascension. Le paysage . . . s'ouvrait de toutes parts, et . . . tournait majestueusement sur lui-même ainsi que la porte d'un autre monde (*JC* 289).

Bernanos' work, which one leaves with the same feeling of purification and enrichment with which one leaves a Racinian tragedy, is in its subject matter and style a typical work of the generation of *entre-les-deux-guerres*. It has as its general theme the moral and social disintegration of the contemporary world no more and no less than have the works of Pirandello, James Joyce or Marcel Proust. Bernanos is however the first to see our epoch in an even more catastrophic decay, exemplified by the lifeless parish, particularly in *Monsieur Ouine*.

Bernanos' means of expression are a kind of interior monologue, contemporary with the kindred attempts of Valéry Larbaud, and the fragmentation of the story into simultaneous layers as seen in André Gide's *Faux monnayeurs* and in the *romanciers surréalistes*. Concerned with the rôle of the Church and of Catholic society in this disintegrating world, Bernanos has in a way done better than François Mauriac by inserting the very essence of his spiritual engagement into the center of the plots, the fascinating imagery and the strikingly diversified sentence types. At the same time he reduces the element of human love to a minimum, making the love of God appear as the paramount means of healing a dying civilization. To the objection that his non-comprehensive grasp of the world is limited to clerical milieu, one might answer that the world of the artists, the workers, the soldiers, the outcasts, as attempted by others, suffers from the same limitation and gains likewise in depth as it loses in breadth, whereas the all-embracing broad *romans-fleuves* from Roger Martin du Gard to Jules Romains have certainly proved a failure. The clerical mileu, furthermore, is justified by the mystical purpose. Mysticism has attracted other authors, too—Alphonse de Chateaubriant, Louis Artus, even Aldous Huxley—but they were incapable of handling it from within. The work of younger authors who may be considered as influenced by Bernanos, like Graham Greene, is morally too unrestrained to compete with his novels in which the moral and the spiritual appear convincingly as the two sides of the same reality.

The novel *Augustin ou le Maître est là* (1933) by Joseph Malègue (1876-1940) deserves consideration as an attempt at making anti-secularism a subject, stressing as it does the purifying influence of the closeness of death on the mentality of an educated young Catholic in post-modernist times. Augustin Meridier had been exposed since his college days to religious doubts. These doubts, however, were counterbalanced by the Pascalian concept of the unshakable reality of Christ-God, even in his days of the Ecole Normale where biblical criticism was everything. He goes through the experience of a chaste love for his pupil Anne de Prefailles and having to renounce her because of his incurable tuberculosis finds with his growing spirit of sacrifice also a living faith again.[14] His interior struggles between what he thinks "rational" versus "sentimental" or "pragmatic" belief are pathetically described.[15] He sees his intellectual situation, however, as becoming clarified by his love for Anne where he experiences that there are phenomena where reason without emotion cannot exist,[16] an insight supported by the heroic behavior of his believing mother and sister Christine and by the faith of his friend Largilier.

The presentation of this novel is meandering and lengthy, abundant in dialogues and descriptions and somehow faulty in psychology, since the critical interference of the author, if only by a strong epithet of subjective blame, is at odds with a deeper analysis. Furthermore the analysis of love is couched unnecessarily in a romantic, almost absurd preciosity, e.g.: "La poignée de main d'Anne . . . déposa sur l'épiderme d'Augustin la douceur mortelle de son effleurement de velours." (*Augustin*, edit. Spes, II, p. 141). Stiltedness characterizes even the nature impressions given: "La nappe des grands phares domina la lune, montra une route rugueuse, alluma des feuilles vertes" (*ib.*, p. 267). If Malègue despite his romantic style still keeps a certain interest, it is for the anti-modernist character of his novels which imply an answer to the modernist challenge of Martin du Gard's *Jean Barois* (see chapter one). The closer relationship to the didactic-apologetic novels of Paul Bourget (see chapter three) cannot be overlooked. Therefore Malègue also decidedly belongs to a past generation.

The Christian existentialist Gabriel Marcel (1887-   ) represents a link between Catholics and those non-Catholics who are sympathetic to the core of Christianity. He is aware that the non-Catholic world has become deaf and blind not only to the Catholic truths of faith and morals, but also to the traditional scholastic method of conveying these truths to the people. Catholics may repeat in vain the technical proofs for the existence of God or the immortality of the soul. Consequently, says Marcel, believers and unbelievers alike have to agree that there are certain mysteries in life in which we are all so deeply and passionately involved that we are not able to treat them as merely academic problems. We have to embrace them in mutual love and understanding. All great tragedies of life contain such mysteries. Marcel, consequently, dramatizes mysterious cases very similar to the themes of Mauriac and Bernanos, cases which give primacy to spiritual and religious values.[17]

The drama *Le Mort de demain* (1931) which we have already considered in chapter three as an answer to Raynal's liberal drama, *Le Tombeau sous l'Arc de Triomphe,* truly represents such a challenge for the primacy of the spiritual. The married woman, Jeanne Fromont, tries to refuse herself to her soldier-husband on furlough from the battle front because she believes that procreation has no place in face of death. She renounces her hope of a higher spiritual level for him only when he, the dead man of tomorrow, refuses to understand the mystery concerning him and her. Challenging the liberal interpretation of Jeanne's behavior as a pathological inhibition, Marcel seems to make clear that mysteries of this sort do exist—the mystery of death and its undeniable promises and menaces, the mystery of chastity as a predisposition to confront God in full detachment.

Two other plays of G. Marcel confront hypocrisy with genuine saintliness. In *Le Chemin de crête,* a poor consumptive woman writes a diary of renunciation and forgives her husband and his mistress, but then this curious "saint," still living, lets a reporter get hold of the diary and proves by this that she is simply a ridiculous and proud woman in a pitiful situation. This disillusioning plot has, according to Marcel himself, an importance in principle: it is in a negative way a reflection about saintliness with all its concrete attributes; it is the introduction to ontology because only through true saintliness is the threatening presence of death nullified in this life and changed into a plenitude which is participation in the true Being itself. The real saint is Mireille in *La Chapelle ardente* (1926). Out of pure charity Mireille yields to the request of her mother-in-law to become, after her husband is killed in action, the wife of the incurable André Verdet. Without loving him, she becomes his guardian angel until he dies, although the world scoffs at her. Her mother-in-law pursues her with jealousy even after André's death.

Since the dramas of Gabriel Marcel are infrequently staged and less read despite their undeniable qualities,[18] we will summarize a few more. In *Le Monde cassé* (1923) marriage breaks down because Laurent Chesnay refuses his unconditioned love to Christiane, deprives her of his trust and confidence and drives her into the desperate vanity of society life. But the real reason is that she is inconsolable about the loss of her first love Jacques Decroy who left her to become a Benedictine monk. His prayers and sacrifices, however, as Christiane's sister reveals to her, after his death, restored the peace in the family. This again is a mystery, not a problem. In *Le Regard neuf,* Etienne Jordan, returning from the war, discovers the split in the marriage of his highly educated father, Maurice, and his rich but poorly educated mother, Elise. Siding with his father, he sees his foolish mother try to "solve the problem" by introducing in the house the well-educated Agathe as a more intellectual common friend. But Agathe, who would have been dangerous to both father and son, decides of her own free will to retire to her country home at the right moment. In *Le Quatuor en fa dièse* (1925) the problem of the transcendence of human relations is presented as a mystery of communion. Since Stéphane is not faithful, Claire divorces him and marries his brother Roger. But Roger continues his brotherly relations with Stéphane. It is the love of music which chains them spiritually together. Claire understands that she is between them and with both of them and cannot decide to which of the two her love belongs. Not only Claire, Stéphane and Roger but all of Marcel's characters show the importance of communication and communion, i.e., the rôle of love in family and human relations and the curse of the depersonalization of human contacts, if true love is lacking.

Love is so precious that according to Marcel it even contains the guarantee of an afterlife, as hatred and sham love preludes Hell by human self-destruction. It is by inordinate love and jealousy that in *L'Iconoclaste* (1920), Abel undermines Jacques' confidence in the fidelity of his dead wife Viviane and makes him unhappy; Abel loved Viviane before her marriage to Jacques and considers her memory soiled by his remarriage. He does not know, however, that Jacques in remarrying believed he was acting according to the request of his dead wife—to give a mother to his children. Thus Gabriel Marcel's play reveals again the Christian existentialist's belief that the mysteries of life and death cannot be analyzed[18] because every human being is here "engaged." No one is in a position to remove himself from them by a cool and objective judgment. In *Le Coeur des autres* (1921) this view of Marcel comes most drastically to the foreground. The dramatist Daniel betrays mystery, love, and confidence by exploiting the mother-child relation of his wife Rose and an adopted boy for a drama. In the drama he retells this delicate relation with intimations that lead to the destruction of the three-fold love between himself and Rose, the boy and his foster parents, and particularly the boy and Rose. Daniel, entirely lacking the sense of communion with Rose, says in an awkward and stiff fashion to his wife who is on the point of leaving him: "Je t'ai associé à ma vie." She answers: "Tu m'as annihilée."[19] It is regrettable that the existentialist refinement of Marcel as a dramatist has been almost forgotten to the advantage of the technically superior dramatists among the *existentialistes brutaux*.

A test case for what Gabriel Marcel calls a "mystery" is the high ranking spiritual approach of one of the greatest strugglers with Christ (to use a slogan of Karl Pfleger), namely, Simone Weil (1909-1943), the Jewish intellectual who, despite superior guidance by Father Perrin, O.P., and Gustave Thibon, never entered the Church. But her writings, *Cahiers* (1951), *Esquisse d'une histoire de la science grecque* (1941), particularly *La Pesanteur et la Grâce* (1947), *Attente de Dieu* and *La Connaissance surnaturelle* (1950), have a Pascalian flavor and reveal two things: the enormous tension between her acceptance of the most austere asceticism and her burning love for Christ on one hand and the refusal to accept dogmatic truths on the other. Her own unyielding and stubborn kind of logic mixed up with a misled and misplaced charity made it impossible for her to admit a divine Redeemer who is not for a pre-Christian world.

The style of Simone Weil is a relentless antithesis offered alternatively in chiastic or anaphorical form. On two consecutive pages from *Attente de Dieu* one finds:

> Ce n'est pas nous qui aimons les malheureux en Dieu,
> C'est Dieu en nous qui aime les malheureux.
>
> Soit en lui faisant du bien   avec justice,
> Soit en lui faisant du mal   avec justice.
>
> Le don de la vie—le don de la mort—sont équivalents.

The depth of the aphorisms of Simone Weil outranks her contradictions and hesitations. Her view on spirituality certainly is realistic when she writes:

Dans tous les problèmes poignants de l'existence humaine,
il y a le choix seulement entre le bien surnaturel et le mal.

Her unified, simple style never obscures her thought. Rhetorical
flowers are unbearable to her. Her place on the whole, however,
is not in the history of literature.

The failure of the individual priest-worker is the theme of
Les Saints vont en Enfer (1952), a novel by Gilbert Cesbron
(1913-   ). The merit of this novel consists in its anticipating
by literary means the ecclesiastical solution of the problem. Cesbron's interests are partly spiritual, as may be seen from his recent
debatable novel, *Vous verrez le ciel ouvert* (1956), partly social as
is evident from another novel of his, *Chiens perdus sans collier*
(1954). Cesbron understands by *Enfer* the communistic-anti-
clerical suburbs of Paris which the Jesuit Father Lhande had
already evoked at the beginning of the century in his book *Le
Christ dans la banlieue*. Cesbron describes the superhuman and
apostolic activities of a priest-worker in workshop, settlement and
chapel, but also the dangers to his dignity, chastity and piety.
Admired for his zeal by the Cardinal himself (in whom the
person of Cardinal Suhard is easily recognizable), he is nevertheless called back from his dangerous assignment among cursing
men and unprincipled women who exposed him to communism
as the only "solution" of the social question. Since the priest-
worker problem has considerably aroused public opinion in
France, we are not surprised that less talented authors, too, have
tried to write priest-worker novels, e.g., Roger Bésus, *Cet homme
qui vous aimait,* Bruno Gay-Lussac, *La Mort d'un prêtre,* and
—a literary monument to the admirable Abbé Pierre—Boris
Simon, *Les Chiffonniers d'Emmaus.*

Beggars and proletarians are introduced not only from the
sociological viewpoint but also from the psychological and religious angle in the novels of the Catholic poet from Bordeaux,
Jean Cayrol (1911-   ), particularly in his trilogy, *Je vivrai
l'amour des autres* (1947-50). Cayrol is much closer to reality than
the more allegorical novels and dramas of the bum by Samuel

Beckett who became famous with his play *En attendant Godot* (1952). In Cayrol's work a delicate psychology dignifies the suffering and erotic aberrations of men who knew concentration camps, poverty and dereliction. The key to the Catholicity of Jean Cayrol's novels are his tragic poems, *Poèmes de la nuit et du brouillard* (Paris: Seghers, 1946), where his faith comes clearly into the open. His novels are surrealistic as to their structure which copies the type of André Breton's *Nadja* (1928) and Aragon's *Le Paysan de Paris* (1926). Cayrol's main asset, comparable to that of the priest-workers, is the preservation of human dignity, even in a debased proletarian world. The hero of the trilogy is first a shapeless figure in volume I: *On vous parle*, a Lazarus-like, almost lifeless beggar. He lives in a room to which access is gained through other rooms occupied by men or women. He comes sometimes with, sometimes without his Suzy. Were he not talking also about love and death with his acquaintances Guillaume or Luc, one would think he is eager for one thing only, a cigarette, which serves as a leitmotif of his desire for calm. In volume II, *Les Premiers jours*, this beggar assumes a name, Armand, together with human traits; he learns to love, to be jealous, to be fair, to suffer with and for others. Being now a roomer in the attic of his friend Albert, he falls in love with the common-law wife of the latter, Lucette. After a terrible quarrel with Albert, Lucette decides to follow Armand. In the third volume, *Le Feu qui prend* (1950), Armand and Lucette get married, and when pressed for his family name, Armand remembers that he was called Parmentier. After having lived on black-market transactions, Armand abandons Lucette, leaving her to prostitution. He finds his family, a guilty mother, a drunkard stepfather, a criminal half-brother and a high-strung half-sister, Francine, to whose sinful love he becomes a prey after Jim, one of the gangster adversaries, has shot Lucette to death. The tragedy of Armand is that he cannot live without a protecting love. The priest who hurries to his mother's deathbed gives Armand some hope, however, saying to him: "Mon enfant, si vous avez encore un peu d'amour en vous, c'est parce que Dieu n'est pas mort."

It seems that Cayrol, a Catholic Sartre, wants to show the extremely slow process of changing a "salaud" into a responsible person. With Cayrol, however, there is the feeling that one is not really confronted with "salauds" but with *pauvres pécheurs* who actually do elicit our deep compassion; for he has a fundamental Christian concern for human beings who seem far away from God.

It is certainly from the fusion of reality and dream, typical of an erstwhile prisoner of war, as was Cayrol himself, that his unusually strong stream-of-consciousness technique is derived. Cayrol explains this fact himself in his essay *Lazare parmi nous*. Unfortunately, when he leaves proletarian subjects his technique becomes artificial. This is the case with the novel of the mysterious manuscript and the estranged wife (*Le Vent de la mémoire,* 1952), and with the story of François visiting his father and finding him dead *(L'Espace d'une nuit)*. This latter novel is too close a copy of the adventure of Donissan in Bernanos' *Sous le soleil de Satan*. Bernanos, it is true, is Cayrol's idol. He talks much of him in his essays. It is in these essays that his catholicity breaks through vigorously, unhampered, full of a charitable fire. He is comparable to Mauriac whose novels become more Christian in the light of his essays. In *Les Mille et une nuits du chrétien* (Téqui, 1952) Cayrol tells us how the wounds of Christ bleed anew because of the cruelty and lack of charity in our epoch, and because of our guilt in remaining silent, conniving with evil and shunning the opportunities of being saints and martyrs. The modern hero and saint, however, seem to have a greater Christ-likeness than ever in history. Such a hero Cayrol met in the concentration camp of Mauthausen. It was Father John Gruber whom he calls "mon plus que père . . . ," and of whom he says:

> il subit les campagnes de discipline les plus dures, . . . il fut supplicié durant la semaine sainte de 1944 pour m'avoir nourri, protégé, secouru. . . . Il fut torturé durant trois jours, abattu le Vendredi-Saint après avoir proclamé la joie de son sacrifice pour nous, et pendu afin que sa mort parût ignominieuse . . . , le saint confidentiel qui n'a pas de légende (p. 31).

Cayrol is creating with his style a contagious *angoisse* based on two leitmotifs: *Lazare* and *Samedi Saint*. In his creeping into the destitution of the *clochard* and his yearning for love, he rejects all sounding words. He avoids images also but bathes his objects in a painful psychological illumination. He enumerates, and creates progressively "une tonalité affective" (see Robert Kanters, "Jean Cayrol" in *Des Ecrivains et des hommes,* Paris, Julliard, 1952, p. 234-254).

On a lower literary and spiritual level appears the work of Maxence Van der Meersch (1907-1951). He wrote novels concerning the workers of the industrial centers *(Quand les sirènes se taisent),* and the smuggling problems on the French-Belgian border *(La Maison dans la dune).* They are all based on strict Catholic morals. Among his best is the three volume story *La Fille pauvre* (1944), reminiscent of Léon Bloy, the patriotic *Invasion 14* (1935), and his conversion story *Car ils ne savent ce qu'ils font.* Van der Meersch stirred some controversy by his lengthy biography of *Sainte Thérèse de Lisieux.* Here he revealed his literary and his Catholic shortcomings. Convinced of the necessity of religion as a *libération* and proof of *santé morale,* he lacked the understanding of such central points as contemplation, cloister, celibacy of the priest, importance of the sacraments. A modern Erasmus, he added to his critical intellectualism an interest in social problems which culminated in his high esteem for Canon Cardijn and his work. The controversial Van der Meersch is perceptively discussed in the study by Robert Reus, *Portrait morphopsychologique de Maxence van der Meersch* (Clairac, 1952). In the novels Van der Meersch avoids many of his own problems simply in order not to make spiritual difficulties for his readers, who certainly will be edified by his later stories such as *L'Elu* and *Pêcheurs d'hommes,* the first dealing with the conversion of Siméon Bramberger, the second with the apostolic spirit of the *Jeunesse Ouvrière Catholique.*

Among the themes which younger Catholic authors derived from the years of horror and disintegration are two which elicit particular interest; one is the problem of facing death with a

Christian serenity as treated by Noel Devaulx (1905-   ) in *Le Pressoir mystique* (1948); the other is the healing of the temptations of sexual perversion by means of grace offered by the Church, as is seen in the novel *Jean Paul* (1953), by Marcel Guersant.

Spirituality and apostolic charity stressed in the literary figure of the priest since Bernanos appear more distinct against the background of the pre-Bernanosian type of the moralistic-intellectual priest and humanist who still was the ideal of Maurice Brillant in his well-written novel full of erudition and culture, *Années d'apprentissage de Sylvain Briollet* (1921). It is the story of the seminarian Sylvain whose doubts and scruples are apparently allayed when he comes to live in his uncle's rectory in the rural parish of Guinoiseau. There a rich library, an elegant aristocratic neighborhood, and the storehouse of Greco-Roman analogies to Christian customs in the pastor's memory make the folly of the Cross as harmless as possible. For the whole problem one ought to consult J. L. Prevost, *Le Prêtre, ce héros de roman, De Claudel à Cesbron* (Téqui, 1952).

A new type of priest novel after Bernanos seems at present impossible. Nevertheless the priest who administered the last rites to Bernanos and buried him, Father Daniel Pézeril, tried another mitigated *Sous le soleil de Satan* with his short novel *Rue Notre-Dame,* the living place of the seventy-eight-year-old Canon Serrurier. The Canon, confronted with a young priest-worker in overalls, Abbé Robert, recognizes that his own comfortable life as a priest was a failure. This new Menou-Segrais dedicates himself at the eleventh hour to the pastoral care of criminals and dies in the Sacré-Coeur Church where he tries to spend a night in prayer for a man condemned to death who had declared himself guilty in order to spare the life of others. Thus existentialist ethics catholicized and combined with the social question represents the legacy of Bernanosian high spirituality.

Pierre Molaine (1906-   ) has imitated Bernanos too closely in *Satan comme la foudre* (1954). Here Anne-Marie, the half-sister of the priest Jacques, seems possessed, so occupied is she by her lust, perversity and sacrilegious behavior. She almost seduces Jacques' friend, the attorney Michel, but Jacques' sacrificial life brings his friend back to a state of grace and rectitude.

The priest as a man entangled in the world comes up again in the heavily attacked novel[20] of Luc Estang (1911-   ), *Les Stigmates* (1949). His other novel, *Cherchant qui dévorer* (1951), shows priests as educators at the College de Saint-Wandrille together with the problem of the psychological and moral difficulties of youth. But Luc Estang has not the spirit of Bernanos although he wrote a monograph on him. This spirit seems even a caricature in Abbé Riche of the already mentioned *La Mort d'un prêtre* (1953) by Bruno Gay-Lussac. Abbé Riche is closer related to the whisky priest of Graham Greene.

Béatrice Beck (1914-   ), on the other hand, has created the type of the modern priest faced by the rather independent Catholic woman who first appears in *Barny* (1947), and remains also the heroine of *Léon Morin, prêtre* (1952). She falls in love with her *convertisseur* who simply urges her in a saintly manner to confess this sin of concupiscence to him or, if she feels inhibited, to another priest. The story is made pathetic by the setting in the French resistance movement. The spiritual aspects sketched are of a rather doubtful, latitudinarian and liberal kind. The humanistic Catholicism of Karl Adam and the liturgical movement find an enthusiastic echo in this novel. Father Morin lacks prudence, Barny lacks decency. Béatrice Beck does not quite exemplify the *sentire cum ecclesia*.

Among the Catholic lyricists the almost forgotten Francis Jammes (1868-1938) and the never too-well-known Marie Noël (1883-   ), with her *Rosaire des Joies* (1920) and *Chants d'Automne* (1947), seem to be replaced now by the more spiritual, but too complex, Patrice de La Tour du Pin (1911-   ). In his collection *La Quête de Joie* (Gallimard, 1933), the main topics are detachment, love of Death, the closer approach to Christ. New within his obscure and medieval symbolism, reminiscent of Claudel, is his concept of the poet as a dedicated life in the personalistic sense of Emmanuel Mounier. Seeking the community of mankind beyond the single egocentric person, however, he searches for true love by casting doubt generally on what man considers to be love. He stresses the danger of any form of human passion like ambition and desire, as well as human satisfaction with earthly things like possession, power, honor, conjugal happiness. This dilemma produces Patrice de La Tour du Pin's Faust-like *Une Somme de Poésie* (1946). The work, not finished as yet, includes all his earlier poems, particularly *La Quête de joie, Psaumes* (1938), *La Vie récluse en poésie* (1938). Here he embodies his cravings in the characters of Lorenquin, Laurent de Cayeux, Philippe, Aldine, the brothers Gorphoncelet, none of whom finds grace before him, each one being condemned to Hell. But a revisional judgment of God finds some good points in the dialectics by which they defend their weaknesses. Many parts of the stilted hieratic poems come very close to prose; in others the poet reveals, in a language captivating by its simplicity, his admirable attitude toward his wife Annie whose lips were the only ones he ever kissed. And yet, does she belong to him or to God?:

> Je justifierai celle que j'ai prise,
> Et Dieu sait pourtant que nul ne l'accuse.

Small wonder that he rushes often from his happy family life in Le Bignon to retreats at Solesmes, saying with Laurent de Cayeux:

> Il n'est pas d'achèvement avant la mort,[21]

and proving that he is "le poète christique."

Less complicated is the Catholic patriot and revolutionary poet Pierre Emmanuel (1916-   ), who became famous through his poems inspired by the résistance, *La Liberté guide nos pas* (1945), and *Memento des vivants* (1946). He wrote his life story and spiritual development in a prose volume which represents him in the Thomistic sense as a particularized concrete universal: *Qui est cet homme? Le singulier universel* (1947).

According to the principles of quality, importance and spiritual originality, I am compelled to do no more than mention some well-regarded lyricists such as René Fernandat, author of the serious collection *Les Signets du missel* (Gallimard, 1939) and *Signes avant l'aurore* (Grenoble, 1952), or Fr. Ducaud-Bourget, Henriette Charasson, Raïssa Maritain, Camille Melloy, R. Vallery-Radot.

If there is anyone among the literary critics who bases judgment primarily on the deepest spirituality, it is Charles Du Bos (1882-1939), the essence of whose ideas must be looked for in his *Journal* (six volumes have appeared up to 1957), and in his volumes of *Approximations* (1922-37). He does along the line of practical criticism what Jacques Maritain (1882-) did along the line of literary theory *(Frontières de la poésie)*. Both stress the primacy of spiritual matters *(Primauté du spirituel, 1927)*, leaving, however, to literature its full autonomy. Other Catholic critics, such as Henri Massis, Daniel-Rops, Martin-Chauffier, Albert Béguin, Jacques Madaule, R. P. Bruckberger, Claude Mauriac, Luc d'Estang, Jean Onimus, Charles Dédéyan, André Rousseaux, Pierre-Henri Simon have a respectable range and enjoy almost the same popularity as Pierre de Boisdeffre, Roger Caillois, Georges Poulet, Claude-Edmonde Magny, Paul Guth, Armand Hoog.

CHAPTER VII

ABSTRACT ART AND PURE POETRY

THE NOVEL and drama which have been stressed so far are too closely related to the sociological and psychological conditions of life to be abstracted from them. Poetry, however, since Mallarmé and Rimbaud, has been considered a realm apart from life, like Plato's ideas, where obscurity and ambiguity are not only permissible but required qualities. This is the reason why desperate attempts were made to attain a symbolism, called motif-symbolism, where the whole poem stands for something which cannot be logically assessed but only prismatically contemplated. Many possible meanings hovering around a not clearly perceptible concept, clad in a motley imagery, is the main principle of this pure or hermetic, cryptic or surrealistic poetry. The more rational supporters of this poetry (Valéry, St.-John Perse) actually have their roots in the *fin-de-siècle* symbolism of the nineteenth century. Disputable as their case may be, they are the more acceptable ones. The irrational pioneers of futuristic, cubistic, dadaistic attempts (André Breton, Apollinaire, Carco) try to reproduce dream-worlds through word metaphors, as we have seen in our discussion of literary infantilism (chapter four). Despite their alleged competition with science, they take too much delight in playing with language and words to be really serious in their poetic creation. Since they are the easier to understand, let us start with them and consider first some mixed forms which leave us with a logical guide to the purer but more complicated forms.

The simplest form of ambiguity consists in reducing the surrealistic stream of consciousness to ordinary language in rhythmical wholes while neglecting punctuation. This is the stylistic recipe of ambiguity of Paul Eluard (1895-1953). He applies it endlessly, as we saw in chapter three, to the theme of the love of the couple of which he and his "Nusch" were the prototypical representatives. Here is an example of his ardent love poems in this style:

> Cherchez la nuit
> Il fait beau comme dans un lit
> Ardente la plus belle des filles adorantes
> Se prosterne devant les statues endormies de son amant
>
> Elle ne pense pas qu'elle dort
> Il fait de plus en plus beau nuit et jour
>   *(La Rose Publique).*

It has been observed that one of Eluard's procedures is, by means of similes, to create one reality, then destroy it with another. This procedure has been put into the form of an equation: Creation A means Destruction B:

> La fleur qui a été belle comme un enfant
> Est livrée au soleil comme le bois aux flammes.[1]

Eluard has well seen that his method is that of the later Picasso and qualifies it in the following way:

> Mêler baigneuse et rivière
> Cristal et danseuse d'orage
> Aurore et la saison des seins
> Désirs et sagesse d'enfance.[2]

Eluard's political poetry (see chapter one) as poetry is a failure; his excellence is in the love poetry which he continued to write even after the death of his wife:

> Je suis mal amputé j'ai mal j'ai froid je vis
> En dépit du néant je vis comme on renie.

Of the fairy tale type, though gruesomely stylized like old-fashioned ballads of robber chiefs, are some obscure poems such as *Paroles* by Jacques Prévert (1900-   ) in which the man who played the *orgue de barbarie* kills those who play more modern instruments. He then marries the girl of the wealthy music patron. He sleeps under a piano and dreams meanwhile of beautiful things; but he will not continue those idle dreams:

> Moi je jouais au cerceau
> à la balle au chasseur
> je jouais à la marelle
> je jouais avec un seau
> . . . . . .
> mais c'est fini, fini, fini
> je veux jouer à l'assassin
> je veux jouer de l'orgue de barbarie.[3]

The same absurd conglomeration of images is found in the poem *Hygiène* by Raymond Queneau (1908-   ):

> Le coq lave sa casquette
> la poule sa liquette
> le canard ses gants beurre frais
> . . . . . .
> la maison lave ses carreaux
> le train ses hublots
> le camion ses pneus et ses crics
> le café lave son billard
> l'école ses têtards.[4]

Jean Cocteau believes in the beauty of the idiot world and claims that opium dreams yield a magic language of uncouth associations which represent the core of surrealistic poetry. Thus he asserts that the idea of singing birds trilling in a cage appeared to him clad in the following verbal-musical form:

> Huit, huit, huit ! colifichet des cages,
> huit, huit, huit ! collets du bocage,
> huit, huit, huit ! boucles des ciseaux,
> huit, huit, huit ! circuit d'hirondelles,
> huit, huit, huit ! chiffre ayant des ailes,
> huit, huit, huit ! disent les oiseaux.[5]

More essential than the origin of this kind of language is its nervous and surprising baroque-like exchange of scarcely suggested visual and auditory associations such as gewgaw-like yellow canaries, invisible singing throats in the woods, shrill sounds like hair-cutting scissors which make the curls fall. It is known how much Giraudoux—though in a humorous way—enjoys this most typical dream language because: "L'analogie porte sur des ressemblances morales des choses . . . et plus le lien qui les unit, est immateriel et abstrait, plus le tour de force est remarquable."[6] But Cocteau uses no tricks as Giraudoux does. His language is "transparently beautiful . . . the gift of . . . the most remarkable talker . . . [who] seemed to create loveliness out of nothing."[7]

Not only the surrealists, however, but also the most serious poets of the twentieth century were looking for pure art as a superior realm of beauty, attainable by the artist only by excluding all impure, i.e., rational, discursive, prosaic, practical elements. In the parallel case of abstract painting, the object as such was likewise eliminated so that pure beauty (objectless beauty) might reveal a reality which cannot be grasped by means other than art, certainly not by science or philosophy. As to music, at least, we may remember what Marcel Proust said about its timeless beauty and spaceless eternity. As to the dance, since Isadora Duncan, Jacques Dalcroze, Leonid Massine and Roger Richard discovered the typical objectlessness of this particular type of art, the tendency has been to make of it a "language of the body." Paul Valéry (1871-1945), in his dialogue: *Eupalinos, précédé de l'âme et la danse* (1923), gives the decisive philosophy of this problem: "Par les dieux, les claires danseuses! . . . Quelle vive et gracieuse introduction des plus parfaites pensées." (*Eupalinos,* p. 19). In another treatise: *Degas, Danse-Dessin,* he calls the dance an "état . . . qui nous met hors ou loin de nous-mêmes, et dans lequel l'instable pourtant nous soutient, tandis que le stable n'y figure que par accident, nous donne l'idée d'une autre existence" (edition 1938, p. 29). Pure dances are "d'ephémères architectures" . . . , choreographically independent of music, where "d'acte familier, automatique, la marche devient écriture."[8] They are pure movement in a pure space, "des étoiles de mouvement, et de magiques ententes" (Valéry, *L'Ame et la danse,* p. 4). The dance is not the imitation, representation, or expression of anything, but "l'art pur des métamorphoses" (*ib.,* p. 41). "Ni la figuration, ni l'expression! La pure fonction."[9]

A poised personality like Charles Du Bos (1882-1939) once received a similar impression from Isadora Duncan:

> A côté de cette femme, dont chaque geste a l'air de dénouer ou de trancher une énigme, tous nos efforts abstraits paraissent tant soit peu nigauds. . . . Je commence à croire en effet qu'elle est capable de danser n'importe quoi.[10]

The riddle of all this enthusiasm for the dance is solved by the fact that the dance alone fulfills by definition what all the other arts in the twentieth century vied with one another to do: to be objectless and pure or functional form, or, as Alain, i.e., the esthetician Emile Chartier (1868-1952), puts it: "La danse qui est toujours mimique est une émotion produite par nous, par nos mouvements, sans objet."[11] From the dance, it seems, one can best understand what "purity" and "abstractness" in all the other arts mean. The realms of art "sont des êtres singuliers . . . qui participent de la vue et du toucher—ou bien de l'ouie—mais aussi de la raison, du nombre et de la parole" (*Eupalinos*, p. 135).

Pure art is something like mathematics. It is therefore not without reason that it was the mathematician Paul Valéry (1871-1945) who became most interested in pure and abstract poetry, and whose central concern is "l'intelligence sollicitée de se connaître et de prendre conscience de sa nature et de sa fonction."[12] Now we understand easily how a music with intellectual and discursive motives in the sense of Richard Wagner seemed unbearable to a composer such as Claude Debussy, who replaced the clear-cut motives by melodious, vague suggestions. Igor Stravinsky comes very near to pure music by making it a kaleidoscope of rhythms, melodies and cacophonies. Still purer is, of course, the merely atonal music of Arnold Schönberg, which, however, has been repudiated by the "melodious" French who were content with "une musique plus nue" (Debussy), instrumental only and detached from song, opera or ballet purposes. The real representatives of *musique pure* became Maurice Ravel and Paul Dukas. Their music is intended to be "une plénitude changeante, analogue à une flamme continue, éclairant et réchauffant tout ton être par une incessante combustion de souvenirs, de pressentiments, de regrets et de présages, et d'une infinité d'émotions sans causes précises, . . . danses sans danseuses . . . , statues sans corps et sans visage (et pourtant si délicatement dessinées), . . . la présence générale de la Musique" (Valéry, *Eupalinos,* pp. 125-26).

Pure poetry wants to achieve almost the same purpose, but represents a problem of greater complexity. Let us first say that *poésie pure*[13] means the ideal of a poetry which is as free as possible from prose elements, a poetry which is made more of hints than of precisions, more of suggestions than of definitions, more of feeling than of meaning, more of associations than of explanations. Consequently, the language of the most modern poet, in spite of his highly developed art, must be related somewhat to the so-called primitive, mythic, or folk poetry. But it is not absolutely necessary for the poet to render visions, dreams, intuitions or ecstasies by casting them into a sort of new myth. Although the theologian Abbé Henri Bremond (1865-1933) compares true poetry to mysticism and prayer[14] because of its intuitive and direct vision of reality, the mathematician Paul Valéry avows that when writing poetry he proceeds by mere reason and logic. Nevertheless he applies the theory of the "alchemy of words" which he learned from his masters Stéphane Mallarmé and Arthur Rimbaud. Both Bremond and Valéry, however, agree on one point, namely, that the language of the poet is absolutely different from the language of a prose writer. The two adversaries Bremond and Valéry have thus enabled us to turn our attention exclusively to the poetic language as such, not to the possible sources of its inspiration, nor to its possible psychological effect on the readers.

Poetical language, in the sense of pure poetry, is a language of a special order of words in the sentence, tending to give them a magic spell, a language of unexpected word sequence and word rhythm, a language which balances pure thought by graphic imagery.[15] It is also a language of euphemisms and ellipses,[16] a language of verbal paradox. It "translates" abstract ideas into images, or rather substitutes the latter for the former, and renders conversely a material object by abstract but not scientific words. All poetic words have besides their precise meaning, some special associations, connotations, overtones and emotional values; and they rarely lack magic sound and a far-reaching resonance. Poetic language embraces furthermore evocative epithet, and mysteriously obscure allusions, musical harmony and onomatopoetic rhythm, symbolic metaphorical condensations and fairy-tale-like exaggerations. All these elements are lacking not only in shapeless everyday speech, but also in the emotional speech of the orator and in the plain reports of the narrator.[17] Poetical language is fresh and virginal. According to T. E. Hulme: "Prose is a museum, where all the old weapons of poetry are kept," while "Poetry is always the advance guard in language," "the progress of language," "the absorption of new analogies."[18] Such is the linguistic prerequisite of *poésie pure*.

Pure poetry evidences better than any other poetry what Jacques Maritain calls creative intuition as the expression of unknown natural realities and their interrelations. Even the rationalist Paul Valéry believed that he found with his *Cimetière marin* the mysterious ratio between the "noumena" and the "phenomena," the *être* and the *non-être*. He hoped with his artifact to answer Pascal's question, why man, the *roseau pensant,* crushed by a little dust or drop of water, is greater than the mighty sun: "Because he knows that he is going to die," was Pascal's answer. Valéry, on the contrary, separating thought from life, tries to suggest that man, by looking both at nature and at himself, recognizes his perishable destiny in front of the "eternal" phenomena of nature. This, he claims, is wisdom. Wisdom, however, in contradistinction to knowledge, can only be obtained and expressed by intuition, the form of which is *poésie pure.* Valéry is right in so far as his "poetic" presentation of the mystery of life and death leaves man with that inquietude which is the prerequisite of faith. Valéry's unfinished *Mon Faust* (1946) leaves no doubt that his poetry is restlessness toned down. Pure poetry thus actually seems a necessary creation even against the intention of the poet, since it stresses the mystery without solving it. Pure dance, in Valéry's concept, had, as we have seen, a similar function.[19] To Bremond, pure poetry links man to something that cannot be reached by discursive means. The requirements of pure poetry as established by Valéry[20] and Bremond, with the critic Paul Souday (1869-1929) participating in the debate, coincide essentially with the conditions of André Breton in his non-rational or anti-rational surrealism: 1. the magic search for a superior insight not attainable by science, 2. the systematic dislocation of the conventional order of things, at least syntactically, 3. the associations of words as a means of natural revelation.[21]

In practice, Valéry by his imagery always changes the appearance of things into a mental picture which, to him, reveals the essence of a reality non-existing in the material sense. Like a sorcerer he changes naked reality into the poet's world, true in the limited sense in which the human mind is able, by surprising analogies, to change the *non-être* into *être*. The calm sea covered with some moving sails is: "Ce toit tranquille où marchent les colombes," or even more veiled: "Ce toit tranquille où picoraient des focs." These poetic pictures are difficult for the reader since the sails stand for the ships on the sea, as doves on a roof, so that it may be said of the sails that bird-like they pick up grains. Only in one point opposed to the surrealists, Valéry ascribes his poetical discoveries not to troubled unconscious feelings, but, on the contrary, to "a kind of lucidity which is almost painful."[22] This lucidity finds highly poetic, unanalyzable formulas. Poets have sung for centuries that the zephyr, the spring winds with their fertile, warm breath and gentle perfume will break up the last ice of winter. Valéry in his masterpiece *La Jeune Parque,* dealing with the antinomy flesh-spirit, changes this whole traditional treasury into a poetical novelty:

> Demain, sur un soupir des bontés constellées,
> Le printemps vient briser les fontaines scellées
> *(La Jeune Parque).*

What psychologists have written about temptations and physico-psychical reactions has been condensed by Valéry in *Ebauche d'un serpent* into an image of poorly veiled sensuality. White, blonde Eve begins to react to the serpent's temptation in a visionary fusion of picture and thought which comprises her very existence:

> Le marbre aspire, l'or se cambre!
> Ces blondes bases d'ombre et d'ambre
> Tremblent au bord du mouvement.

The language of *poésie pure* was a linguistic discovery. As Emilie Noulet says, Valéry discovered "le velouté de l'abstraction, . . . une langue sensuelle et précieuse, pressée d'images, dotée de notes élues et de toute façon si harmonieuse et si pleine que sa beauté paraît se séparer de son contenu."[23] But *poésie pure* is condemned to failure just as is the mystical language because: "How describe in human language . . . realities, too concrete to be expressed in abstractions, too spiritual to admit of imagery, too far above nature to endure the use of analogies?"[24]

Nobody has yet been able to decide whether Paul Valéry is a great poet or a philosophizing highly mannered craftsman whose artifacts, although well constructed, lack nevertheless an inner compulsion. How can a person with the interior attitude of the more than prosaic *Monsieur Teste* be a poet? Nonetheless, innumerable analyses have been made of Valéry's poems. Only a few critics, such as Jean Venettis, condemn them as a burlesque formalism which circumscribes ideas instead of casting them into convincing symbols. But even so, one would have to account for the gracefully arranged trill of his vowels, as Ernst Bendz has said. And the symbols, as Hans Sörensen has demonstrated for *La Jeune Parque,* are so artistically chosen that ambiguous, almost contradictory groups of them like *fruit de velours* and *étoiles,* standing for the flesh, receive their meaning only from the opposite groups such as *cygne* and *soleil,* standing for the spirit. Such symbols, helped by the musical essence of the unheard-of melodious arrangement of words, are said by Henri Parize to be capable of transmitting an idea into that region of the spirit where an immediate, intuitive and non-analytical comprehension becomes possible. Not everyone will agree, however, that Valéry's metaphors are calculated to evoke a transfigured reality without laborious analysis on the part of the reader.

New and detailed vocabulary counts by Pierre Guiraud and very intensive studies by Hytier and Bémol may help to solve this decisive question: Is Valéry a poet or a skillful craftsman?

It will be difficult to find a poet who can be called a successor of Valéry or can be said to belong to his "school." If stress is laid on the rhetorical elements which poetry ought not to have, traces of Valéry may be found in the poetry of Robert Ganzo (1898-   ) and Jacques Audiberti (1899-   ), perhaps even in Henri Michaux (1899-   ).

The preserver of a certain *poésie pure* which continues Valéry's burning intellectual transfigurations of experience is St.-John Perse, the great diplomat Léger de Saint Léger (1887-   ). In his self-made exile in Washington he wrote, long after his *Eloges* (1907) and *Anabase* (1924), the greatest poem in this transfigurative symbolism: *Exil* (1946) where appear the lyrical fragments *Pluies, Neiges, Vents,* recently followed by *Et vous, mers.*[25] St.-John Perse belongs to the line of Mallarmé in so far as his highest art concerns a motif symbolism of such a strong centripetal power that the snow symbol in *Neiges* connotes not only moral purity but also the pure race of his mother and the pure languages quoted and philologically commented on in part IV of the poem.[26]

St.-John Perse's verse form is a secular competitor of Claudel's versicle and of his daring imagery. Moreover, like Claudel, St.-John Perse is under the spell of Rimbaud's hallucinations and of diplomatic assignments and travels. Accents of beauty are placed on things which appear only "archeologically" and exotically beautiful, but almost repulsive to the modern western reader. The epic elements fuse into a rhapsodic drama, particularly in *Anabase.*[27] Powerfully expressive are the demonstrative pronouns, the elliptic condensations, the refrain-like repetitions and Proust-like parentheses. Tenses shift constantly from present to past and vice versa. Statements are mitigated by the insertion of verbs such as *dire* or *voir* that make the concrete timeless and create strangeness and even the myth of the stranger, almost anticipating St. Léger's historic exile from France.[28] Some think that there are two phases in the poetic development of St.-John Perse; there is an early, more lyrical poetry and a later poetry which is more rhetorical in character.[29] Others believe that in all poems alike the striking features are the same: elegance of circumlocution, juxtaposition of the cultural and the barbaric, elaborate decoration and bare bluntness.[30] Everywhere St.-John Perse is encyclopedic, couples banal adjectives with sublime substantives, grandly replaces the usual grammatical words by others (*par* by *de*), builds lacework of the same pattern around phraseological central points, and thus ends in gigantic structures.[31]

Even more than Valéry, St.-John Perse has a propensity for the solemn, hieratic, sacred side of poetry, for rare words the sound of which dominates a meaning vague and ambiguous not only by arrangement but also because of the lack of knowledge on the part of even a sophisticated reader unless he recurs to the dictionary.[32] The message sometimes is uttered in the name of a hieratic Prince supposed to live in strange climates and environments. In the early poems, inspired by his native Guadaloupe, as well as in the later ones inspired by his exile in Washington, there reigns unabated a myth-creating language with the ceremonial cult of grandeur.[33] But admiring the artisanship of language which, of course, is more than *art pour l'art,* expressing as it does the deeply felt vicissitudes in the life of the author, we must admit that we remain in a cold world of supermen and master races without humility, human warmth, or charitable relations—a world without God, again Valéry's world which pays for pure art by diminishing human dignity. There is no thought of the creator of the "mathématiques suspendues aux banquises du sel!" (*Anabase,* Harcourt-Brace, 1948, p. 28).

Those who set out to moderate purism, hermeticism and surrealism by retaining a minimum of story telling, a minimum of classical tradition and a minimum of discursive thread in lyricism stand out as more solid and acceptable. Among them will remain Jules Supervielle (1884-   ) who crowned his collected *Poèmes* (1939-45) by an *Art poétique* appended to *Naissances* (1951) where he underscores his literary philosophy: "I like the strange only when it is tempered and humanized."[34] Supervielle is reluctant to indulge in a non-communicable poetic surrealism and he therefore mitigates *poésie pure*. "Chez Supervielle on voit . . . que la simplicité triomphe où l'alchimie échoue."[35] Beyond this, the tension between his vague belief in an infinite and a fanatic clinging to the earth makes his poetry genuine. The language into which he casts his feelings and transfigured observations is exquisite from his first mostly rhymed collection *Débarcadères* (1922) to the unrhymed collection *Naissances*. His main originality consists in having revealed to Europe the Uruguayan Pampa (he was born in Montevideo) and in having used it as a storehouse of symbolism for his life and aspirations:

> J'azure, fluvial, les gazons de mes jours,
> Je nacre les neigeux leurres de la montagne
> Aux collines venant à mes pieds de velours,
> Tandis que les hameaux dévalent des campagnes.
> (La Sphère, *Débarcadères*).

As has been shown by an extensive study of his style[36] his novelty consists in the creation of functional metamorphoses based on metaphorized actual impressions:

> La bave marine
> A la plage fait un mouvant collier
> (*Débaracadères*).

Supervielle avoids surrealistic obscurity, he uses substantives derived from verbs as appositions explaining previous statements, and exploits the euphonic sonorities of the ending *euse*, e.g., "la vague . . . cherch*euse* d'ecume, la nuit . . . découch*euse* de hiboux, nuits mang*euses* de soleils, l'âme oubli*euse* de la chair." Typical also are the strong metaphors he derives from tools (*Werkzeugmetaphern*): "La sirène déchire le paysage comme avec un couteau ébréché" (*Débarcadères*); "La mer de ses lames coupe la côte" (*ib.*). The corrections of *Gravitations* make it clear that to Supervielle poetization means condensation and personification. The verbal fields of *faire-changer-devenir; vouloir-chercher; envahir-traverser-pénétrer; comprendre-reconnaître* reveal a serious effort to understand the sense of life and death by confronting human action and a destiny which opposes, transcends and subdues it. Metaphors of fleeting life, of light, of change, offer images, first seen, then understood, and finally comprehended in a vision leaning heavily on symbolization through animal fables. The style thus almost betrays the slogan: "Supervielle, familier de l'au-de-là," the "Hors-venu," "Plus grave que l'homme et savant comme certains morts. . . ."[37] Supervielle's technique in poetry corresponds to his moving along in a world without seams, it is cinema-like, or as the French say, "le glissement par fondus enchaînés."[38]

There are other forms of pure literature, namely "pure theatre" and "pure prose," which I shall mention briefly.

Benjamin Crémieux (1888-1944) coined the term *le théâtre pur*. This is not the theatre of the pure word but a stagecraft independent of literature. The tendencies of the Théâtre de l'Oeuvre and its director, Lugné-Poe (1869-1940), or the theatre of the "Vieux Colombier" and its director Jacques Copeau (1879-1949), as well as Gaston Baty (1885-1952) from the Théâtre Montparnasse, author of *Le Masque et l'encensoir,* and Georges and Ludmilla Pitoëff (1886-1939, 1885-1952) of the Théâtre *Les Mathurins,* may give an idea of it. "A Jacques Copeau on doit . . . tout aussi bien que la formation d'un jeu de comédien à la fois simple et stylisé, l'idée que le spectacle de théâtre forme un tout, qu'il est une création. Il n'a pas à copier, mais à interpréter. Il nous impose un monde aussi neuf que le monde de la poésie et de la musique. Tout doit y concourir, décors, acteurs, textes."[39] Others understand by *théâtre pur* rather the condition that a setting is intended to be auxiliary to the actor's activity. The actor is to rely mainly on the poet's word and his own interpreting gesture. Therefore any setting may be replaced by *le tréteau nu* which is practically the equivalent of what modern directors understand by the Shakespearean stage.[40]

Ecstatic authors even dream of an inconceivable *prose pure* or even *roman pur.* "As I sat listening to Schubert or Debussy," says Julien Green, "I imagined strange and beautiful books coming out of my brain, sentences the like of which no one had ever read. . . . When the music stopped, however, this blissful state came abruptly to an end and there only remained an acute longing for the great unwritten masterpieces."[41] Here, by a vicious circle, we fall back on surrealism.

There is still *un cinéma pur* which remains linked to the name of René Clair (1898-   ) who in the twenties introduced surrealism to the movies showing on the screen in *Entr'acte* things never seen in reality. He was followed by Maurice Carné. Since then the cinema and literature have worked together: not only have men of the film industry adapted literary works as Jean Delannoy (1898-) did with Gide's *Symphonie pastorale*, or Robert Bresson (1907-) with Bernanos' *Journal d'un curé de campagne*, but the literary authors themselves have dedicated their efforts to film scenarios. Some examples are Jean Giraudoux's *La Duchesse de Langeais*, Marcel Pagnol's *La Fille du puisatier*, Georges Bernanos' *Dialogues des Carmélites*, Jean-Paul Sartre's *L'Engrenage*, and François Mauriac's *Le Pain vivant*.

CHAPTER VIII

COLLECTIVE STYLISTIC
ACHIEVEMENTS

THE TWO great stylistic achievements of twentieth century literature may be logically derived from two fundamentally new structural devices: first, surrealism as the view of a world to be
recomposed from the fragments into which the author has split
it, and second, the simultaneity of the movie technique reflecting
the speed of modern means of transportation which allow the
same person to be within a matter of hours in different cities,
countries, continents. These surrealistic and unanimistic tendencies, aided by some means of refined sensibility, produced a doubly
transfigured language capable of representing adequately the new
structure of a fanciful world and of telescoping several planes.
This fact becomes clear even if we take the stylistic elements out
of the compounds of the verbal artifacts which has to be done
here anyway, since we cannot analyze a collective style with reference to individual structures; we can only check these new style
elements with the aid of traditional literary language, the linguistic system, and ordinary conversational prose. In other words, we
check on the new literary language deduced from the individual
speeches of the single authors by a fair sampling of passages from
different texts converging towards a general style of fanciful
fusion that deviates considerably from the norm.

Just as impressionistic art at the beginning of this century
turned slowly into expressionistic art, so impressionistic language
slowly developed into expressionistic-surrealistic language. The
initial situation is this: the simple past becomes rare, the epithet
moves ahead of the substantive, the word order becomes bold,
the noun reigns sovereign.[1] We do not need, therefore, extremist
artists like the Comte de Lautréamont (Isidore Ducasse), or

Arthur Rimbaud for a pedigree for the style of twentieth century literature. It is sufficient to take as a starting point Verlaine's impressionism, theoretically expounded in his *Art poétique* and practiced in his poetry, to make understandable the new style of the twentieth century with all its features.

Verlaine's great asset was a kind of dream language by which he translated reality into poetry. Verlaine has indeed introduced the dream element into nature description by his evaluation of the *exquis* and of the moment "Où l'Indécis au Précis se joint" (*Art poétique*), where things get a hue and a mood together, be it impressionistic: "Le bleu fouillis des claires étoiles" (*ib.*), or expressionistic with a metaphorical shift to sensibility: "Le gai Guadalquivir rit aux blonds orangers" (*Nocturne Parisien*). Reason, senses, and feeling share equally, almost "existentially" in these fine sentimental transfigurations and shades. The reason for these poetic cravings was seen by Henri Bergson who formulated the problem negatively: "Le mot aux contours bien arrêtés, le mot brutal emmagasine seulement ce qu'il y a de stable, de commun et par conséquent d'impersonnel dans les impressions délicates et fugitives de notre conscience individuelle."[2]

Robert Brasillach has gathered from the works of Mme Colette prose expressions rendering sensations in such a refined way that in spite of their "naturistic" tendencies, the selected euphonic and imagistic details evoke a transfigured reality, e.g.: "l'amère saveur de la tranche d'orange"; "la pêche qui mûrit ses joues d'un fard trop lent"; "la biche aux longs yeux qui lève un sabot craintif"; "une vague molle de parfum qui guide les pas vers la fraise sauvage."[3] A little more "activity" and personification than is the case in "le parfum qui 'guide'" and such images become the most daring expressions of an enchanting nature: "Les cerisiers fleuris attachaient des brouillards duveteux et nacrés aux pentes des collines."[4]

It is instructive to choose such examples from both major and minor writers because the minor writers are inclined to overdo the pattern which then appears like a drastic *pastiche*. Ramuz uses more exaggerated elements in his type of magic realism: "On devinait le lac plus qu'on ne le voyait, à une espèce de luisant qu'avait l'air, et une espèce de papier d'argent collé sur les objects du côté de la lumière."[5] This comparison is designed to be childish, with the effect that nature becomes a modern magic world. With the same intention Marcel Proust can see a snow landscape with trees cast in delicate colors more as an object of art than of nature:

> Les silhouettes des arbres se reflétaient nettes et pures sur cette neige d'or bleuté, avec la délicatesse qu'elles ont dans certaines peintures japonaises . . . (*Le Temps retrouvé* I, p. 62).

Returning to the master stylist Colette, we easily discover that her style does not just continue the tradition of Verlainean impressionistic style which tries to see nature through culture and to enhance it by surprising features. When Colette describes for instance a serpent, she evokes at the same time in the manner of Rimbaud all the fiendish nightmares imaginable, i.e., she includes different layers of sensibility which are reflected by the different layers of imagery, but all of them are telescoped into an expression of strangeness and horror:

> C'est le python qui a bougé, . . . ainsi la marée avance sur les longs sables, suspendue à la lune. Ainsi le poison se propage dans la veine, ainsi le mal dans l'esprit. . . . Il remue et c'est l'univers solide qui chavire. . . . Il remue, il aggrave la confusion de ses lacs, enfle, déforme ses monogrammes et m'abuse: c'est l'O qui est un C, et le G un Z. Il se liquéfie, coule le long de l'arbre et d'autre part se retracte, il s'efforce, il présage je ne sais quelle éclosion—aux plus épais des spires qui luttent et se malaxent, baille enfin un étroit abîme, qui expulse une tête (*Prisons et Paradis. Serpents*. Anthol. P. Clarac, Paris, p. 274).

This fanciful description of a python in a zoo makes us feel as if we were carried off into the circles of Dante's hell. But the arrangement and selection of details to produce a fascinating mood makes Colette successful also with less exciting topics. She can describe a rainy summer evening, followed by a rainy night, by producing a special summer atmosphere without the beaming features of sun and brightness. She selects intriguing details and presents them in a gradation culminating in synaesthetic effects:

> Ils avaient trouvé à Crausac la pluie, le soleil couchant, un arc-en-ciel au-dessus de la rivière, les lilas alourdis, la lune levante dans un ciel vert, de petits crapauds vernissés sous les degrés du perron, et pendant la nuit ils avaient entendu choir, du haut de la futaie, les averses ralenties et des chants de rossignols en larges gouttes (*Duo*, p. 19, quoted in Yves Gandon, *Le Démon du style*, p. 213).

Transfiguration of nature by selected and rearranged details is so natural with Colette that when she describes her country, she evokes a lost paradise by a combination of visual and acoustic elements affecting the very lifestream of man:

> Si tu suivais, dans mon pays, un petit chemin . . . jaune et bordé de digitales d'un rosé brûlant, tu croirais gravir le sentier enchanté qui mène hors de la vie. . . . Le chant bondissant de frelons fourrés de velours t'y entraîne et bat à tes oreilles comme le sang même de ton coeur, jusqu'à la forêt, là-haut, où finit le monde. . . . C'est une forêt . . . toute pareille au paradis (*Les Vrilles de la vigne: Jour gris*).

The younger generation striving for a more restrained and less showy language sticks nevertheless to the stylistic transfusion of nature into a magic reality. Even Albert Camus, the most moderate and "classical" of all the younger authors, cannot help metaphorizing in an unusual manner, the acutely experienced natural landscape, by an exaggerated metamorphosis of his sense impressions:

> Sous le soleil qui nous chauffe un seul côté du visage, nous regardons la lumière descendre du ciel, la mer sans une ride, et le sourire de ses dents éclatantes (*Noces*, p. 13).

Paul Eluard surrealistically pictures tropical Africa as it trembles in all colors under the heat by dovetailing the real and the moral climate of the burning sun and the bodies burning in desire:

> Le feu jaune, rose, mauve, pourpre foisonne. . . . La nudité de l'homme et de la femme est si chaude qu'elle humilie le ciel, qu'elle laisse une tache dans la prunelle de l'espace (*Donner à voir*, NRF, 1939, p. 59).

Joseph Malègue, although with less fancy, lends Parisian streets the biting teeth which Camus had reserved for the sea:

> L'automobile fuyait sur un boulevard Saint Germain désert où mordaient les bouches noires des rues latérales (*Augustin,* Paris: Spes, 1933, I, p. 369).

For stronger transpositions of first impressions one may go to the boundless synaesthetic imagery of Julien Gracq:

> L'aube spongieuse et molle était trouée par moments de louches passées de lumière, qui boitaient sur les nuages bas comme le pinceau tâtonnant d'un phare (*Le Rivage des Syrtes,* Paris: Corti, 1951, pp. 19-20).

*   *   *

Moving from the transfiguration of nature to the presentation of events, actions and ideas, a similar strange metamorphosis will surprise us. It seems deeply rooted in Jules Romains and his countless imitators. When *Père* Godard in *Mort de quelqu'un* is traveling with other people to Paris, the cars of the night train absorbing all these travelers with the common aim of speedily attaining Paris are described as a herd of animals: "Le compartiment n'allait pas seul à travers la nuit; il courait au milieu de sa bande, pareille à une migration de bêtes." This herd changes into a group of spirits or hobgoblins teasing the sleeping travelers:

> Les voyageurs avaient le train entier présent à leur sommeil; il palpitait sous leurs talons, secouait les planches de ses battements qui passaient dans la chair, envahissaient les jambes, remontaient les veines et se heurtaient aux battements des coeurs.

They produce the phantom of a monster of will power extending to the engine to push it forward: "Et chaque homme allongeait une volonté jusqu'à la machine." By an extreme condensation of thought, image and reality coincide here in an almost uncanny fashion and result in a poetization that makes reality psychologically still more real.

Jules Romains' concept that things create and destroy groups has produced a metaphorical language which, easier to grasp than

Colette's imagery, has been imitated by the greatest and even most "classical" writers.[6] André Gide, for instance, describes a park concert at night as a roaring of instruments grouping the listeners close to them and holding night aloof. The dark struggles against the electric light which is caught on some nearby trees:

> Sous un kiosque illuminé se tenait le petit orchestre où les instruments de métal sévissaient. Tout autour du kiosque, la nuit écartée comme un voile, ne laissait retomber ses plis qu'au-delà du peuple en arrêt que groupait ici la musique. Une partie des arbres voisins accrochait encore a l'extrémité d'un rameau la lumière; le reste s'enfonçait dans la nuit.[7]

This process of stylization becomes clearer in minor authors. Marcel Arland in his *Monique* (1926) adopts the unanimistic-expressionistic style more as an inner necessity than as a *pastiche*. Nightfall for him means that "Le soir se glissait dans les rues" (p. 101); a path narrowing at certain points is described as follows: "Entre les remparts et les maisons, le sentier s'étranglait parfois" (p. 88). The devout worshippers in a church are presented by a keen impressionistic metonymy: "L'église était pleine de génuflexions" (p. 99); the watering of a garden by a magic metaphor: "Les arrosoirs lançaient sur la terre de grandes et simples fleurs d'argent" (p. 156).

Paul Morand's description of a flight in the morning fog is entirely unanimistic and assumes an experimental truth: the earth seems to repel the plane; the factories devour people like a monster:

> La terre parut se détendre comme un ressort et projeter les voyageurs loin d'elle. L'avion . . . se mit a découper des arcs dans le vide. Ogresses, les usines du Rhin, aux toits dépliés comme des paravents, aspiraient des faubourgs entiers, les privant d'hommes et de femmes.[8]

One can easily see that the unanimistic language was bound to become in literature the normal language of the flyer, who, as he approaches the earth feels that he is absorbing the countries and the men on its surface. Antoine de Saint-Exupéry therefore describes his first bird's-eye view of Tangier as follows:

> Je ramenais au jour une ville engloutie et qui devenait
> vivante . . . et à cinq mètres du terrain cet Arabe qui labourait,
> que je tirais à moi, dont je faisais un homme à mon échelle, qui
> était vraiment mon butin de guerre ou ma création ou mon jeu.
> J'avais pris un otage et l'Afrique m'appartenait (*Courrier Sud*,
> p. 61).

The flyer-poet feels the villages in the plain to be a flock and himself to be "the shepherd of the little towns below him" (*Vol de nuit*).

François Mauriac can use Romains' language though with him it is less effective: "Le métro absorbait et vomissait des fourmis à têtes d'homme" (*Le Mystère Frontenac*, p. 274). Georges Duhamel, in spite of his resolute separation from the unanimistic movement, says in 1924: "un cinéma engloutit ses dernières gueulées de public" (*Deux hommes*, p. 174). André Malraux pictures rays of light invading a dark room like solid bars: "Deux grands prismes de soleil criblés d'atomes, que projettent les fenêtres, plongent comme des barres obliques dans l'ombre de la salle" (*Les Conquérants*, p. 188). Henri Bosco transforms the house in which the hero of *Malicroix* protects himself against a nocturnal thunderstorm into a living and sympathetic animal:

> L'être déjà humain, où j'abritais mon corps, ne céda rien
> à la tempête. La maison se serra sur moi, comme une louve, et par
> moments je sentais son odeur descendre maternellement jusque
> dans mon coeur.[9]

The existentialists took over from Romains not only his practice of animating the inanimate but also his vocabulary, with the key word *exister*. Thus in Simone de Beauvoir's *L'Invitée* the heroine Françoise, wandering through the empty theatre building during the night, transforms the hall into a living being:

> Elle descendit un étage et poussa la porte de la salle . . . ,
> il fallait la faire exister, cette salle . . . pleine de nuit . . . ; les
> fauteuils de peluche rouge s'alignaient, inertes, en attente . . . et
> ils tendaient leurs bras. Ils regardaient la scène masquée par le
> rideau de fer, ils appelaient Pierre [her actor husband] (*L'Invitée*,
> NRF, p. 10).

Albert Camus' technique of recombining fragments of reality is different, as can be seen from a passage of *L'Etranger*. The activities outside the prison cell of Meurseault, who is condemned to death, reach him as sense impressions evoked by sounds. These fragmentary impressions clash with his craving for a *vie unanime* from which he is going to be cut off. They suggest a despairing *paysage d'âme* as he confides his emotions to his diary and induces a unique mood of melancholy:

> Le cri des vendeurs de journaux dans l'air déjà détendu, les derniers oiseaux dans le square, l'appel des marchands de sandwiches, la plainte des tramways dans les hauts tournants de la ville et cette rumeur du ciel avant que la nuit bouscule sur le port, tout cela recomposait pour moi un itinéraire d'aveugle que je connaissais bien avant d'entrer en prison.[10]

But Camus' forte is the presentation of a weird landscape which has actually absorbed and devoured man, assumed his functions and petrified his picture in the mock and sham existence of his monuments. Thus the abandoned city of Oran is presented during the plague, with her ghostly and deserted streets after the curfew hour:

> La ville était de pierre. Sous les ciels de lune, elle alignait ses murs blanchâtres et ses rues rectilignes, jamais tachées par la masse noire d'un arbre, jamais troublées par le pas d'un promeneur ni le cri d'un chien. . . . Les effigies taciturnes de bienfaiteurs oubliés ou d'anciens grands hommes étouffés à jamais dans le bronze s'essayaient seules, avec leurs faux visages de pierre ou de fer, a évoquer une image dégradée de ce qui avait été l'homme, . . . ordre ultime, celui d'une nécropole où la peste, la pierre et la nuit auraient faire taire enfin toute voix (Camus, *La Peste,* p. 192).

Camus, by showing with overwhelming enumerations of details and changing verbs the fiendish, all destroying action of the enemy Plague, creates an uncanny pseudo-unanimistic style: "Pendant le mois de décembre, elle flamba dans les poitrines de nos concitoyens, elle illumina le four, elle peupla les camps d'ombres aux mains vides" (*La Peste,* p. 282). Here the metaphorical verbal allusions *(flamber, illuminer, peupler)* are of a truly ghastly condensation.

The elements of prose style inherited from *naturisme* and unanimism and used to transform efficiently a banal reality into a magic one are not enough, however, to present time relations as space relations, and to concretize ideas poetically through language. Contemporary French prose receives, in addition, help from pure and surrealistic poetry.

The main device of this transfiguring style is the handling of the abstract as though it were concrete and vice versa, an accepted procedure since Baudelaire. Magic realism links an oneiric language to the world of ideas, as is the case with the language of Paul Valéry, described by E. Noulet as follows:

> Rendre l'abstrait voluptueux sans qu'il perde rien de son austérité, de lui créer une plasticité sans qu'il perde rien de sa profondeur, et de le faire bruire et chatoyer comme une étoffe moirée.[11]

Peculiarly enough, François Mauriac also shares this dream language: "Le grand émotif n'écrit qu'en 'état second,' et les fluctuations d'un tel état retentissent discrètement sur son mode d'expression."[12]

One of the great pioneers of oneiric language is Léon Paul Fargue (1876-1947). He appears as the Vincent van Gogh of literature when he says: "Ton cou si droit, serré du collier, flambe tes cheveux comme une fumée grasse" or as its Modigliani: "De fausses oranges dans les têtes bleues aux trous noirs de bouches ouvertes."[13]

Giraudoux succeeds in masterly fashion in combining "naturistic," unanimistic and oneiric processes. He wantonly revises nature in order to make it artistically more splendid. Starting from the most banal things in the world, he makes a wondrous phenomenon out of the prosaic action of shoe shining:

> Et le cireur le laissa, les pieds étincelants, et la tête perdait de plus en plus d'éclat. Et il s'avançait vers l'ascenseur les regards perdus dans l'or de ses pieds; sur les dalles de verre bleu il avait l'air de marcher sur le ciel (*Choix des Elues,* p. 285).

Giraudoux himself very cleverly describes the process of transforming abstract reality into a concrete dream:

> Au nom seul du Jour, je le sentais onduler silencieusement entre ses deux nuits comme un cygne aux ailes noires. Au nom du Mois, je le voyais s'échaffauder, arc-bouté sur ses Jeudis et ses Dimanches.[14]

Impressed by a Catholic funeral, he remarks humorously that "la mort est si ancienne qu'on lui parle latin" (*Provinciales,* ed. Livre Modern Illustré, p. 34). We find daring associations of the real and the psychological, with no ironical intention, in an "adieu" to a parting ship in Roger Allard's (1885-   ) poem *Histoire d'Yvonne:*

> Et je vis le bateau passer
> Traînant des cygnes de vapeur
> Et tous les voyageurs
> Agiter des adieux comme des mains coupées.[15]

The realist André Malraux, without himself recurring to oneiric language, nevertheless presents certain scenes from real life as weird and dreamlike. Thus he comments on four corpses leaning against a wall: "Ces corps droits ont quelque chose, non de fantastique mais de surréel, dans cette lumière et ce silence" (*Les Conquérants,* Pleïade, p. 135).

The mark of genius is evident when the oneiric and the realistic style fuse by an interior necessity without any surrealist experimentation involved. Those authors who cultivate the oneiric style as a matter of principle are not the most perfect ones, but rather those who use it only when it fits the subject matter. The classical peak of fusion seems to be reached in Camus' description of the invasion of rats carrying the germs of the plague. Here reality is evoked as a nightmare by a chaotic accumulation of details characteristic of Rabelais. In an ominous sequence of shocking elements the description of the rising menace assumes onomatopoetic overtones, while fantastic details make the tableau weird and overpowering:

> Des réduits, des sous-sols, des caves, des égouts, ils [les rats] montaient en longues files titubantes pour venir vaciller à la lumière, tourner sur eux-mêmes et mourir près des humains. La nuit, dans les couloirs ou les ruelles, on entendait distinctement leurs petits cris d'agonie. Le matin, dans les faubourgs, on les trouvait étalés à même le ruisseau, une petite fleur de sang sur le museau pointu, les uns gonflés et putrides, les autres raidis et les moustaches encore dressées. . . . Ils venaient aussi mourir isolément dans les halls administratifs, dans les préaux d'école, à la terrasse des cafés. . . . La Place d'armes, les boulevards, la promenade du Front-de-Mer, de loin en loin étaient souillés. . . . On eût dit que la terre même où étaient plantées nos maisons se purgeait de son chargement d'humeurs, qu'elle laissait à la surface des furoncles et des sanies qui jusqu'ici, la travaillaient intérieurement (*La Peste,* Gallimard, 1947, p. 27).

When the painter Gomez in Sartre's *Les Chemins de la Liberté,* having looked at the pictures of the Museum of Modern Art in New York, sees everything in a new light and movement as an inspiration for his own canvas, it is as though oneiric realism were describing itself:

> Les couleurs battaient à grands coups dans les choses, comme des pouls affolés; . . . les objects allaient se rompre ou tomber d'apoplexie et ça criait, ça jurait ensemble, c'était la foire (Sartre, *La Mort dans l'âme,* p. 25).

It is with this same oneiric realism that Sartre starts Chapter XI of *L'Age de Raison:* "Une grande fleur mauve montait vers le ciel, c'était la nuit" (p. 171).

Oneiric style is easily traceable in animistic atmosphere descriptions such as electric storms in the making, e.g., in Henri Bosco, *Antonin* (NRF, 69):

> L'orage . . . laissait pendre presque au sol ses livides nuées. Elles avançaient lentement. Par dessus s'élevait le monumental édifice de la tempête. Par un calme déroulement de volutes énormes qu'il tirait solennellement du sein de ses vapeurs, l'orage construisait cet édifice.

At this juncture it may be well to explain how the magic-oneiric style assumes the two-level dimension referred to above.

* * *

Changing life into a magic reality ends logically in a mythical and highly metaphorical language where life and its intended myth come together. A simple example from Mauriac would be the headlight of a streetcar which in the morning or evening mist appears as a cyclop's eye, but remains at the same time the trolley light: "Presque toujours l'oeil de cyclope du tramway émergeait d'un brouillard épais" (*Chemins de la mer*, p. 115). For Claudel persons out of Christ's parables and out of modern life melt together into a modern picture of hedonistic behavior: "L'enfant prodigue qui traite le mauvais larron et les employés du comput, se divertit chez le rôtisseur avec les joueuses de flûte" (*Corona benignitatis*, p. 154). This kind of association is comparable to the arbitrary method of "M. Stravinsky in his later chamber-music. . . . He produces a succession of combinations which you must follow, if you can."[16] It coincides with Cézanne's "affective deformation of reality"[17] and in more outspoken cases with Braque's and Picasso's "dissociation and recombination."[18] The combination of dissected impressions, rearranged on different levels, seems to me the very secret of Claudel's poetic language in its higher spheres as well as in its ordinary procedures. The motif of "A foreboded dying" is split as to the soul's destiny (*autre porte*) and the body's decay (*odeur*) and recombined more metaphorically on these two levels:

> Le temps viendra bientôt
> qu'une autre porte se dissolve . . .
> et que les encensoirs de la nuit se mêlent
> à l'odeur de la mèche infecte qui s'éteint
> (*L'Annonce faite à Marie*, p. 19).

In this mixture of extinction, beatitude and decomposition there is still ambiguity in that the door to eternal life becomes earthly life's dissolution and the smell of decomposition is shifted to that of the candles of the wake.

Even the lucid Paul Valéry likes the myth-style with its two planes. He describes his own nightly walk under the stars with a friend as a close participation in cosmic "animal" life: "Nous marchions, fumeurs obscurs, au milieu du Serpent, du Cygne, de l'Aigle et de la Lyre,—il me semblait maintenant d'être près, dans le texte même de l'univers silencieux" (*Variété* II, p. 197).[19]

The triumph of Proust's dissection and new combination is that "On dirait qu'il ne peut faire apparaître l'objet qu'en le déformant. . . . Ici la transposition est essentielle, et c'est pourquoi elle ne se voit d'abord, . . . les souvenirs au lieu de se superposer, se juxtaposent." That is, according to Alain, the poetic deformation in Proust.[20] The higher reality of Proust rises from a constant juxtaposition of exterior and interior worlds, of nature and culture, but most of all of past and present, in all possible analogies taking on the rôle of parallels or similes. There is no description of a landscape without an oblique reference to a painter or engraver who grasped it artistically before him, and no mention of a place name without speculation on its etymology: Honfleur is the holm-fjord of the Normans and Lyons is the Lug-dun-um of the Celts, with the same stem "dun" which appears also in Châteaudun and London. The procedure is similar to the new polyphonism in music as represented by Hindemith, where melodious strings are superimposed on one another in order to provoke a tremendous depth of harmonies.

The mature Montherlant has a habit of whirling pictured realities together with their metaphorical interpretations, thus producing agreeable associations of different worlds such as land—sea—arena in competition:

> Les autobus naviguaient comme des paquebots sur une mer étale. Elle héla un taxi, arrêtée au milieu de la chaussée, la main levée, les pieds joints, comme un banderillero qui "cite" de loin le taureau; la voiture, comme une houle, vint expirer à ses pieds.[21]

Structurally the modern novel is also as a whole a narration on different planes: dialogues, reflections, interpolated letters and documents, mere facets of people, incomprehensible events, appearances, guesswork, probable explanations, but never a complete story entirely satisfying the curiosity of the reader. The *Journal des faux monnayeurs* is a strange sequel to the novel in that it expounds the thesis that introducing logic into literature is a paradox because it tries to make sense out of a fragmentary, absurd and unpredictable world. The *Histoire de Mouchette* in *Sous le soleil de Satan* is a most challenging introduction to Donissan's mosaic-like history. Composition and language alike reflect the esthetics of a multiple plane arrangement or the "esthétique de la discontinuité."[22] Giraudoux and Morand are the masters of this esthetics of disharmony which in modern music is called "atonal."

Sartre even goes so far as to use a *monologue intérieur à rebours,* hiding from the reader which subjects on which planes he is concerned with, since he uses the pronoun *il* without any previous referent. "Il [Pierre] aurait voulu être à Tours, dans la maison de ses parents, et que ce fût le matin et que sa mère vînt lui porter son petit déjeuner au lit! Eh bien, vous descendrez dans le salon des journalistes, dit-il [Chamberlain] à Neville Henderson, et vous voudrez bien faire savoir que, déférant à la demande du chancelier Hitler, je me rendrai a l'hôtel Dreesen aux environs de vingt-deux heures trente" (*Le Sursis,* p. 47).[23] Here the absurdity of the world comes to the fore in a chaotic two-plane presentation merging into radical *simultanéisme.* There is no distinction of time anymore as to the events referred to despite the mentioning of hours of the day. The prototypes for this *procédé* are to be looked for in Dos Passos and Faulkner, particularly in the latter's *The Sound and the Fury* (1929).

The radical consequence of the language of *simultanéisme* is the stream-of-consciousness, or flux of consciousness. With this technique the boundaries between outside world and thought disappear, everything being based on the barbarian extension of the *style indirect libre,* eternalized in its greatest exaggeration in James Joyce's *Ulysses.* The French with their sense of *mesure* use this technique merely for the purpose of characterization, as for example, Duhamel for his Salavin who cannot distinguish between reality and imagination. Another application of the stream-of-consciousness technique is found in Valéry Larbaud's *Mon plus secret conseil.* This work, says Bouvier, "n'est que le monologue intérieur d'un voyageur au lendemain d'une rupture sentimentale; et les incidents les plus menus du voyage y font comme la trame, le feutre aux mille brins sur lequel court la broderie d'une idée fixe."[24] The different planes of a flux of consciousness generally are: 1. the story, 2. the thoughts, and 3. the interfering memories buttressing the thoughts. The memories themselves may take a "dialectic" form causing an anacoluthic tension as in the following example from Jules Romains:

> De quoi pourrait se plaindre Gambaroux. . . . Il y a bien la mort. . . . Et il faut avouer que lorsque par hasard, seul, l'après-midi, sur le siège de son cabriolet, on pense à la mort (cela peut venir d'un glas qu'on entend dans la campagne, ou d'une nouvelle qu'on vous a dite le matin sur le marché: "Vous savez un tel, de Mazergues, vous le connaissez?—Parbleu, je lui ai acheté un veau, ça ne fait pas trois semaines.—Eh bien, il est mort!") Il faut avouer donc, que cette idée sait aller vous pincer dans des replis, où nulle autre n'irait vous atteindre (*Les Hommes de bonne volonté* VIII: *Province*).

Malraux in his *Conquérants* finds an exciting fragmentary style by combining discussions, broadcasts, and telegrams arriving from revolutionary Canton. These three sources of information make it possible to piece together the material for a first picture of what is going on. This method, however, remains too close to *reportage*.

The James Joyce type of stream-of-consciousness-writing is well shown by François Mauriac:

> Jean Louis . . . fut distrait par la vue de cette barrière démolie. . . . Il fallait dire à Burthe de la réparer. Il monterait demain matin. . . . Il irait à Léojats, il verrait Madeleine Cazavieilh. . . . Le vent tournait à l'est et apportait l'odeur du village. . . . Il marchait dans l'herbe déjà trempée, etc. (*Le Mystère Frontenac*, p. 55).[25]

The multiple-plane technique has still another function in modern French fiction, that of character delineation. What the persons say about themselves is supposed, by definition, to be a lie, or an illusion; what the others observe in them is assumed to be superficial and mischievous if true at all. The author attempts on the basis of these unreliable sources of information to pierce at least the thinnest mask of the individual concerned. Besides this, however, the character revealing himself or noticed by others is never consistent, but continuously changing. The consequence is many fragments of characterization and criticism, contradictory and inconsistent and only temporarily valid, so that they never will make a real personality, but a bundle of traits of behavior. This is according to Jacques Rivière a tremendous achievement due to Dostoevsky who took seriously the *Insondable* and depicted *créatures* instead of *individus*.[26] A characteristic face which one remembers in this literature is only "un visage formé par l'union de ses visages successifs" (Malraux, *Les Conquérants,* p. 85). This characterization again corresponds to the type of music initiated by Claude Debussy in which there is no theme, no line, no sequence of motives, but only fragmentary suggestions. It is comparable to the dances of Borodine, whose beauty arises from the violent and the abrupt.[27] Syntactically the fragmentary style is characterized by an excessive use of the *phrase invertébrée,* a kind of clause without verb; it is a most extreme nominalistic style, very much cherished by Duhamel and Malraux.

The psychology of the fragmentary style corresponds to the disconnected images of nervous persons who see things only in detached portions and are incapable of a comprehensive scheme incorporating the detached details.

* * *

Contemporary style is extremely tense and almost always ambiguous; we can only make sense of the ambivalent language if we recognize its unity with the life stratum behind it or, better, within it. J. Romains says: "La vérité peut se loger tout près de l'enveloppe des idées, ou dans leur enveloppe même, comme tels organes de très haut prix se logent dans le tégument" (*Les Hommes de bonne volonté,* v. XII: *Les Créateurs,* Anthol. Coidreau, p. 282).

The most decisive point in the overlapping and fusion of planes may be a tendency expressed theoretically by André Breton:

> Je crois à la résolution future de ces deux états, en appar-
> ence si contradictoires, que sont le rêve et la réalité, en une sorte
> de réalité absolue, de surréalité, si l'on peut ainsi dire (*Les Mani-
> festes du surréalisme,* 1946, p. 28).

Thus surrealism is in the narrower and wider sense, to use a word
of Duhamel, *rêvogène.* This means that poetic creation starts
from dreamy vagueness: Proust's *A la recherche du temps perdu*
begins with hovering recollections, developing through the whole
book but due to the half-conscious moment of Marcel's awaking
from sleep to *souvenir.* Then the recollections stream arbitrarily
from the subliminal over the threshold of conscience (theoretic
remarks about this state are to be found in *La Prisonnière,* I,
p. 167). The third book, chapter 8 of Duhamel's *Cécile Pasquier,*
reveals the same secret: "Out of the black darkness of sleep a
little glimmer appears. Like a silvery bubble rising from the depth
of the water, the soul emerges from its abyss, etc." Colette knows
about it, too: "Avant de m'éveiller, avant le moment lucide du
souvenir, il y a un remous confus de rêves en lambeaux, de
réalité fumeuse" (*L'Entrave,* p. 263). Proust would like to pierce
this secret in the chapter entitled *La regardant dormir* concerning Albertine, and Valéry, too, pondering on *La dormeuse* and
La fausse morte. Marcel Arland shows *Monique* "restant sans
penser, s'écoutant vivre" (p. 185), and "jusqu'à ce que sa lucidité
lui revenait, porteuse de souffrance" (p. 165). A similar transi-
tional state is described conversely by Bernanos when the "dream"
of consciousness fuses with the greater "reality" of mystic invasion.
Valéry's *Jeune Parque* has been interpreted, though clumsily, as
"the revery of the poet awakening early one morning in bed and
lying more or less awake till dawn."[28] In a half-trance a woman
in J. Romains' *Montée des perils* "entend des phrases, comme un
noyé les entendrait arriver étrangement à travers l'eau, où il
s'engloutit" (p. 78). Bernanos says about the moment of mystic
invasion, that the last ringing of the bell is replaced by a soft
call (*Sous le soleil de Satan,* p. 125), that it is an awakening in
never seen landscapes (*ib.,* p. 193), and most wonderfully, that
a false note arises from the orchestra. The director is aware of it,

but is not able to check it (*ib.*, p. 126). This mysterious possibility of moving from one level to another (levels bridgeless in life) which is clear in mysticism and less clear in poetry is the main concern of contemporary writers in general.

Valéry's *Eupalinos* explains the passing from the stage of analytical thinking to the stage of artistic inspiration with another simile: "Je ne puis te parler que des approches d'une si grande chose. Quand elle s'annonce, cher Phèdre, je diffère déjà de moi-même, autant qu'une corde tendue diffère d'elle-même qui était lâche et sinueuse" (p. 113).

*   *   *

The stress on the elusive moment of passage from the unconscious to the conscious is sometimes replaced by a more extensive consideration of the transparency of life. According to Bernanos, earth and heaven are two fluids mixed together, but of different specific weights (*Sous le soleil* . . . , p. 299). Death is always present in life like a face under clear, deep water (*ib.*, p. 326).

The conception of the inseparability of dream and life, sleep and waking, normal life and ecstasy, life and death with the point of interrogation as to the true reality and the higher one, thus constantly appears condensed in comparisons and metaphorical forms. France for the first time in history allows herself such a "Calderonianism," e.g., the interchange of planes which are facets of time and eternity, prismatic appearances of being.

Everything is transparent: Marcel Proust finds the sadness motive of Debussy's *Pelléas* in the "cris des marchands de Paris" (*La Prisonnière* I, p. 160), Giraudoux explains the double idea in the verb *captiver* (1. obsolete: to capture, 2. modern: to impress someone) and takes it as an equivalent of "passer une corde au cou." With this bold double plane of a self-constructed synonymics he writes: "O Ulysse, il n'est qu'une corde solide, celle que la parole passe au cou de tes auditeurs, et pour jamais ils sont tes prisonniers" (*Elpénor*, p. 61).[29] Giraudoux makes as a matter of principle an ironic juxtaposition of life and humanism, as his *Simon le Pathétique* does seriously: "Je leur [aux professeurs] devais, en voyant un bossu, de penser à Thersite, une vieille ridée, à Hécube."[30] In Paul Valéry's *Ebauche d'un serpent,* "la férocité, le défi, l'insulte, l'ironie, la séduction, l'éloquence, l'orgueil, la tendresse . . . tous les tons de la voix humaine y alternent que ne cesse d'accompagner un sifflement":[31] moral evil is present in all passions.

When in Bernanos' novels possessed persons begin to speak, they, too, hiss like a fiendish serpent. When in Julien Green's *Le Visionnaire,* Manuel sees Marie-Thérèse going to denounce him to her mother, he feels like an accused delinquent and superimposes his imagination on reality: "En voyant cette enfant immobile devant nous, et les mains derrière le dos, j'eus l'impression fugitive d'un tribunal. La table où nous étions assis occupait en effet une estrade qui la surélevait d'un pied au-dessus du sol et ajoutait . . . a l'aspect . . . solennel de la longue salle basse" (p. 88).

The superimposed-plane style may be based on shocking clashes. Thus we better understand the hidden brutality in certain comparisons. Albertine, linked closely to Marcel's life, appears to him like a bomb which one holds in his hands and cannot drop without committing a crime.

Some of these comparisons are offensive just because of their necessary vulgarity: Montherlant sees people massed in a square as "collés les uns sur les autres comme des mouches sur une blessure" *(Les Célibataires).* It is as though mortal dangers ahead were involved in the harsh comparison. The same holds true for Claudel who adds crude, unnecessary details to underline a sinister situation heading toward catastrophe. The following comparisons accompany a conversation on the high seas between Amalric and Mesa who are both on the verge of an adulterous love affair with the same woman, Ysé *(Partage du midi):*

> Amalric: On se sent horriblement visible, comme un poux entre deux lames de verre.
> Mesa: La mer à l'échine resplendissante est comme une vache terrassée que l'on marque au fer rouge.[32]

Many may consider such images extravagant, particularly the images of Breton, Delteil, Soupault, and all the genuine *Surréalistes*. This is not the point. "Ces images, pour extravagantes qu'elles paraissent, sont justes, exactes, collent à l'objet autant que les métaphores de Donne, de Gongora, de Shakespeare."[33] We see here stated that the multiple-plane style is a new baroque. It is in harmony, too, with opposing characters, e.g., husband and wife, clashing together in their ideas and speeches as Jean-Louis Frontenac and Madeleine:

> —Penses-tu qu'après beaucoup d'efforts, on puisse transformer . . . la destinée d'un homme?
> —Qu'est-ce que ça peut faire, chéri?
> —Après la cène, ces paroles tristes et douces du Sauveur à Judas . . .
> —Sais-tu l'heure qu'il est?

The famous *Théâtre de l'inexprimé,* as best represented by Jean Jacques Bernard's *Martine,* consists essentially in stichomythic clashes of two speakers whose underlying thoughts are too delicate to be expressed:

> C'est moins par les répliques mêmes que par le choc des répliques que doivent se révéler les sentiments le plus profonds. Il y a sous le dialogue entendu comme un dialogue sousjacent qu'il s'agit de rendre sensible.[34]

Lenormand's technique consists in introducing detours in order to avoid by a smoother conduct of the action premature explanations and indiscrete anticipations.[35] The clash of different planes, especially in the comparisons, can be still very important to characterization, even if there is a certain banality implied. Paul Morand speaks of "Un ancien Président du Conseil qui se tenait modestement dans un coin comme un crachoir" (*Lewis et Irène,* p. 31).

The clash can be the reflection of a vulgar political reality, as is the case when the Franco functionary in Avila tells a political adversary: "Va te faire voir, salaud. Vive le Christ-Roi!" (A. Malraux, *L'Espoir:* Gallimard, 1937, p. 8).

The whole style of André Gide, being an imitation of *classicisme pur,* when expressing troubled ideas is a clashing style for it involves "une pensée hardie, brûlante, batailleuse, et une forme timide, un style d'une blancheur inquiétante."[36]

The juxtaposition of planes in a clashing sense characterizes also what might be called the modern Homeric simile. Here the psychological ingredient helps to make the simile drastic. A white plane tree evokes the association of the white skin of a woman, and thus Ramuz dreams on: "Les platanes ont une peau trop blanche et trop lisse, qui fait qu'on détourne les yeux de sa blancheur, comme quand une femme ôte sa robe" (*Les Signes parmi nous,* p. 6). By a similar comparison Thierry Maulnier makes the houses of Mantua appear in the moonlight like snow, milk, flesh:

> Les médiocres palais de Mantoue recueillent sur leur surface tout ce qui reste épars de lueurs dans l'espace, veuf du soleil, ils brillent doucement comme la neige, comme le lait, comme la chair d'une femme dévêtue dans une chambre presque obscure. . . . L'obscurité nous vient du ciel. La clarté nous vient de la terre (*Le Profanateur,* acte IV, sc. 2, Ed. Gallimard, 1952, p. 195).

Sartre hazards the drastic "Homeric" simile that "Oreste . . . s'est embrouillé dans sa destinée comme les chevaux éventrés, s'embrouillent leurs pattes dans leurs intestins; et maintenant, quelque mouvement qu'il fasse, il faut qu'il s'arrache les entrailles" (*Les Mouches,* acte 2, Théâtre I: NRF, p. 57).

Jules Romains speaks of the new attraction of crime, when remorse has become silent, in an almost Baudelairian simile:

> Mais ce poids enlevé de la poitrine, c'était comme une de ces grosses pierres un peu enterrées. Quand on les soulève, on voit s'agiter et partir à l'aventure d'horribles bestioles que la pierre retenait, qui étaient emprisonnées sous la pierre (*Le Drapeau Noir,* Flammarion, 1931, p. 151).

Another form of a more camouflaged simile concerns the parental lack of watchfulness as far as the children are concerned: "Une mère [Mme Maieul] savait qu'elle avait à surveiller sa fille, tout le temps. . . . Quand on lâche le volant de sa voiture, peut-on se plaindre qu'au bout d'un moment elle aille dans le fossé?" (Romains, *Naissance de la bande*, p. 47).

Claudel even goes so far as to add to the picture associations which do not clarify the object compared but simply help the reader to dream on, exactly as in the extended Homeric similes: "Pensées, actions qui dorment, comme les nouveau-nés qui ramènent les cuisses vers le ventre" (*Tête d'or* in *Théâtre* I, p. 19). Giono, who is consciously Homeric, tells in a broadly spun story his myth of the thundercloud as an escaped bellowing bull:

> L'orage comme un taureau fouetté d'herbes; il s'est arraché à la boue des plaines; son dos musculeux s'est gonflé; puis il a sauté les collines, et il s'est mis en marche dans le ciel.[37]

These similes, however, compared to those of Homer himself are not sufficiently expansive. There is a more "spacious" example offered by Alphonse de Chateaubriant, *La Réponse du Seigneur:* The narrator enters unaware a room where silent mourners are surrounding a casket; the text runs as follows:

> Une foule noire, de paysans et de paysannes, de métayers et de métayères, tous en costumes de dimanche, et tous regardant du même côté. . . . Dans les ventes publiques, on assiste parfois ainsi à des instants sans bruit. C'est le moment où le commissaire -priseur se livre à un difficile calcul professionnel au milieu de la plus profonde attention de l'assistance. Et je pensai que je tombais là peut-être sur quelque pathétique liquidation. . . . Mais à peine avais-je passé la porte . . . (Ed. Grasset, 1933, p. 32).

This very detailed explanation is not "poetic." Poetry begins in this field of similes when a very slight idea is submerged in a series of surrounding images. This is prototypically the case when Marcel Proust describes his discovery of a single poppy and some cornflowers on a slope, heralding the cornfield on the top. Proust steeps the whole situation in the parallel of the progressive pattern of a tapestry and then of a slow approach to the sea, but in such a way that sea metaphors are telescoped, i.e., first used for the slope itself and then for the simile:

> Je poursuivais jusque sur le talus . . . quelque coquelicot
> perdu, quelques bluets . . . qui le décoraient de leurs fleurs comme
> la bordure d'une tapisserie . . . où apparaît clairsemé le motif
> agreste qui triomphera sur le panneau; rares encore, espacés, . . .
> comme les maisons isolées qui annoncent déjà l'approche d'un
> village, ils m'annonçaient l'immense étendue où déferlent les blés
> . . . et la vue d'un seul coquelicot . . . hissant au bout de son
> cordage et faisant cingler au vent sa flamme rouge, . . . au-dessus
> de sa bouée graisseuse et noire . . . me faisait battre le coeur . . .
> comme au voyageur qui aperçoit sur une terre basse une première
> barque échouée . . . que répare un calfat . . . et s'écrie, avant de
> l'avoir encore vue: "La Mer!" *(Du Côté de chez Swann, La Haie
> d'aubépine).*

Marcel Proust discovers in the Guermantes library a copy of
George Sand's *François le Champi,* a book of no great value, but
once read to him by his mother. This emotional remembrance
strikes him so deeply that it suggests to him the simile of the
trumpet disturbing the mourner at a burial as the work of George
Sand disturbs the literary connoisseur. But since he remembers
that the book was liked by his mother, he is moved like the
mourner who realizes that the trumpet of the soldier is a military
honor for his dead father:

> Tel à l'instant que dans la chambre mortuaire les em-
> ployés des pompes funèbres se préparent à descendre la bière, le
> fils d'un homme qui a rendu des services à la patrie serrant la main
> aux derniers amis qui défilent, si tout à coup retentit sous les fenê-
> tres une fanfare, se révolte, croyant à quelque moquerie dont on
> insulte son chagrin, puis lui qui est maître de soi jusque-là ne
> peut plus retenir ses larmes, lorsqu'il vient à comprendre que ce
> qu'il entend c'est la musique d'un régiment qui s'associe à son
> deuil et rend honneur à la dépouille de son père. Tel, je venais de
> reconnaître la douloureuse impression que j'avais éprouvée en lisant
> le titre d'un livre dans la bibliothèque du Prince de Guermantes
> *(Le Temps retrouvé* II, p. 31).

It seems that imagery within modern literary art has reached
its peak in this type of the epico-lyric simile, one of the main
proofs of the vanishing frontiers between prose and poetry.

as counseled by an equally desperate desire for Him. Although
he speaks about, the arts studied ocity that He is present by
implication in every literature, but there is not a trace. Since
this atheistic and anarchistic society with all its anti-theistic revolt

EPILOGUE

SINCE IT IS the function of literature to penetrate the problems
of life by means of artifacts, we first logically turned our attention to the problems presented in contemporary French literature;
then we analyzed the style which was used to transform these
problems into motives of art. The differences between artistic
genius and talent taken for granted, it would seem that those
works which try to lay bare the secret depths of the soul are
bound to have greater artistic form than those which analyze
primarily sociological problems. The moral factor, for instance,
an attitude in which connivance with evil is excluded, fuses
easily with the psychological into an artistic unit, while it clashes
often with presentations of a merely accepted but deficient social
and factual order. Many aspects of this literature, therefore,
despite all the "transfiguring" tendencies of language, are so
brutal and obscene that they have weakened all the healthy
reticencies of a sound society.

The preponderance of the problem novel or rather the novel-
essay seems to the historian of literature an incontestable proof that
he is confronted with what might be called an arguing literature.
The nineteenth century enjoyed mere novelistic fiction. In the
France of Louis XIV, the novel lived on the margin of literature.
It may be that a technical age was bound to try to reverse all
values, an occurrence we observe in the whole domain of art.
Consequently it was sometimes very unpleasant to discuss these
contemporary quasi-artifacts which contain so much moral poison. Under the filth, dirt and mud, however, one finds often not
mere wantonness but the sincere analysis of the human condition
and the tragic plight of modern man. One finds even something
more than in the conventional literature of the nineteenth century
which sidetracked the metaphysical problem and was too "humanistic" and "romantic" to be true. One discovers nothing less
than the desperate revolutionary denial of God; but this denial is

accompanied by an equally desperate desire for Him. Although He seems absent, the texts studied reveal that He is present by implication in every line written. But there is much more. Since this atheistic and apostate society with all its anti-theistic revolt cannot cut itself off from its Christian roots, the God searched for in this literature is still as Baudelaire says: "Jésus, des Dieux le plus incontestable."

NOTES

Introduction

[1] All three manifestoes (1924, 1930, 1942) are published together, Paris: Sagittaire, 1946. See also Michel Carrouges, *André Breton et les données fondamentales du surréalisme*, Neuchâtel: La Baconnière, 1950.

[2] Louise Delpit, *Paris-Théâtre contemporain: Rôle prépondérant des scènes d'avant-garde depuis trente ans* (Smith College Studies in Modern Languages, vol. VI, Northampton, Mass., 1924-1925), p. 122.

[3] André Gide, *Nouveaux prétextes*, Paris: Mercure de France, 1911, p. 315.

[4] John Palmer, *Studies in the Contemporary Theatre*, London: Secker, 1927, p. 63.

[5] *Le Temps retrouvé*, Paris: Gallimard, vol. II, p. 72.

[6] Henri Massis, *Réflexions sur l'art du roman*, Paris: Plon, 1927, p. 5.

[7] Georges Lemaître, *From Cubism to Surréalism*, Cambridge: Harvard Univ. Press, 1941, p. 203.

[8] A. J. Dickman, "Le Mal, force dramatique chez M. Lenormand," *The Romanic Review*, XIX (1928), p. 218.

[9] John Palmer, *op. cit.*, p. 41.

[10] Maurice Martin du Gard, *Impertinences*, Paris: Bloch, 1924, p. 30.

[11] Pierre Trahard, *L'Art de M. Proust*, Paris: Dervy, 1953, p. 14.

[12] Louis Carrette, *Naissance de Minerve*, p. 72, quoted in Claude-Edmonde Magny, *Histoire du roman français depuis 1918*, Paris: Seuil, 1950, p. 62.

[13] Jean de Pierrefeu, *Les Beaux livres de notre temps*, Paris: Plon, 1938, p. 43.

[14] May Daniels, *The French Drama of the Unspoken*, Edinburgh: Univ. Press, 1953.

[15] G. Lanson et P. Tuffrau, *Histoire de la littérature française depuis cent ans*, 1850-1950, Paris: Hachette, 1953, pp. 1328-29.

[16] See C.-E. Magny, *L'Age du roman américain*, Paris, 1949.

[17] Gaétan Picon, *Panorama de la nouvelle littérature française*, Paris: Gallimard, 1949, p. 43.

[18] R.-M. Albérès, *L'Aventure intellectuelle du XXᵉ siècle*, Paris: La Nouvelle Edition, 1950, p. 59.

[19] Georges Lafourcade, *Notes sur le roman français contemporain*, The University of Buffalo Studies, vol. VI, Ap. 1939, no. 2, p. 88.

[20] G. Lemaître, *op. cit.*, p. 183.

[21] H. A. Barnes, *The History of Western Civilization*, New York: Harcourt, Brace, 1945, vol. II, p. 1035.

[22] H. A. Barnes, *op. cit.*, p. 1038 ff.; Lanson-Tuffrau, *op. cit.*, p. 1314, and Pierre de Latil, "Notre galaxie, cité d'étoiles," *Le Figaro littéraire*, 29 janvier 1955, p. 9.

[23] Georges Duhamel, *Vue de la terre promise*, Paris: Mercure de France, 1934, pp. 79-80.

[24] Cp. Jacques Maritain, *Metafísica de Bergson*, Buenos-Aires: Instituto de Filosofía, 1938, passim.

[25] G. Turquet-Milnes, *Some Modern French Writers*, New York: McBride, 1921, p. 60.

[26] Jacques Maritain, *Creative Intuition in Poetry and Art*, The Bollingen Series, 1953.

[27] John Palmer, *op. cit.*, pp. 13 and 45.

[28] G. Lemaître, *op. cit.*, p. 33.

29 Herbert Read, *Art Now*, London, 1933, p. 67.

30 Marcel Proust, *Le Temps retrouvé*, Paris: Gallimard, 1925.

31 Paul Valéry, *Degas, Danse, Dessin*, Paris: Gallimard, 1938, p. 217.

32 J. Isaacs, *An Assessment of Twentieth Century Literature*, London: Secker and Warburg, 1951.

33 See Georges Michaud, *Vingtième siècle*, New York: Harper, 1933, pp. 421 ff.

34 M. Proust, *Sodome*, vol. I, Paris: Gallimard, p. 177.

35 M. Proust, *Le Temps retrouvé, op. cit.*, vol. II, p. 217.

36 M. Proust, *Le Temps retrouvé, ib.*, vol. II, p. 98.

37 Jean E. Ehrhard, *Le Roman français depuis Marcel Proust*, Paris: Nouvelle Revue Critique, 1932, p. 16.

38 John Palmer, *op. cit.*, p. 99.

39 H. R. Lenormand, "Pourquoi j'ai écrit les ratés," in *Le Gaulois*, 3 juillet, 1920.

40 Jean Giraudoux, *Juliette au pays des hommes*, Paris: Grasset, 1924, p. 156.

41 Georges Duhamel, *Essai sur le roman*, quoted by Achille Ouy, *Georges Duhamel. L'Homme et l'oeuvre*, Paris: Olivier, 1935, p. 20.

Chapter One

1 See Louise Hubbard, *The Individual and the Group in French Literature since 1914*. Diss. Catholic University, Washington, D. C., 1955.

2 *The Inferno*, transl. by Edward J. O'Brien, New York, 1918, p. 207.

3 Felix Klein, *Madeleine Sémer*, New York: Macmillan, 1927, p. 107, Letter of July 14, 1919.

4 Leo Spitzer, "Der Unanimismus Jules Romains im Spiegel seiner Sprache," in *Stilstudien*. II: *Stilsprachen*, Muenchen: Hueber, 1928, pp. 208-300.

5 Leo Spitzer, "Explication linguistique et littéraire de deux textes français," *Le Français moderne* III (1935), pp. 315-23.

6 André Cuisenier, *Jules Romains et l'Unanimisme*. 2 vols. vol. II: *L'Art de Jules Romains*, Paris: Flammarion, 1948. See also Madeleine Berry, *Jules Romains, sa vie, son oeuvre*, Paris: Conquistador, 1953, and Noel Martin-Deslias, *Jules Romains*, Paris: Nagel, 1951.

7 Alfonso Reyes, "L'Esthétique de Jules Romains," in *Hommage à Jules Romains*, Paris: Flammarion, 1945, p. 131.

8 Yves Gandon, *Le Démon du style*, Paris: Plon, 1938, pp. 73-89.

9 1. *Le Cahier gris, Le Pénitencier* (1922); 2. *La Belle saison* (1923); 3. *La Consultation. La Sorellina* (1928); 4. *La Mort du père* (1929); 5.-7. *L'Eté* (1936); 8. *L'Epilogue* (1940).

10 1. *Le Notaire du Havre* (1933); 2. *Le Jardin des bêtes sauvages* (1934); 3. *Vue de la terre promise* (1934); 4. *La Nuit de la Saint Jean* (1935); 5. *Le Désert de Bièvre* (1937); 6. *Les Maîtres* (1937); 7. *Cécile parmi nous* (1938); 8. *Le Combat contre les ombres* (1939); 9. *Suzanne et les jeunes hommes* (1945); 10. *La Passion de Joseph Pasquier* (1945).

11 Pierre-Henri Simon, *Georges Duhamel ou le bourgeois sauvé*, Paris: Temps présent, 1946.

12 César Santelli, *Georges Duhamel. L'Homme. L'Oeuvre*, Bordas, 1947, p. 128.

13 Lucien Pierre Bernheim, *Georges Duhamel. Le Clinicien dans l'art du roman*, Paris: Lapied, 1939, p. 27.

14 Paul Claudel, *Art poétique*, quoted by René Groos et Gonzague Truc, *Les Lettres*, Paris: Denoël, 1934, p. 45.

15 ———— *Art poétique*, Paris, 1907, pp. 72-73.

[16] Frédéric Lefèvre, *Une heure avec*, VIe série, Paris: Flammarion, 1933, p. 9.

[17] Excellent surveys of Malraux's novels in Marcel Savane, *André Malraux*, Paris: Masse, 1946: *Les Conquérants*, pp. 27-44, *La Condition humaine*, pp. 61-82.

[18] R. M. Albérès, *La Révolte des écrivains d'aujourd'hui*, Paris: Corrêa, 1949, p. 47.

[19] Robert Brasillach, *Portraits*, Paris: Plon, 1936, pp. 218-23.

[20] Pierre Brodin, *Les Ecrivains français de l'entre-deux-guerres*, Montréal: Valiquette, 1942, p. 346.

[21] André Malraux, *Romans. Le Temps du mépris*, Paris: Gallimard, 1951, p. 342.

[22] René Girard, "L'Homme et le cosmos dans 'L'Espoir' et 'Les Noyers de l'Altenburg' d'André Malraux," *PMLA*, XXVIII (1953), pp. 208-14.

[23] Bert M.-P. Leefmans, "Malraux and Tragedy: The Structure of *La Condition humaine*," *Romanic Review*, XLIV (1953), pp. 208-14.

[24] G. O. Rees, "Types of recurring similes in Malraux's Novels," *Modern Language Notes*, LXVIII (1953), pp. 373-77.

[25] W. M. Frohock, "Notes on Malraux's Symbols," *Romanic Review*, XLII (1951), 274-281, and *André Malraux and the Tragic Imagination*, Stanford Univ. Press, 1953.

[26] Charles Bruneau, *La Prose littéraire de Proust à Camus*, Oxford: Clarendon, 1953, p. 18.

[27] Henry de Montherlant, *Mors et Vita*, Paris: Grasset, 1932, pp. 61-62.

[28] *Ib.*, p. 72.

[29] Jacques Bompard, "Trois témoins du temps présent: Henry de Montherlant," *La Grande Revue* (mars-juin, 1928), pp. 203 ff.

[30] Maxwell Geismar, *Writers in Crisis*, Boston: Houghton-Mifflin Co., 1942, p. 56.

[31] Yves Gandon, *Le Démon du style*, Paris: Plon, 1938, p. 200.

[32] Marcel Cohen, *Grammaire et Style*, Paris: Editions Sociales, 1954, p. 130.

[33] Quoted from "L'Appel des armes" by Jean de Pierrefeu, *Les Beaux livres de notre temps*, Paris: Plon, 1938, p. 130.

[34] Georges Lemaître, *Four French Novelists*, London: Oxford Univ. Press, 1938, p. 250.

[35] Marcel Thibaut, *Evasions littéraires*, Paris: Gallimard, 1935, pp. 34-35.

[36] Louis Chaigne, *Notre littérature d'aujourd'hui*, Paris: De Gigord, 1949, p. 156.

[37] Pierre Fabricius (ed.), *Lebendiges Frankreich. Eine Anthologie*, Zürich: Oprecht, 1950.

[38] Erich Heller, *André Gide*, New Haven: Yale Univ. Press, 1954, p. 57.

[39] Georges Duhamel, *Le Voyage de Moscou*, Paris: Mercure de France, 1928, p. 213.

[40] Otto Fest, *Stilistische Untersuchungen zu Romain Rolland's 'Pierre et Luce,'* Diss. Jena, 1935.

[41] Luise Krauche, "Zur künstlerischen Gestaltung des Jean Christophe," *Zeitschrift für französische Sprache* LV (1931), 194-218, and Maria Jäger, "Die Erzählungstechnik Romain Rollands in 'Jean Christophe,'" *Arbeiten zur Romanischen Philologie*, vol. 4, Münster, 1933.

[42] Leo Spitzer, "Zu Charles Péguy's Stil," *Stilstudien* II, München: Hueber, 1928, pp. 301-364.

[43] Henri Massis, *Notre ami Psichari*, Paris: Flammarion, 1936, p. 76.

[44] Henry de Montherlant, *Mors et Vita, op. cit.*, p. 27.

Chapter Two

[1] Jean Larnac, *Colette*, Paris: Kra, 1927, p. 216; see Margaret Crosland, *Madame Colette. A Provincial in Paris*, London: Owen, 1953, passim.

[2] Maurice Martin du Gard, *Impertinences*, Paris: Bloch, 1924, p. 64.

[3] Henry Bordeaux, *De Baudelaire à Soeur Marguerite*, Paris: Flammarion, s.d., p. 23.

4 Jean Giraudoux, *Bêtes,* Paris: Firmin-Didot, 1931, p. X.

5 Fernand Desonay, *Le Roman français d'aujourd'hui,* Tournai: Casterman, s.d., p. 50.

6 Yves Gandon, *Le Démon du style,* Paris: Plon, 1938, pp. 203-24.

7 Irene Frisch-Fuglsang, "Le style de Colette," *Orbis Litterarum,* III (1945), pp. 1-29; 200-82; IV (1946), pp. 95-123.

8 Pierre Trahard, *L'Art de Colette,* Paris: Renard, 1941; Jean Larnac, *Colette,* Paris: Kra, 1927; Paul Reboux, *Colette ou le génie du style,* Paris: Rasmussen, 1925.

9 Quoted from Pierre-Henri Simon, *Témoins de l'homme,* Paris: Colin, 1952, p. 25.

10 *Ib.,* p. 31.

11 René Cros et Gonzague Truc, *Tableau du XXe siècle,* IV: *Les Lettres,* Paris: Denoël, 1934, p. 27.

12 Jean Schlumberger, *Essais et dialogues,* Paris: Gallimard, 1937, p. 216.

13 Robert Brasillach, *Portraits,* Paris: Plon, 1936. Chapter: "Barrès vivant," p. 57.

14 *Le Démon du style, op. cit.,* pp. 129-30; see also H. Groh, *Der publizistische Stil des Léon Daudet,* Diss. Heidelberg, 1935.

15 Richard Aldington, *The Spirit of Place. An Anthology from the Prose of D. H. Lawrence,* London: Heinemann, 1935, pp. 207-209.

16 See Christian Michelfelder, *Jean Giono et les religions de la terre,* Paris: Gallimard, 1938.

17 Henri Clouard, *Histoire de la littérature française du symbolisme à nos jours,* vol. II, Paris: Michel, 1949, p. 327.

18 Charlotte Dietschy, "Natur und Mensch in Giono's Sprache," *Festschrift Ernst Tappolet,* Basel: Schwabe, 1935, p. 73; see also Romée Villeneuve, *Jean Giono, ce solitaire,* Paris: Presses universitaires, 1955.

19 Bernard Vodenne, *C.F. Ramuz ou la sainteté de la terre,* Juillard, 1948.

20 Henri Peyre, *The Contemporary French Novel,* New York: Oxford Univ. Press, 1955, p. 150.

21 Marcel Girard, *Guide illustré de la littérature française moderne,* Paris: Seghers, 1954, p. 111.

22 Henri Clouard, *op. cit.,* vol. II, p. 323.

23 Erich Brock, "Das Magische im Stil von C.F. Ramuz," *Trivium,* I (1942), pp. 16-33.

24 Klara Pasch, *Charles Ferdinand Ramuz. Motive und Sprache seiner Romane als Ausdruck seiner waadtländischen Heimat,* Diss. Rostock, 1938.

25 Pierre Kohler, *L'Art de Ramuz,* Genève, 1929.

26 Werner Günther, *C.F. Ramuz. Wesen-Werk-Kunst,* Bern: Haupt, 1948.

27 Nelly Lauchenauer, *Ramuz' Verhältnis zum Gegenständlichen,* Diss. Zürich, 1937.

28 Alexander Hartmann, *C.F. Ramuz. Mensch, Werk und Landschaft,* Diss. Leipzig, 1937, pp. 90-145.

29 Clarence Reuben Parsons, *Ch.F. Ramuz et la peinture,* Diss. Toronto, 1953.

30 Cp. Jérôme Tharaud, *Mes années chez Barrès,* Paris: Plon, 1928.

31 *Le Chemin de Damas,* Paris: Plon, 1923, p. 45.

32 *Ib.,* p. 71.

33 For the Jewish question in contemporary French literature see Ferdinand Baldensperger, *La Littérature française entre les deux guerres,* Los Angeles: Lymanhouse, 1941, pp. 65-68.

34 Marcel Thibaut, *Evasions littéraires,* Paris: Gallimard, 1935, p. 121.

Chapter Three

1 J. M. Manly and Edith Rickert, *Contemporary British Literature,* New York, 1935, p. 22.

[2] Raoul Celly, *Répertoire des thèmes de Marcel Proust,* Paris: Gallimard, 1935, p. 24.

[3] E. R. Curtius, *Marcel Proust,* Paris, 1928, new edition, Berlin, 1952.

[4] Stilstudien II, *Stilsprachen,* München: Hueber, 1928.

[5] Hermann Blackert, *Der Aufbau der Kunstwirklichkeit bei Marcel Proust. Aufgezeigt an der Einführung der Personen,* Berlin: Juncker, 1935.

[6] Louis Emié, *Langage et humour chez M. Proust,* Paris: Le Rouge et le Noir, 1931.

[7] Lester Mansfield, *Le Comique de Marcel Proust,* Paris: Nizet, 1953.

[8] Florence Hier, *La Musique dans l'oeuvre de M. Proust,* New York: Columbia Univ. French Institute, 1933.

[9] John H. Morrow, "The Comic Element in 'A la recherche du temps perdu,' " *French Review,* XXVII (1953), pp. 114-121.

[10] Germaine Brée, *Du temps perdu au temps retrouvé,* Paris: Les Belles Lettres, 1950.

[11] Charles N. Clark, "Love and Time. The Erotic Imagery of M. Proust," *Yale French Studies,* XI (July, 1953), pp. 80-90.

[12] Frederick Charles Green, *The Mind of Proust. A detailed interpretation of "A la recherche du temps perdu,"* Cambridge: Univ. Press, 1949.

[13] Jean Mouton, *Le Style de M. Proust,* Paris: Corrêa, 1948.

[14] Léon Guichard, *Sept études sur M. Proust,* Le Caire: Horus, 1942.

[15] R. Etiemble, "Le Style de Proust," *Temps Modernes,* May, 1947.

[16] Käte Zaeske, *Der Stil M. Prousts.* Diss., Münster, 1937.

[17] Robert Vigneron, "Structure de Swann; Balzac, Wagner and Proust," *French Review,* XIX (1946), pp. 370-84.

[18] John W. Kneller, "The Musical Structure of Proust's 'Un Amour de Swann,' " *Yale French Studies,* no. 4, II (1949), pp. 55-62.

[19] Emeric Fiser, *Le Symbole littéraire de Marcel Proust, etc.,* Paris: Corti, 1941.

[20] Irma Tiedtke, *Symbole und Bilder im Werke Prousts,* Hamburger Studien zu Volkstum und Kultur der Romanen, XXI (1936).

[21] Antun Polanscak, *La Peinture du décor et de la nature chez Marcel Proust.* Thèse Paris, 1941; R. Ironside, "The Artistic Vision of Proust," *Horizon,* IV, no. 19 (1941), pp. 28-42.

[22] J. Murray, "Marcel Proust and John Ruskin," *Mercure de France,* vol. 189 (1926), pp. 86-100.

[23] Maurice E. Chernowitz, *Proust and Painting,* New York: Intern. Univ. Press, 1945.

[24] Frances V. Fardwell, *Landscape in the Works of Marcel Proust.* Diss. Catholic Univ., Washington, D. C., 1948.

[25] René Huyghe, "Affinités électives: Vermeer et Proust," *Amour de l'Art,* XVII (1936), pp. 7-15.

[26] Sylvia Narins Lévy, "Proust's Realistic Treatment of Illness," *French Review,* XV (1942), pp. 233-38; 324-29; 421-24.

[27] "Note et digression," in *Variété,* quoted by E. Noulet, *Paul Valéry,* Paris: Grasset, 1938, p. 29.

[28] E. Noulet, *Paul Valéry,* Paris: Grasset, 1938, p. 149.

[29] Marcel Proust, *Past Recaptured,* vol. I, New York: Boni, 1932, p. 218.

[30] The great enigma behind the creation of Albertine seemed to receive a disappointing elucidation as to the abnormalcy of Proust himself through the diary of André Gide (*Journal* [1889-1939], Paris: Gallimard, 1939, pp. 692-694). See André Maurois, *A la recherche de Marcel Proust,* Paris: Hachette, 1949, p. 145.

[31] T. W. Earp, *The Modern Movement in Painting,* London (New York): The Studio Publication, 1935, Plate 16.

[32] Albert Thibaudet, *Réflexions sur la littérature,* Paris: Gallimard, 1938, p. 199.

[33] Cp. Alfons Wegener, *Impressionismus und Klassizismus im Werke Marcel Prousts,* Diss. Frankfurt am Main, 1930.

34 Gladys Dudley Lindner, *Marcel Proust. Reviews and Estimates in English*, Stanford Univ. Press, 1942, p. 186.

35 Henri Bonnet, *Le Progrès spirituel dans l'oeuvre de M. Proust*. Vol. I: *Le Monde, l'amour et l'amitié*. Vol. II: *L'Eudémonisme esthétique de Proust*, Paris: Vrin, 1944-49.

36 Jean-Richard Bloch, *Destin du Théâtre*, Paris: NRF, 1930, p. 58.

37 *L'Oeuvre de François Mauriac*, Paris: Hartmann, 1927.

38 Amélie Fillon, *François Mauriac*, Paris: Malfère, 1936.

39 Pierre Brodin, *Présences contemporaines*, New York: Univ. Française, 1954, p. 25.

40 Details of character in James Schwarzenbach, *Der Dichter des zwiespältigen Lebens François Mauriac*, Einsiedeln: Benziger, 1938, pp. 128 ff.

41 Donat O'Donnel, *Maria Cross: Imaginative Patterns in a Group of Modern Catholic Writers*, London: Chatto and Windus, 1954, pp. 14 ff.

42 Robert J. North, *Le Catholicisme dans l'oeuvre de François Mauriac*, Editions du Conquistador, 1950, p. 60.

43 O'Donnel, *ib.*

44 Quoted by Nelly Cormeau, *L'Art de François Mauriac*, Paris: Grasset, 1951, p. 228.

45 Raymond Ritter, *Radio-Parnasse. A la manière de François Mauriac, Léon Daudet, Francis Jammes, et d'autres*, Paris: Michel, 1933.

46 Ernst Bendz, *François Mauriac, Ebauche d'une figure*, Göteborg: Elander, 1945.

47 Sister Ann Gertrud Landry, *Represented Discours in the Novels of François Mauriac*. Diss. Cath. Univ., Washington, D. C., 1953.

48 Milton H. Stansbury, *French Novelists of Today*, Philadelphia: Univ. of Pennsylvania Press, 1935, p. 155.

49 Marc Eigeldinger, *Julien Green ou la tentation de l'irréel*, Paris: Portes de France, 1947; and particularly Hans Taeschler, "Julien Green, 'Minuit,' " *Trivium*, IV (1946), pp. 153-165.

50 A. J. Dickman, "Le mal, force dramatique chez M. Lenormand," *The Romanic Review*, XIX (1928), pp. 220.

51 Daniel Rops, *Notre inquiétude*, Paris: Perrin, 1927, p. 111.

52 Marcel Proust, *The Past Recaptured, op. cit.*, p. 207.

53 François Mauriac, *Les Chemins de la mer*, Paris: Grasset, 1939, pp. 146, 241.

54 François Mauriac, *Plongées*, Paris: Grasset, 1938, p. 23.

55 See Emile Baumann, *La Symphonie du désir*, Paris: Grasset, 1933, p. 71.

56 José María Monner Sans, *El teatro de Lenormand*, Buenos Aires, 1937.

57 Pierre Clarac, *Textes choisis de Colette*, Paris: Grasset, 1936, Introduction, p. 14.

58 Ginette Guitard-Auviste, *La Vie de Jacques Chardonne et son art*, Paris: Grasset, 1953, pp. 118-28.

59 John Palmer, *Studies in the Contemporary Theatre*, London: Secker, 1927, p. 156.

60 Paul Géraldy, *L'Amour. Notes et Maximes*, Paris: Hachette, 1922, p. 58.

61 —————, *Toi et Moi*, Paris: Stock, 1931, p. 99.

62 About this whole problem see Sr. Francis Ellen Riordan, *The Concept of Love in the French Catholic Literary Revival*. Diss. Cath. Univ., Washington, D. C., 1952.

63 François Mauriac, *Dieu et mammon*, Paris: Capitole, 1920, pp. 192-93.

64 More Proust quotations on love in Raoul Celly, *op. cit.*, s.v. *amour*.

65 See Henri Clouard, *Histoire de la littérature française du symbolisme à nos jours*. Vol. II. Paris: Albin Michel, 1949, pp. 85-86.

66 Louis Parrot et Jean Marcenac, *Paul Eluard*, Paris: Seghers, 1953.

67 Klaus Mann, *André Gide*, New York: Creative Age Press, 1934, p. 120.

68 An exhaustive structural analysis of *Les Faux monnayeurs* can be found in Jean Hytier, *André Gide*, Charlot, 1946, pp. 246-315. Another detailed study: P. Lafille, *André Gide, Romancier*, Paris: Hachette, 1954, pp. 179-258.

69 A. Gide, *Le Journal des faux monnayeurs*, Paris: Ed. Eos, 1926, p. 143.

[70] *Ib.*, p. 83.

[71] Philo M. Buck, *Directions in Contemporary Literature,* New York: Oxford Univ. Press, 1942, p. 89.

[72] Elisabeth N. Monroe, *The Novel and Society,* Chapel Hill, 1941.

[73] Ernst Bendz, *André Gide et l'art d'écrire,* Paris: Messageries du livre, 1939.

[74] R. Etiemble, "Le Style du *Thésée* d'André Gide," *Temps Modernes,* II (1947), pp. 1032-38.

[75] Justin O'Brien, "Gide's fictional Technique," *Yale French Studies,* VII (1951), pp. 81-90.

[76] Pierre Lafille, *André Gide, Romancier,* Paris: Hachette, 1954.

[77] Ramon Fernandez, *André Gide,* Paris: Corrêa, 1931, p. 153.

[78] Ph. M. Buck, *Directions in Contemporary Literature, op. cit.,* p. 247.

[79] Henry de Montherlant, *Le Songe,* Paris: Grasset, 1922, p. 171.

Chapter Four

[1] Georges Lafourcade, *Notes sur le roman français contemporain,* The Univ. of Buffalo Studies, vol. XVI, 1939, no. 2, p. 77.

[2] Carlos Lynes, "Northern Africa in André Gide's Writing" in *PMLA,* LVII (1942), pp. 851-866, 852.

[3] *Ib.*, p. 854.

[4] Cp. W. L. Schwartz, *The Imaginative Interpretation of the Far East in Modern French Literature,* Paris: Champion, p. 225.

[5] Amédée Guiard, *Antone Ramon,* Paris: Bloud, 1928, p. 288.

[6] Georges Lemaître, *Four French Novelists,* London: Oxford Univ. Press, 1938, p. 369.

[7] *Ib.*, p. 370.

[8] See W. M. Frohock, *André Malraux and the Tragic Imagination,* Stanford: Univ. Press, 1952, p. 17.

[9] *Ib.*, pp. 46-54.

[10] Paul Gaultier, *L'Adolescent,* Paris: Bloud et Gay, 1914, pp. 22, 35.

[11] Henri Peyre, *Hommes et oeuvres du XXe siècle,* Paris: Corrêa, 1938, p. 204.

[12] *Ib.*, p. 197.

[13] Raoul Celly, *Répertoire des thèmes de Marcel Proust,* Paris: Gallimard, 1935, p. 119.

[14] Fernand Desonay, *Le Grand Meaulnes,* Bruxelles: Ed. des Artistes, 1941, pp. 229-52.

[15] Walter Jöhr, *Le Rêve et la réalité dans la vie et dans l'oeuvre d'Alain-Fournier,* Neuchâtel: Les Cahiers du Rhône, 1945, p. 31.

[16] Alain-Fournier, *Correspondance avec Jacques Rivière,* vol. IV, Paris: Gallimard, p. 293.

[17] Robert Gibson, *The Quest of Alain-Fournier,* New Haven: Yale Univ. Press, 1954, p. 268. See also Robert Champigny, *Portrait of a Symbolist Hero,* Bloomington: Indiana Univ. Press, 1954.

[18] François Mauriac, *La Vie et la mort d'un poète,* Paris: Grasset, 1924, p. 56.

[19] David G. Larg, *André Maurois,* London: Shaylor, 1931, p. 26.

[20] André Maurois, *Méïpe ou la délivrance,* Paris: Grasset, 1926, p. 13.

[21] Jean Calvet, *L'Enfant dans la littérature française,* Paris: Lanore, 1930, 2 vols., esp. vol. II, pp. 203-31; and Justin O'Brien, *The Novel of Adolescence in France,* New York: Columbia Univ. Press, 1937, p. 164.

[22] J. J. Bernard, *Théâtre,* vol. V, Paris: Michel, 1936, p. 17.

[23] Georges Lafourcade, *op cit.,* p. 83.

[24] John Palmer, *Studies in the Contemporary Theatre,* London: Secker, 1927, p. 118.

[25] Pierre Brodin, *Les Ecrivains français de l'entre-deux-guerres,* Montréal: Valiquette, 1942, p. 151.

[26] Georges Lemaître, *op. cit.,* p. 241.

[27] Albert Thibaudet, *Réflexions sur le roman,* Paris: Gallimard, 1938, p. 87.

[28] Robert Brasillach, *Portraits,* Paris: Plon, 1936, p. 126.

[29] Guido Meister, *Gestalt und Bedeutung der Frau im Werk Jean Giraudoux',* Diss. Basel, 1951, p. 104.

[30] See Jacques Houlet, *Le Théâtre de Jean Giraudoux,* Paris: Ardent, 1945, p. 86.

[31] See Gaëtan Picon, *Panorama de la nouvelle littérature française,* Paris: NRF, 1949, p. 41.

[32] Morton M. Celler, *Une Etude du style métaphorique de Jean Giraudoux,* Thèse Sorbonne, 1952, rev. by Ch. Bruneau in *Le Français Moderne,* XXI (1953), pp. 66-67.

[33] Ruth Elizabeth McDonald, "Le Langage de Giraudoux," *PMLA,* LXIII (1948), pp. 1029-50.

[34] Gabriel du Genêt, *Jean Giraudoux, ou un essai sur les rapports entre l'écrivain et son langage,* Paris: Vigneau, 1945.

[35] Henri Lemaître, "L'Art de Jean Giraudoux," *Confluents,* III (Jan. 1943, no. 16), pp. 81-85.

[36] Bengt Hasselrot, "Technique et style de Jean Giraudoux, auteur dramatique," *Studia Neophilologica,* XVIII (1945-46), pp. 249-268.

[37] Anne Chaplin Hansen, "Les Deux univers de Jean Giraudoux," *Orbis Litterarum,* VI (1940), 1-51.

[38] Hans Sörensen, *Le Théâtre de Jean Giraudoux. Technique et style,* Copenhagen: Munksgaard, 1950.

[39] G. Lemaître, *Four French Novelists, op. cit.,* p. 294.

[40] Laurence LeSage, "Jean Giraudoux, Prince des Précieux," *PMLA,* LVII (1942), pp. 1196-1204.

[41] Jean Ehrhard, *Le Roman français depuis Marcel Proust,* Paris: Nouvelle Revue Critique, 1932, p. 131.

[42] René Boylesve, *Opinions sur le roman,* Paris: Plon, 1929, p. 211.

[43] G. Lemaître, *Four French Novelists, op. cit.,* p. 383.

[44] See Yves Le Hir, *Fantaisie et mystique dans Le Petit Prince de Saint-Exupéry,* Paris: Nizet, 1954.

[45] Quoted in Jean Lambert, *Un Voyageur des deux mondes. Essai sur l'oeuvre d'Henri Bosco,* Paris: Gallimard, 1951, p. 161.

[46] John Palmer, *op. cit.,* p. 48.

[47] Georges Lemaître, *From Cubism to Surrealism,* Cambridge, Mass., 1941.

[48] *Ib.,* pp. 150-151.

[49] André Breton, *Manifeste du surréalisme,* Paris: Le Sagittaire, 1925, p. 58.

[50] Laurence LeSage, "The Cliché Basis for some of the Metaphors of Giraudoux," *Modern Language Notes,* LVI (1941), pp. 435-39.

[51] Clive Bell, *Since Cézanne,* London: Chatto and Windus, 1923, pp. 12, 15, 116-146, 223.

[52] Arnaud Dandieu, *Marcel Proust; sa révélation psychologique,* Paris: Didot, 1930.

[53] Pierre Lasserre, *Les Chapelles littéraries,* Paris: Garnier, 1920, pp. 26, 56-57.

[54] Francesco Casnati, *I drammi cristiani di Claudel,* Milano, 1933, p. 25.

[55] M. E. Coindreau, *La Farce est jouée,* New York: Maison Française, 1942, p. 187.

Chapter Five

[1] See Herbert Dieckmann, "French Existentialism before Sartre," *Yale French Studies,* Spring-Summer 1948, pp. 33-41; Pierre de Boisdeffre, *Métamorphose de la littérature,*

II: *De Proust à Sartre,* Paris: Alsatia, 1953, pp. 211-30, and Robert Campbell, *J.-P. Sartre,* Paris, 1945.

2 Robert G. Cohn, "Sartre's first Novel: *La Nausée,*" *Yale French Studies,* Spring 1948, p. 62.

3 Excellent analysis of *L'Age de raison,* by Wallace Fowlie, "Existentialist Hero: a study of L'Age de Raison," *Yale French Studies,* I (1948), pp. 53-61.

4 Analysis in Carlo Falconi, *Jean-Paul Sartre,* Parma: Guanda, 1949, 156-181. See also Jean Bruneau, "Existentialism and the American Novel," *Yale French Studies,* Spring 1948, pp. 66-72.

5 Nelly Cormeau, *Littérature existentialiste. Le roman et le théâtre de Jean-Paul Sartre,* Liège: Thone, 1950, p. 90.

6 Raymond Picard, "L'Art de J.-P. Sartre et Les hommes de mauvaise volonté," *La France libre* (Feb. 15, 1946), pp. 289-96.

7 Robert Champigny, "L'Expression élémentaire dans l'Etre et le Néant," *PMLA,* LXVIII (1953), pp. 56-64.

8 R. M. Albérès, *Jean-Paul Sartre,* Paris-Bruxelles: Editions Universelles, 1953, p. 109.

9 Roger Garaudy, *Literature of the Graveyard,* New York: Internat. Publishers, 1948, p. 60.

10 Th. Spoerri, *Die Herausforderung des Existentialismus,* Hamburg: Furche Verlag, 1954, p. 43.

11 Jean-Paul Sartre, "Explication de L'Etranger," *Situations,* I, Paris: NRF, 1947, pp. 99-121.

12 Pierre de Boisdeffre, *Métamorphose de la littérature,* I: *De Proust à Sartre,* Paris: Alsatia, 1951, pp. 264-74.

13 Charles Bruneau, *La Prose littéraire de Proust à Camus,* Oxford: Clarendon, 1953, pp. 19-22.

14 See Robert de Luppé, *Albert Camus,* Paris: Temps Présent, 1951, passim.

15 Germaine Brée, "Albert Camus and the Plague," *Yale French Studies,* no. 8, pp. 93-100.

16 Charles Bruneau, *op. cit.,* see note 13.

17 S. John, "Symbol in the work of Camus," *Yale French Studies,* no. 9 (1955), pp. 42-53.

18 W. M. Frohock, "Camus: Image, Influence and Sensibility," *Yale French Studies,* no. 2 (1949), pp. 91-99.

19 Criticus, *Le Style au microscope. Jeunes Gloires,* Paris: Calmann Lévy, 1951, pp. 25-42.

20 G. Pons, "Das Theater von Jean Anouilh," in Emile Calot, *Frankreichs zeitgenössische Literatur,* Stuttgart: Schmiedel, 1949, pp. 72-99; and, with all plays analyzed, Edward Owen Marsh, *Jean Anouilh,* London: Allen, 1953.

21 Pierre de Boisdeffre, *op. cit.,* pp. 185-207.

Chapter Six

1 Albert Chabanon, *La Poétique de Péguy,* Paris, 1948; and Leo Spitzer, "Zu Charles Péguy's Stil," *Stilstudien* II, München: Hueber, 1928, pp. 301-64.

2 Sister Clare Marie Gallenstein, *The Treatment of Suffering in Catholic Novels of Baumann and Bernanos,* MA Diss. Catholic Univ., Wash., D. C., 1945.

3 Herbert Dieckmann, *Die Kunstanschauung Paul Claudels,* Diss. Bonn, 1931.

4 Paul Imbs, "Etude sur la syntaxe du *Soulier de Satin,*" *Le Français Moderne,* XII (1944), pp. 243-79.

5 Klara Maurer, *Die biblische Symbolik im Werke Paul Claudels,* Diss. Zürich, 1941.

[6] Marcel Castay, *Entretiens Exemplaires*, Paris: Les Lettres, 1950.

[7] Fernan Vial, "Symbols and Symbolism in Paul Claudel," *Yale French Studies*, no. 9 (1952), 93-102.

[8] Helmuth Petriconi, "Das Meer und der Tod in drei Gedichten von Mallarmé, Rimbaud, Claudel," *Romanistisches Jahrbuch*, II (1949), pp. 282-95.

[9] Leo Spitzer, "Interpretation of an Ode by Paul Claudel," *Linguistics and Literary History*, Princeton: Univ. Press, 1948, pp. 193-236.

[10] The contents of the novels may be found in Pierre Brodin, *Maîtres et témoins de l'entre-deux-guerres*, Montréal: Valiquette, 1943, pp. 193-199; Bibliography, p. 243. J. M. Carrière in *Columbia Dictionary of Modern European Literature*, New York, 1947, pp. 84-85, has a condensation of the political writings. An interpretation approved by Bernanos himself, is Luc Estang, *Présence de Bernanos*, Paris: Plon, 1947. A great *Hommage à Bernanos* is A. Béguin (ed.) *Georges Bernanos*, Cahiers du Rhône, 1949; and Charles Moeller, "Bernanos," in his *Littérature du XXᵉ siècle et Cristianisme*, vol. I, Tournai: Casterman, 1953, pp. 371-400. Abbreviations: *Sous le soleil de Satan*=S; *L'Imposture*=I; *La Joie*=J; *Journal d'un Curé de campagne*=JC.

[11] *Les Deux sources de la morale et de la religion*, Paris: Alcan, 1932.

[12] Gabriel Marcel, *Journal métaphysique*, Paris: Gallimard, 1927.

[13] John Tucker, *Bernanos Romancier*, Thèse Sorbonne, 1953.

[14] See Sister Francis Ellen Riordan, *The Concept of Love in the French Catholic Literary Revival*, Diss. Catholic Univ., 1952, pp. 31-33.

[15] See Charles Moeller, *Littérature du XXᵉ siècle et Christianisme, op. cit.*, pp. 217-302.

[16] Bibliography of critical studies of *Augustin* in Yvonne Malègue, *Joseph Malègue*, Tournai: Casterman, 1947, pp. 198-201.

[17] Joseph Chenu, *Le Théâtre de G. Marcel et sa signification métaphysique*, Paris: Aubier, 1948.

[18] G. Fessard, "Théâtre et mystère," Introduction à *La Soif*, Paris, 1938.

[19] J-P. Dubois Dumée, "Solitude et communion dans le théâtre de Gabriel Marcel," in *Existentialisme chrétien: Gabriel Marcel*, ed. E. Gilson, Paris: Plon, 1947, pp. 269-289.

[20] See R. P. Valentin Breton, Luc J. Lefèvre, François Ducaud-Bourget, *Claudel, Mauriac et Cie, Catholiques de littérature*, Paris: L'Hermite, 1951, pp. 139-155.

[21] Biéville-Noyant, *Patrice de La Tour du Pin*, Paris: Nouvelle Revue Critique, 1948, p. 203.

Chapter Seven

[1] Lotte Thiessing-Specker, "Zur Lyrik Paul Eluard's," *Trivium*, III (1945), pp. 99-120.

[2] *Paroles peintes*. Paul Eluard, *Selected Writings*, New York: New Directions, 1951, p. 39.

[3] Quoted in Léon Verriest et Marie Louise Michaud Hall, *Variétés Modernes*, Boston: Houghton Mifflin Co., 1952, p. 194.

[4] See Jean Paulhan, *Poètes d'aujourd'hui*, Paris: Clairefontaine, 1947.

[5] Jean Cocteau, *Opium. The Diary of an Addict*, New York: 1932, pp. 148 ff.

[6] Jean de Pierrefeu, *Les Beaux livres de notre temps*, Paris: Plon, 1938.

[7] Julien Green, *Memories of Happy Days*, New York: Harper, 1942, p. 288.

[8] André Levinson, *Paul Valéry, Philosophie de la danse*, Les Cahiers Valéry I, Paris: La Tour d'Ivoire, 1927, pp. 17, 37.

[9] *Ib.*, p. 27.

[10] Charles Du Bos, *Extraits d'un Journal*, 1908-1928, Paris: Pléiade, 1929, pp. 13-15 (1909, Mercredi 17 fevrier).

[11] Fr. Lefèvre, *Une heure avec . . .*, 2ᵉ série, Paris: NRF, 1924, p. 136.

[12] E. Noulet, *Paul Valéry*, Paris: Grasset, 1938, p. 11.

[13] See Henri Bremond, *La Poésie pure*, Paris, 1926.

[14] Henri Bremond, *Poésie et prière*, Paris, 1926.

[15] See the quotations from Jean Bouchary, Paul Claudel, René Guilleré in Régis Michaud, *Vingtième siècle*, New York, 1933, pp. 389-99.

[16] Frédéric Lefèvre, *Entretiens avec Paul Valéry*, Paris, 1926, p. 258.

[17] See Theodora Bossanquet, *Paul Valéry*, London, 1933, p. 106.

[18] T. E. Hulme, *Notes on Language and Style*, Seattle: Univ. of Washington Book Store, 1929.

[19] André Levinson, *op. cit.*

[20] See Gustave Cohen, *Essai d'explication du Cimetière Marin*, Paris: N.R.F., 1933.

[21] Georges Lemaître, *From Cubism to Surrealism*, *op. cit.*, p. 48.

[22] Theodora Bossanquet, *Paul Valéry*, London, 1933, p. 82.

[23] E. Noulet, *op. cit.*, p. 57.

[24] Félix Klein, *Madeleine Sémer*, New York: Macmillan, 1927, p. 195.

[25] See Maurice Saillet, *Saint-John Perse, poète de la gloire*, Paris: Mercure de France, 1952; Alain Bosquet, *Saint-John Perse*, Paris: Seghers, 1953.

[26] Arthur J. Knodel, "The Imagery of Saint-John Perse's 'Neiges,' " *PMLA*, LXX (1955), pp. 5-18.

[27] Renato Poggioli, "The Poetry of St.-John Perse," *Yale French Studies*, I (1948), pp. 5-33.

[28] Gerda Zeltner-Neukomm, "St.-John Perse als Dichter der Fremdheit," *Überlieferung und Gestaltung. Festgabe Spoerri*, Zürich: Speer, 1950, pp. 187-206.

[29] Maurice Saillet, *op. cit.*, pp. 190 ff.

[30] Wallace Fowlie, "The Poetics of St.-John Perse," *Poetry* LXXXII (1953), pp. 345-50.

[31] Roger Caillois, *Poétique de St.-John Perse*, Paris: Gallimard, 1954.

[32] There are such words as *jaubert*, swab (a sea-term); *hongre*, gelding, emasculated; *cocculus*, an Indian fruit; *lé*, "largeur d'une etoffe entre ses lisières"; *engoulevent*, "large peaked sparrow"; *bale*, husk; *écobuages*, tracts of burnt-over-land; *corymbe*, cluster.

[33] Georges Emmanuel Clancier, *Panorama critique de Rimbaud au Surréalisme*, Paris: Seghers, 1953, p. 354.

[34] Wallace Fowlie, *Mid-Century French Poets*, New York: Twayne, 1955, p. 71. See also Claude Roy, *Jules Supervielle* (Etudes et Textes), Paris: Seghers, 1949.

[35] Gaétan Picon, *Panorama de la nouvelle littérature française*, Paris: Gallimard, 1949, p. 155.

[36] Lotte Specker, *Jules Supervielle. Eine Stilstudie*, Diss. Zürich, 1942.

[37] Christian Sénéchal, *Jules Supervielle, Poète de l'univers intérieur*, Paris: Flory, 1939.

[38] Claude Roy, *Jules Supervielle*, Paris: Seghers, 1949, p. 47.

[39] Lina Morrino, *La Nouvelle Revue Française dans l'histoire des lettres*, Paris: Gallimard, 1939, p. 201.

[40] See Phyllis Aykroyd, *The Dramatic Art of La Compagnie des Quinze*, London: Eric Partridge, 1935, p. 13.

[41] Julian Green, *Memories of Happy Days*, New York: Harper, 1942, p. 221.

Chapter Eight

[1] L. C. Harmer, *The French Language Today. Its Characteristics and Tendencies*, London: Hutchinson House, 1954, esp. chapter VI: *The Literary Language*, pp. 236-318.

[2] Henri Bergson, *Essais sur les données immédiates de la conscience*, Paris: Alcan, 1926, p. 99.

[3] Robert Brasillach, *Portraits*, Paris: Plon, 1936, pp. 7-18.

4 Jeanne Galzy, *Sainte Thérèse d'Avila*, Paris: Rieder, 1927, p. 52.

5 C. F. Ramuz, *Les signes parmi nous*, Paris: Grasset, 1931, p. 1.

6 This statement will be supported by the forthcoming dissertation of Mrs. Kathryn Day Wyatt, *The stylistic imitation of Jules Romains' Unanimism*, Catholic Univ., Washington, D. C.

7 André Gide, *Caractères*, Paris: A l'enseigne de la Porte étroite, 1925, p. 21.

8 *Flèche d'Orient*, Paris: N.R.F., 1931, p. 46.

9 Quoted in Jean Lambert, *Un Voyageur des deux mondes. Essai sur l'oeuvre d'Henri Bosco*, Paris: Gallimard, 1951, p. 48.

10 Camus, *L'Etranger*, Paris: Gallimard, 1944, p. 128.

11 E. Noulet, *Paul Valéry*, Paris: Grasset, 1938, p. 56.

12 Yves Gandon, *Le Démon du style*, Paris: Plon, 1938, p. 64.

13 Quoted by Yves Gandon, *ib.*, pp. 111-12.

14 *L'Ecole des indifférents*, p. 39.

15 *Anthologie des poètes de la NRF*, Paris: Gallimard, 1936, p. 40.

16 John Palmer, *Studies in the Contemporary Theatre*, London: Secker, 1927, p. 15.

17 Georges Lemaître, *From Cubism to Surrealism*, Cambridge: Harvard Univ. Press, 1941, p. 66.

18 *Ib.*, p. 77.

19 Quoted by Yves Gandon, *op. cit.*, pp. 29-30.

20 Frédéric Lefèvre, *Une heure avec . . .* 6ᵉ série, Paris: Flammarion, 1924, p. 140.

21 H. de Montherlant, *Les Célibataires*, Paris: Grasset, 1934, p. 155.

22 Jean Thomas, *Quelques aspects du romantisme contemporain*, Paris; Les belles lettres, 1928, p. 11. Gide's explanation in *Le Journal des faux monnayeurs*, Paris: Edition Eos, 1926, p. 59.

23 Quoted by Nelly Cormeau, *Littérature existentialiste. Le roman et le théâtre de Jean-Paul Sartre*, Liège: Thone, 1950, p. 41.

24 Emile Bouvier, *Initiation à la littérature d'aujourd'hui*. Cours élémentaire, Paris: La Renaissance du Livre, 1927, p. 145.

25 See Sister Ann Gertrude Landry, *Represented Discourse in the Novels of François Mauriac*, Diss. Catholic University, Washington, D. C., 1953.

26 Elisabeth Geertruida de Roos, *Het essayistisch Werk van Jacques Rivière*, Proefschrift, Amsterdam: H. J. Paris, 1931, pp. 129 ff.

27 See Jacques Rivière, *Etudes*, Paris: Gallimard, 1925, pp. 155-166.

28 Edmund Wilson, *Axel's Castle. A study in imaginative literature*, New York: Scribner's, 1931, p. 70.

29 Laurence LeSage, "The Cliché Basis for some of the Metaphors of Giraudoux," *Modern Language Notes*, LVI (1941), 435-39.

30 J. Giraudoux, *Simon le pathétique*, Paris: Grasset, 1918, p. 25.

31 E. Noulet, *op. cit.*, p. 75.

32 Quotes from Joseph de Tonquédec, *L'Oeuvre de Paul Claudel*, Paris: Beauchesne, 1917, p. 13.

33 Georges Lafourcade, *Notes sur le roman français contemporain*, Buffalo: Univ. of Buffalo Studies, vol. XVI, 1939, no. 2, p. 82.

34 Jean Jacques Bernard, *Témoignages*, Paris: Masques, Cahiers d'Art dramatique, ed. G. Baly, Cahier XXV, 1933, p. 25.

35 José María Monner Sans, *El teatro de Lenormand*, Buenos Aires: Imprenta López, 1937, p. 113.

36 Yves Gandon, *op. cit.*, p. 17.

37 Quoted by J. Ehrhard, *Le Roman français depuis Marcel Proust*, Paris: Editions de la Nouvelle Revue Critique, 1932, p. 241.

GENERAL BIBLIOGRAPHY

I *Bibliographies. Literary Histories. Anthologies.*

Complete bibliographical references will be found in H. P. Thieme, *Bibliographie de la littérature française* (1800-1930), Paris: Droz, 1933, and its very valuable continuations by S. Dreher and M. Rolli (1930-39), Droz, 1948, and by Marguerite L. Drevet (1940-49), Droz, 1955, for the most recent years in Douglas W. Alden, A. S. Crisafulli and others, *Critical and Biographical References for the Study of Contemporary French Literature,* New York: Stechert, 1949-57, 9 volumes (to be continued).

Sketches of authors and photographs are found in Marcel Girard, *Guide illustré de la littérature française moderne,* Paris: Seghers, 1954; complete lists of works, analyses and appreciations of the most important authors in Pierre Brodin, *Présences contemporaines,* Editions Debresse et Université française de New York, vol. I, 1954, vol. II, 1955; sketches of lives and works of all the minor novelists known since 1940, and a complete list of American translations of contemporary French novels with indication of the publishing houses in Henri Peyre, *The Contemporary French Novel,* New York: Oxford University Press, 1955; current productions of the French book market are listed in two monthlies: *Le Bulletin critique du livre français* and *Les Livres du mois.* The most important titles are found in the current bibliography of the *Revue d'histoire littéraire de la France.*

Among the many general literary histories of the whole contemporary French literature which try to cover more ground than Girard, Brodin and Peyre the most valuable are:

Lalou, René, *Histoire de la littérature française contemporaine,* 2 vols., Presses Universitaires, 1941.

Clouard, Henri, *Histoire de la littérature française du symbolisme à nos jours,* 2 vols., Albin Michel, 1947-49.

Billy, André, *L'Epoque contemporaine* (Histoire de la vie littéraire), Tallandier, 1956.

Simon, Pierre-Henri, *Histoire de la littérature française contemporaine,* 2 vols., Colin, 1956.

Picon, Gaëton, *Panorama de la Nouvelle littérature française,* Gallimard, 1949.

Nathan, Jacques, *Histoire de la littérature française contemporaine, 1920-1953,* F. Nathan, 1954.

Brée, Germaine and Margaret Guiton, *An Age of Fiction: The French Novel from Gide to Camus,* New Brunswick: Rutgers University Press, 1957.

As far as anthologies are concerned, contemporary poetry may well be studied in:

Hackett, C.-A., *Anthology of Modern French Poetry,* Oxford: Blackwell, 1952.

Clancier, Georges Emmanuel, *De Rimbaud au surrealisme,* Seghers, 1953.

Fowlie, Wallace, *Mid-Century French Poets,* New York: Twayne Publishers, 1955.

Those interested in contemporary French drama may consult:

Pillement, Georges, *Anthologie du théâtre français contemporain,* 3 vols., Editions du Bélier, 1945-48.

Lumley, Frederick, *Trends in Twentieth Century Drama,* London: Rockliff, 1956.

For an over-all appraisal of the present situation of French Letters, there is:

Albérès, R. M., *Bilan littéraire du XXe siècle,* Aubier, 1956.

II. *Trends.*

Hubbard, Louise Jones, *The Individual and the Group in French Literature since 1914,* Diss. Washington, D. C., Catholic University, 1955.

Guisan, Gilbert, *Poésie et collectivité,* Lausanne, 1938.

Riordan, Sister Francis Ellen, *The Concept of Love in the French Catholic Revival,* Diss. Washington, D. C., Catholic University, 1953.

Edel, Leon, *The Psychological Novel, 1900-1950,* New York, Philadelphia: J. B. Lippincott Co., 1955.

Trignon, Jean de, *Histoire de la littérature enfantine,* Hachette, 1950.

Paribatra, Marsi, *Le Romantisme contemporain. Essai sur l'inquiétude et l'évasion de 1850-1950,* Editions Polyglottes, 1954.

Wahl, Jean, *Petite histoire de l'existentialisme,* Club Maintenant, 1947.

Mounier, Emmanuel, *Introduction aux existentialismes,* Denoël, 1947.

Barjon, Louis, S.J., *Le Silence de Dieu dans la littérature contemporaine,* Editions du Centurion, 1955.

Blanchet, André, *Le Prêtre dans le roman d'aujourd'hui*, Desclée de Brouwer, 1955.

Du Bos, Charles, *François Mauriac ou le problème du romancier catholique*, Corrêa, 1933.

Georgin, René, *La Prose d'aujourd'hui*, André Bonne, 1956.

S. Ullmann, *Style in the French novel*, Cambridge Univ. Press, 1957.

III   Single Authors.

Alain-Fournier

Delettrez, Jean-Marie, *Alain-Fournier et le Grand Meaulnes*, E. Paul-Frères, 1954.

Borgal, Clément, *Alain-Fournier*, Editions Universitaires, 1955.

Anouilh

Gignoux, Hubert, *Jean Anouilh*, Editions du Temps présent, 1947.

March, Edward Owen, *Jean Anouilh*, London: Allen, 1953.

Apollinaire

Rouveyre, André, *Amour et poésie d'Apollinaire*, Editions du Seuil, 1955.

Aragon

Roy, Claude, *Aragon*, Seghers, 1945.

Audoux

Lanoizelée, Louis, *Marguerite Audoux, sa vie, son oeuvre*, Plaisir du bibliophile, 1954.

Barrès

Lalou, René, *Maurice Barrès*, Hachette, 1952.

Mondor, Henri, *Maurice Barrès . . .*, Ventadour, 1956.

Beauvoir

La Vouldie, *Madame Simone de Beauvoir et ses "Mandarins,"* La Librairie française, 1955.

Bergson

Delattre, Floris, *Bergson et Proust*, A. Michel, 1948.

Maritain, Jacques, *Bergsonian Philosophy and Thomism*, New York: Philosophical Library, 1955.

Arbour, Roméo, *Henri Bergson et les lettres françaises*, Corti, 1955.

Bernanos

Estang, Luc, *Présence de Bernanos*, Plon, 1947.

Béguin, Albert, *Bernanos. Essais et témoignages*, Seuil, 1949.

Gaucher, Guy, *Le Thème de la mort dans les romans de Georges Bernanos*, Lettres Modernes, 1955.

Urs von Balthasar, Hans, S.J., *Le Chrétien Bernanos*, Seuil, 1956.

Scheidegger, Jean, *Bernanos romancier*, Neuchâtel: Attinger, 1956.

Bourget
Feuillerat, A., *Paul Bourget. Histoire d'un esprit sous la 3ᵉ République,*
Plon, 1937.
Brasillach
Vandromme, Pol, *Robert Brasillach, l'homme et l'oeuvre,* Plon, 1956.
Breton
Mauriac, Claude, *André Breton,* Paris, 1949.
Bosco
Lambert, Jean, *Un Voyageur des deux mondes,* Gallimard, 1951.
Camus
Luppé, R. de, *Albert Camus,* Temps présent, 1951.
Maquet, Albert, *A. Camus ou l'invincible été,* Debresse, 1955.
Quilliot, Roger, *La mer et les prisons. Essai sur A. Camus,* Gallimard,
1956.
Céline
Denoël, Robert, *Apologie de mort à crédit,* Denoël, 1937.
Chardonne
Guitard-Auviste, Ginette, *La Vie de Jacques Chardonne et son art,*
Grasset, 1953.
Claudel
Madaule, Jacques, *Le Génie de P. Claudel,* Desclée de Brouwer, 1933.
Chonez, Claudine, *Introduction à P. Claudel,* Albin Michel, 1947.
Ryan, Mary, *Introduction to Paul Claudel,* Westminster, Md.: Newman
Press, 1951.
Andrieu, Jacques, *La Foi dans l'oeuvre de P. Claudel,* Nouvelle Recherche,
1955.
Guillemin, Henri, *Claudel et son art d'écrire,* Gallimard, 1955.
Hommage à Paul Claudel, No. 33 of *La Nouvelle Revue Française,*
1ᵉʳ sept., 1955.
Madaule, Jacques, *Paul Claudel, dramaturge,* L'Arche, 1956.
Cocteau
Lannes, Roger, *Jean Cocteau; Etude et textes,* Seghers, 1945.
Dubourg, Pierre, *Dramaturgie de Jean Cocteau,* Grasset, 1954.
Crosland, Margaret, *Jean Cocteau,* London: Nevill, 1955.
Colette
Beaumont, Germaine, *Colette par elle-même,* Seuil, 1951.
Crosland, Margaret, *Madame Colette, a provincial in Paris,* New York:
British Book Center, 1954.
Cocteau, Jean, *Colette,* Grasset, 1955.
Le Hardouin, Maria, *Colette,* Editions Universitaires, 1956.
Daniel-Rops
Dournes, Pierre, *Daniel-Rops ou le réalisme de l'esprit,* Fayard, 1949.

Delteil
 Choisie, Maryse, *Delteil tout nu,* Montaigne, 1930.
Desnos
 Berger, Pierre, *Robert Desnos,* Seghers, 1949.
 Buchole, Rosa, *L'Evolution poétique de R. Desnos,* Bruxelles: Académies, 1956.
Du Bos
 Gouhier, Marie-Anne, *Charles Du Bos,* Vrin, 1950.
 Mouton, Jean, *Charles Du Bos, sa relation avec la vie et avec la mort,* Desclée de Brouwer, 1954.
Duhamel
 Santelli, César, *G. Duhamel,* Bordas, 1947.
 Simon, Pierre-Henri, *G. Duhamel,* Editions du Temps présent, 1947.
Durtain
 Chatelain, Yves, *Luc Durtain, Oeuvres représentatives,* 1933.
Eluard
 Parrot, Louis, et Jean Marcenac, *Paul Eluard,* Seghers, 1953.
Ghéon
 Brochet, H., *Henri Ghéon,* Les Presses de l'Isle de France, 1947.
 Deléglise, Maurice, *Le Théâtre d'Henri Ghéon,* Billaudot, 1951.
Gide
 Pierre-Quint, Léon, *A. Gide, sa vie, son oeuvre,* Stock, 1952.
 Brée, Germaine, *A. Gide, l'insaisissable Protée,* Les Belles Lettres, 1953.
 Beigbeder, Marc, *André Gide,* Editions Universitaires, 1954.
 Dauvigny, Alain, *A. Gide ou l'impossible morale,* Bordeaux: Impr. de Samie, 1954.
 Starkie, Enid, *André Gide,* New Haven: Yale Univ. Press, 1954.
 Delay, Jean, *La Jeunesse d'André Gide,* Nouvelle Revue française, 1956.
 Schlumberger, Jean, *Madeleine et André Gide,* Gallimard, 1956.
Giono
 Pugnet, Jacques, *Jean Giono,* Editions Universitaires, 1955.
 Villeneuve, R. de, *Jean Giono, ce solitaire,* Paris, 1955.
 Chonez, Claudine, *Jean Giono,* Seuil, 1956.
Giraudoux
 Marker, Christian, *Giraudoux par lui-même,* Seuil, 1953.
 Debidour, Victor-Henry, *Jean Giraudoux,* Editions Universitaires, 1955.
 Bidal, M.-L., *Giraudoux tel qu'en lui-même,* Corrêa, 1956.
Green
 Eigeldinger, Marc, *Julien Green et la tentation de l'irréel,* Au Portes de France, 1947.
 Fongaro, Antoine, *L'Existence dans les romans de Julien Green,* Rome: Signorelli, 1954.

Stokes, Samuel E., *Julien Green and the Thorn of Puritanism*, New York: King's Crown Press, 1955.

Gorkine, Michel, *Julien Green*, Debresse, 1956.

Jammes

Mallet, Robert, *Francis Jammes*, Seghers, 1950.

Dyson, Rose M., *Les sensations et la sensibilité chez Francis Jammes*, Genève: Droz, 1954.

Jouhandeau

Rode, H., M. *Jouhandeau et ses personnages*, Chambriand, 1951.

Larbaud

Aubry, G. Jean, *Valéry Larbaud*, Editions Du Rocher, 1949.

Lenormand

Hernried, Doris E., *L'Expérience de l'univers de H.-R. Lenormand*, Paris: Thèse Univ., 1954.

Maeterlinck

Hardy, Gérard, *La Vie et l'oeuvre de M. Maeterlinck*, Fasquelle, 1932.

Malègue

Varin, Germain, *Foi perdue et retrouvée dans "Augustin,"* Fribourg: St. Paul, 1953.

Michaël, Elisabeth, *Joseph Malègue. Sa vie. Son oeuvre*, Spes, 1957.

Malraux

Boisdeffre, P. de., *A. Malraux*, Editions Universitaires, 1954.

Delhomme, Jeanne, *Temps et destin. Essai sur André Malraux*, Gallimard, 1955.

Marcel

Chenu, Joseph, *Le Théâtre de G. Marcel et sa signification métaphysique*, Aubier, 1948.

Sottiaux, Edgard, *Gabriel Marcel, philosophe et dramaturge*, Louvain: Nauwaelerts, 1956.

Martin du Gard

Lalou, René, *Roger Martin du Gard*, Gallimard, 1937.

Mauriac

Hourdin, Georges, *Mauriac romancier chrétien*, Temps présent, 1945.

North, Robert J., *Le Catholicisme dans l'oeuvre de François Mauriac*, Ed. du Conquistador, 1950.

Cormeau, Nelly, *L'Art de François Mauriac*, Grasset, 1951.

Jarret-Kerr, Martin, *François Mauriac*, Yale Univ. Press, 1954.

Maurois

Fillon, André, *André Maurois, romancier*, Malfère, 1937.

Michaux

Bertelé, René, *Henri Michaux*, Seghers, 1946.

Coulon, Philippe de, *Henri Michaux, poète de notre société,* Neuchâtel: Baconnière, 1949.

Montherlant

Sandélion, Jeanne, *Montherlant et les femmes,* Plon, 1951.

Laprade, Jacques de, *Le Théâtre de Montherlant,* La Jeune Parque, 1950.

Bordonove, Georges, *Henry de Montherlant,* Editions Universitaires, 1954.

Datain, Jean, *Montherlant et l'héritage de la renaissance,* Amiot-Dumont, 1956.

Morand

Guitard-Auviste, Ginette, *P. Morand,* Editions Universitaires, 1956.

Noailles

De la Rochefoucauld E., *Anna de Noailles,* Ed. Universitaires, 1956.

Péguy

Rousseaux, André, *Le Prophète Péguy,* A. Michel, 1947.

Servais, Yvonne, *Charles Péguy. The Pursuit of Salvation,* Oxford: Blackwell, 1953.

Suire, Pierre, *Le Tourment de Péguy,* Laffont, 1956.

Pitoëff

Lenormand, H.-R., *Les Pitoëff,* Lieutier, 1943.

Prévert

Queval, Jean, *Jacques Prévert,* Mercure de France, 1956.

Proust

Bonnet, Henri, *Le Progrès spirituel dans l'oeuvre de M. Proust,* 2 vols., Vrin, 1946-49.

Hindus, Milton, *The Proustian Vision,* New York: Columbia Univ. Press, 1954.

Pierre-Quint, Léon, *Proust et la stratégie littéraire,* Corrêa, 1954.

Brée, Germaine, *M. Proust and the deliverance from time,* New Brunswick, N. J., Rutgers Univ. Press, 1955.

Cocking, J. M., *Proust,* London: Bowes, 1956.

Radiguet

Goesch, Keith: *Raymond Radiguet,* Paris-Genève: La Palatine, 1955.

Ramuz

Vodenne, Bernard, *C. F. Ramuz ou la sainteté de la terre,* Juillard, 1948.

Cingria, Hélène, *Ramuz, notre parrain,* Bienne: Boillat, 1956.

Rolland

Arcos, René, *Romain Rolland,* Mercure de France, 1950.

Starr, William Thomas, *Romain Rolland and a world at war,* Evanston: Northwestern Univ. Press, 1956.

Romains

Figuéras, André, *Jules Romains,* Seghers, 1952.

Berry, Madeleine, *Jules Romains conquistador,* Paris, 1953.

Saint-Exupéry
   Chevrier, Pierre, *Antoine de St.-Exupéry,* Gallimard, 1949.
   Kessel, Patrick, *La Vie de Saint-Exupéry,* Gallimard, 1954.
   Ibert, C. I., *Saint-Exupéry,* Ed. Universitaires, 1956.
Saint-John Perse
   Bosquet, Alain, *Saint-John Perse,* Seghers, 1949.
   Guerre, Pierre, *Saint-John Perse et l'homme,* Gallimard, 1955.
Sartre
   Beigbeder, Marc, *L'Homme Sartre,* Bordas, 1947.
   Dellevaux, R., *L'Existentialisme et le théâtre de J.-P. Sartre,* Bruxelles, Edit. La Lecture au foyer, 1951.
   Jeanson, Francis, *Sartre par lui-même,* Seuil, 1955.
Supervielle
   Roy, Claude, *Jules Supervielle. Etudes et textes,* Seghers, 1949.
Valéry
   Rideau, Emile, *Introduction à la pensée de P. Valéry,* Desclée de Brouwer, 1944.
   Bémol, Maurice, *P. Valéry,* Belles Lettres, 1949.
   Noulet, Emilie, *P. Valéry,* Renaissance du livre, 1951.
   La Rochefoucauld, Edmée de, *Paul Valéry,* Editions Universitaires, 1954.
   Scarfe, Francis, *The Art of Paul Valéry,* Glasgow: University Publications, 1954.
   Walzer, Pierre-Olivier, *La Poésie de Valéry,* Genève: Cailler, 1954.
   Sutcliffe, F. E., *La Pensée de Paul Valéry,* Nizet, 1955.
   Charpier, Jacques, *Essai sur P. Valéry,* Seghers, 1956.
Van der Meersch
   Bordes, Elie, *Le Drame spirituel dans l'oeuvre de Maxence Van der Meersch,* Tourcoing: Frère, 1944.
   Reus, Robert, *Portrait morpho-psychologique de Maxence Van der Meersch,* Aurillac: Clairac, 1952.
Verhaeren
   Christoffe, Lucien, *Emile Verhaeren,* Editions Universitaires, 1955.
   Jones, P. Mansell, *Verhaeren,* London: Bowes, 1957.
Weil
   Perrin, J. M. and Thibon, Gustave, *Simone Weil as we knew her,* London: Routledge, 1953.
   Bugnion-Secretan, P., *Simone Weil. Itinéraire politique et spirituel,* Neuchâtel: Messeiller, 1954.
   Tomlin, E. W. F., *Simone Weil,* New Haven: Yale Univ. Press, 1954.
   Cabaud, J., *L'Expérience vécue de Simone Weil,* Paris, 1957.

INDEX OF CONTEMPORARY AUTHORS AND WORKS